COWBOY and INDIAN TRADER

COWBOY
and INDIAN
TRADER

Joseph Schmedding

Introduction by
Jack Schaefer

UNIVERSITY OF NEW MEXICO PRESS
Albuquerque

Library of Congress Catalog Card No. 73-92994
International Standard Book No. 0-8263-0319-6

INTRODUCTION

When Joe Schmedding wrote about his years as cowboy and Indian trader he was a man in his sixties looking back to the time when both he and this century were young. As he stated in his foreword, he believed he was producing "an American document." He was.

He was also producing a book that is eminently readable, and—precisely because it is so readable—is in one sense somewhat aggravating. It is full of facts and observations and opinions, but it is singularly lacking in facts about Joe Schmedding. True enough, his purpose was less to write about himself, more to record his impressions of cowboying and Indian trading of the period—and to express his personal convictions on a variety of allied subjects. Yet to make his acquaintance through the pages of his book is inevitably to want to know more about him, to be annoyed that he was content to offer only occasional hints, sometimes confusing hints, about other aspects of his career. What manner of man was he? What kind of life as a whole did he shape for himself? Surely such a vital and versatile young man would very likely remain much the same through his later years. He did.

He did, that is, on the basis of a few of his letters that have been preserved, information supplied by a few people who knew him well during his last years, and the scant but often significant

data I have been able to assemble from a few notes about himself
he prepared at the time his book was originally published.

*   *   *

He was born in Bremen, Germany, on October 15, 1887,
presumably of pure North European ancestry. His father, for
whom he was named, was German, his mother Dutch, and they
had at least one other child, a girl named Elise. While the
children were still very young, the family came to this country
and settled in North Carolina. There, with the century too just
beginning, began (as does his book) the American saga of Joe
Schmedding, now in his teens, already on his way to becoming
one-hundred-percent-plus patriotic, working as what he later
labeled a "horsehandler" on a stock farm in Polk County.

He was a fast-growing, self-reliant young one, stretching up
towards the lean, redheaded six feet three or four inches of his
maturity, barely fourteen years of age when he took on that
horsehandling job, and only sixteen when he left North Carolina
bound for the American Southwest completely on his own. At
this stage he might have been just another of the young men still
being drawn westward by the lure of cowboy mythology—but
with this difference: by sheer luck or by intuitive push on his own
part he was fortunate in the employers he found.

For a year or more he was a range rider for Nation's Ranch, an
affiliate of a meat-packing concern with headquarters in El Paso,
Texas. "Old Man" Nation ran a rough-and-ready outfit with a
sound reputation, and young Joe acquired about as thorough an
introduction to ranch work as he could have obtained anywhere
in the Southwest. Then for a brief time he was what he later
described as "ranch-hand, cowboy, bronco-buster" as the Mc-
Donald Ranch near Carrizozo, New Mexico Territory. His
employer this time was William Calhoun McDonald, who has an
honored place in New Mexico history.

Originally a New York Stater, McDonald had come to the
territory back in the 1880s and had shared bachelor quarters for
a time with writer Emerson Hough (who used him as model for a
character in his first published work). McDonald had been a
teacher, lawyer, and civil and mining engineer before becoming

manager of the Carrizozo Cattle Ranch Company, which was owned by a British syndicate. Within a few years he purchased the ranch for himself and took on management of similar property for the huge El Capitan Land and Cattle Company. Through the years he held various public offices in the territory, and in 1912, when it became the forty-seventh state, he won the distinction of serving as its first elected governor.

At the time young Joe worked for him, McDonald was one of the most respected and knowledgeable ranchmen in the Southwest—and one with interests much wider than mere ranching. His influence permeated his home outfit. Young Joe was not a part of this for long—he had simply been lucky enough to be taken on for temporary extra work—but the experience made an enduring impression on him. He was learning that life, even hard-working ranch life, could have compensations beyond merely earning a living out in the great distances of the Southwest, where nature had played artist on a vast scale with a prodigal palette and where human history traced back through many millennia. After a brief episode of lazy sightseeing in Albuquerque, he went to work—again as a ranch hand but again with a difference—for Richard Wetherill.

*   *   *

There is no need here to fill in facts about Richard Wetherill, his father, and his four brothers, all of whom, particularly Richard, played important roles in cowboying and Indian trading—and archaeological exploring—in the Southwest. The whole Wetherill story is thoroughly documented in Frank McNitt's *Richard Wetherill: Anasazi,* and further background, superbly human and atmospheric, is available in *Traders to the Navajos,* by brother John Wetherill's wife, Louisa Wade Wetherill, in collaboration with Frances Gillmor. The point here is that Joe Schmedding, all of an impressionable eighteen years old, had the good luck to go to work for Richard Wetherill during the best years of the Wetherill Ranch in Chaco Canyon, on the edge of the Navajo Reservation, with Pueblo Bonito, the most famous of the canyon's astounding array of Indian ruins, barely a stone's throw from the ranch buildings.

There was plenty of the work for which Joe was qualified. The Triangle Bar Triangle, so known from a major Wetherill brand, ran some cattle but specialized in horses, with some twelve hundred or more head regularly on its range. Horse buyers came from long distances, and delivery drives were made for equal distances. On such occasions Richard Wetherill would turn over the ownership papers to the cowboy in charge, in full trust that the stock would be properly delivered and the payment brought back. Joe went on one of these drives all the way to Goodnight, Oklahoma. Young as he was, at horsehandling he was an old hand. He was also being introduced to other interesting activities.

The Wetherill establishment in Chaco Canyon was only incidentally a working ranch. It had come into being earlier in connection with a unique and fascinating enterprise, the Hyde Exploring Expedition. In 1893 the Hyde brothers, Talbot and Fred, Jr., heirs to a moderate fortune derived from a soap business founded by their paternal grandfather, formed a partnership with Richard Wetherill to explore and study the Indian ruins that Richard and his brothers had been discovering all through what is nowadays known as the Four Corners Region. The Hydes were to provide most of the financing, Richard to be in charge of fieldwork.

The Hyde Exploring Expedition was the first serious and reasonably well organized attempt with definite scientific intent to accumulate data about and artifacts of the early Indian civilizations of the area. It was a large-scale operation for the time and soon outgrew the mere "exploring" aspect of its name. Inevitably, as work progressed, what could be called the general field headquarters was established in Chaco Canyon, the site of the most comprehensive array of ruins. Just as inevitably, given the scope of operations, the need for supplies, and the difficulty of freighting these into what was then a remote, almost inaccessible region, the field headquarters became an ever–more important supply center and trading post. By the time the Hyde Exploring Expedition partnership was amicably dissolved in 1903 (again the full account is documented in Frank McNitt's book), Richard Wetherill had homesteaded the site in the canyon, had his horse ranch operating, was proprietor of a general and Indian trading post serving a large surrounding area, and was establishing smaller outlying posts. With his interest in the early Indian civilizations unabated, he undoubtedly knew more about the whole region and its archaeological possibilities than any other man of the period. In 1905, when Joe Schmedding won acceptance as a Triangle Bar Triangle ranch hand, the Wetherill operations in Chaco Canyon were in full swing.

Handling horses for Richard Wetherill, slogging off on freighting trips for Richard Wetherill, listening to Richard Wetherill talk in the evenings, leafing through the unusually varied newspapers and magazines and books Richard Wetherill always had on hand, watching Richard Wetherill trade with and be a fellow human with Indians, prowling old ruins on his own, seizing the opportunity to attend a Hopi Snake Dance at Walpi, observing the archaeological work sporadically under way by various scientific groups, young Joe was absorbing interests, attitudes, and habits of mind that would remain with him all the rest of his life.

*   *   *

Three years as a Wetherill man (1905–8) and he was coming twenty-one. A letter from a boyhood friend suggesting an extended pack trip revived his wanderlust, a desire to see more of the Southwest. The two of them were exploring parts of Arizona when their trip was cut short by the hurried departure of the friend on news of a death in his family. Immediately following this episode there is a five-to-six-year gap in the continuity of his book, explained only by the statement that he "became a wanderer upon the face of the earth and over the seven seas."

Part of this time, the later record reveals, he was an enlisted man in the Fourteenth U.S. Cavalry. He spent some or most of his service in the Philippines, won sergeant's stripes, and was honorably discharged in June of 1911. What lands and what seas he wandered during the rest of this period remains a mystery. Some hints might be picked out of the listing he gave on pages 31–32 of his book of his "wandering over this world of ours." But so doing he supplied no dates, summing in swift haphazard manner a whole lifetime of varied experience in many places. He was simply citing his qualifications for making the judgment that "the great Southwest of our United States comprises a region of more varied beauty and scenic grandeur . . . than any other portion of the earth."

When the reasonably accurate available record begins again in 1914, we find him once more in the Southwest, living in Albuquerque, drawing on knowledge obtained during the Chaco Canyon period, engaged now in buying and selling Navajo blankets.

Later that same year he shifted into true Indian trading and became proprietor of the post at Sanders, Arizona. About two years later he acquired the famous old Hubbell trading post at Keams Canyon, deep in the Indian reservation. There for the next eight years he was an all-around Indian trader in the Wetherill tradition, establishing a subsidiary post at Low Mountain and also serving as a postmaster, a notary public, and a deputy sheriff.

Sometime following his military service, probably when those mysterious wanderings were over and he had returned to the Southwest, he acquired a wife. Curiously, though he gave her full credit in his book as a trader's helpmeet and the impression is plain that the years with her were well worth the living, he never mentioned her name, either in the book or in later notes. What is recorded is that in July of 1916 she bore a son whom they named another Joseph and in June of 1921 she bore a daughter whom they named Kathryn.

*   *   *

Early in 1923 what he described as the "tranquil existence" at Keams Canyon was interrupted by the sudden notice that his license as a trader was being revoked by order of the secretary of the interior, Albert B. Fall. This was one of the last official acts of Fall, who was under suspicion as one of the principals in the emerging Teapot Dome oil-lease scandal and who would soon be out of office and later be indicted and convicted. In Joe's version of the license matter, which seems accurate in the light of what developed, the revocation order was issued to clear the way for one of Fall's personal friends to take over the trading post.

Joe Schmedding had been lucky before with the employers he found when he was cowboying, and he was lucky now with the friends who helped when he was Indian trading. Foremost among them was advertising executive James B. Young of New York and Chicago, who had been a visitor at Keams Canyon and who now summoned legal aid and publicity for a thorough airing of the case. This was the James B. Young who later retired to New Mexico, where he owned a large apple orchard near Cochiti, and eventually became a generous benefactor of the University of New Mexico, leaving much of his land to it in his will. Politically important aid came from Congressman Carl Hayden and Senator Cameron of Arizona, who managed to take the issue—and Joe Schmedding himself—into the office of President Harding, who promised that Joe would get "justice." He did. His license was renewed.

He was vindicated—but Indian trading had lost some of its savor for him. Moreover, there was the problem of schooling for the children. He put the post up for sale. In 1924 his career as cowboy and Indian trader came to an end—as does the somewhat confused continuity of his book.

*   *   *

Joe Schmedding was now thirty-seven years old, well into his middle years, one kind of a career behind him, another beginning—one that would take him to more far places and immerse him in new interesting activities.

For a few years (James B. Young must have been helpful here) he was a big-city man, manager of the Watson Food Products account for the J. Walter Thompson advertising agency in New York. For a few more he was commercial manager of the Firestone Rubber plantations in Liberia, West Africa. For yet a few more he was in charge of Cuban affairs in Havana for Libby, McNeill & Libby.

In 1931, during the Cuban period, his wife died. This seems to have triggered a change in him, a desire to return to the region of his youth and refashion a life there. Nothing is known of what happened to the children, indeed whether they had even survived to this period. Always reticent about personal matters, even to close friends later in life, he never made mention of them and no record of them can be found. What is known is that by 1933 he had returned alone to the American Southwest, to the California edge of it, and was developing a business as an importer of Mexican goods with outlets in Los Angeles and San Francisco. And in that year he married Margaret E. Anderson of Chicago and settled in Montrose, California, just north of Pasadena.

By 1940 he was into his fifties and slowing down some, beginning to suffer from rheumatoid arthritis in increasingly virulent form, the affliction that would torment him the rest of his life. No more buying jaunts into Mexico. No more shuttling between the Los Angeles area and San Francisco. He became owner and operator of a medical laboratory in Hollywood.

Five more years and, in a physical sense, he had to slow down to a virtual stop. He sold the laboratory and was now confined much of the time to a wheelchair.

The following were hard years for his wife Margaret. She had to be nurse, housekeeper, chauffeur—and though Joe had some income out of the past, she had to obtain outside work to augment their finances. Now she proved her vitality and versatility, capably keeping the household functioning, meanwhile becoming first an efficient private secretary, then an equally efficient businesswoman on her own.

Those must have been even harder years for Joe Schmedding, onetime cowboy and Indian trader, former wanderer upon the face of the earth and over the seven seas, now pinned down to a wheelchair in a suburban home in overcivilized Southern California, dependent in so many ways on his wife. He refused to let his situation defeat him. His body was now a handicap. Not his mind. He plunged into a new occupation. He began writing, endlessly, letters and articles and possible books, in a fine, almost elegant, script.

He joined a local literary group, though attending meetings was difficult, and won respect not only for his own writings but also as both an honest hard-hitting critic and a generous encourager of the talents of others. He wrote long, newsy, opinionated, aptly phrased letters to friends—and concise, strongly worded letters to newspapers and national magazines, whose editors apparently liked to receive them because they usually published them promptly. His articles on cowboying and Indian trading, Indian problems, and his notions of Americanism appeared in various magazines. And he began to pile up book-length manuscripts based on his wanderings in the Southwest, in Mexico, in Liberia, in Cuba. In 1951 he had the satisfaction of seeing the best of these, his *Cowboy and Indian Trader,* achieve permanence as a printed book. He would have been more satisfied if he could have known that in 1974 this would be reprinted in companion format to stand alongside Frank McNitt's biography of Richard Wetherill and Louisa Wade Wetherill's moving account of life among the Navajos.

During these last years his affliction steadily increased its hold on him and surgery became imperative on several occasions, but almost to the end he held to his final practicable occupation, writing, finally able only to dictate to his wife, who typed manuscripts for him, some of which have been preserved and may in their own time also achieve the permanence of print.

His household now included his sister, Mrs. Elise Tenney, who as a semi-invalid herself added to the difficulties of daily living. In the hope that a desert climate might give Joe some relief, the three of them moved to Desert Hot Springs, where Margaret soon established herself again as a businesswoman. On September 2, 1956, Joe Schmedding died in that final desert home. He was approaching his sixty-ninth birthday. In his will he had requested that his body be turned over to the nearby Loma Linda Sanitarium for any possible scientific study of the disease from which he had suffered so long, and that it thereafter be cremated and his ashes scattered in the sanitarium rose garden. They were.

*   *   *

To a fellow writer his book is interesting not only for the material it contains but for its easy, direct, forward-flowing style. Obviously it was written by an intelligent, educated, well-read man with a surprising grasp of literary craftsmanship—surprising, that is, in one who had only two years of so-called high school in the North Carolina of the turn of the century, who went to work at fourteen, who at sixteen started wanderings on his own. But that apparent lack of education presents no problem.

Joe Schmedding had native ability aplenty, and with the impetus given him by association with William Calhoun McDonald and especially with Richard Wetherill he became, among so many other things, an inveterate reader and researcher into subjects that interested him. Along the way he picked up snatches of what could be called more formal education. While in the Philippines he took private tutoring from a professor at Manila University. While in New York he regularly attended public lectures at Columbia University. While in Cuba he studied privately under a professor at Havana University. In later years he noted that he was "fluent" in English and German and Spanish, with a "fair knowledge" of Latin and French. He also noted that he had a "predilection" for early American history and achievements.

This last was what helped impart a strong flavor to his book and underlay many of the opinions he put into it. He was completely of his generation and background, his Americanism founded on old days and old ways. He had a profound distrust of what was happening in the United States during his lifetime, of the influence of what he called "unassimilated aliens" and "cynical elements contemptuous of our cherished institutions." The inevitable movement towards a welfare state appalled him. He vigorously rejected the philosophy of the New Deal, was strongly opposed to organized labor, or at least to labor organizers, and had a rather paternalistic attitude tainted with suspicion towards ethnic minority groups, even towards the Indians whose true "friend" he insisted he was—and in many ways actually was. In the perspective of today he was an old-fashioned, almost reactionary, conservative, the attitudes and prejudices of many—perhaps a majority—of the Americans of his time imbedded in him. In a sense he was a mirror of one important aspect of his passing period in America. He was also a quite decent human being.

Plainly he tried to be honest and fair in his judgments. Inevitably, derogatory clichés, adjectives betraying the attitudes behind them, crept into his pages. But a careful reading shows that he was impartial in making his judgments. He spared no one in his criticism, was quite as caustic about whites as about reds or browns or blacks. He could temper a condemnation with the comment "But, possibly, I was prejudiced." He knew, and tried to remember, that "it is difficult to estimate correctly the conduct of another race."

Nowhere in his book (or in his personal life) did he pretend, when expressing an opinion, to speak for any group or organization or segment of the population—only and always for himself, what he, Joe Schmedding, felt and thought. He believed in free speech and practiced it—and was more than willing that others, however much they might disagree, should do the same. Reprinting of his book implies no agreement or disagreement with the opinions it contains on the part of the present publishers, simply a recognition that it offers good reading, considerable firsthand information about the transition period from frontier to modern times in the Southwest, and frequent insights into aspects of the mental climate of that period.

Joe Schmedding believed that the book he was writing just might qualify as an "American document." It does.

* * *

As a final note on the man as a man I would like to mention a small item that occurs early in his book. It convinced me that he had been no ordinary cowboy and that the rest of the book would be well worth the reading. When he wrote of his ride from El Paso to Carrizozo, he knew that though no one had been with him he had not really been alone. The experience was being shared by a fellow living creature. He remembered the partnership with a horse and used that lovely appreciative little pronoun "we."

Jack Schaefer

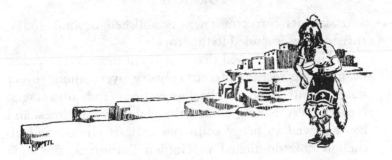

FOREWORD

The generations that watched the United States emerge from the horse-and-buggy age, whose eyes saw the transformation wrought in all phases of life during the years between ox team and airplane, are fast passing into oblivion. Possibly no other people in all recorded history lived through such phenomenal changes as occurred between the last two decades of the nineteenth century and the present.

This narrative records some personal experiences, impressions and observations dealing largely with obscure phases of our national life that the present world knows mostly, if at all, from hearsay. I believe the details presented constitute an American document and I would like to have them considered as such.

My long, on-the-ground experiences enable me to speak with certainty; every fact presented in the narrative is authentic; intentionally, no effort has been made to glamorize or dramatize any incident. My personal experiences I have told as such; other material was obtained from sources that were carefully investigated and cross-checked, and after its correctness was established beyond doubt, this, too, was included in the story.

Let it be understood that this is not intended to praise unduly one section of our country over others; every state has its own peculiar attractions and advantages. Nevertheless, having circled the globe several times, and having lived in many countries and all climes, and although now domiciled in Golden California, nostalgia sweeps me for another ride over the boundless mesas to fill my lungs once more with the sweet scent of pinon, cedar and sage. However, let the tale tell its own story.

JOSEPH SCHMEDDING

TABLE OF CONTENTS

LIST OF ILLUSTRATIONS

Following page 184

COWBOY AND INDIAN TRADER

Chapter 1

GO WEST, YOUNG MAN

The folk on the farm were unanimous in their declaration that anyone starting for New Orleans in the middle of the summer must be daft. It was their firm conviction that only people with their good sense disrupted would think of making such a hot journey, or would consider a further trip into Oklahoma or Texas at that season. However, none of them was able to shake my determination to start for the West, via Louisiana, hot weather or no.

I had been working on a stock farm that specialized in raising thoroughbred horses. The farm was located on the Pacelot River, in Polk County, North Carolina. While the work was very much to my liking, and all-around conditions most pleasant, I had, nevertheless, got the bug, or wanderlust, or whatever it was that made me decide to see the southwestern states. Looking back, I believe it was a post card which arrived from a former acquaintance, then located at Silver City, New Mexico, that kindled my first desires.

New Orleans, as had been predicted, was unbearably hot and humid. Just two days there satisfied me—I left the city before the end of the third day. In various towns, just as the notion took me, I stopped off and sampled the air, but did not make an extended stay anywhere until I arrived at Del Rio, Texas. There was no particular or outstanding attraction to keep me there except a vague and indefinable feeling that I had reached my destination.

Several weeks passed by in delicious loafing, riding saddle horses rented from a local livery stable, acquiring a Western outfit, such as a saddle and other riding equipment, cowboy boots, big Stetson hat, long-shanked spurs, and both a .45 Colt and a Winchester rifle. Then, one day, I met the foreman of a group of riders working an extended stretch of territory north and south of Eagle Pass. I asked him whether he could find a place for me in his outfit, telling him that while I had no experience as a cow hand, I was familiar with horses and riding. Thus, while still in my teens, I was hired as a rider for an El Paso meat-packing concern whose cattle ranged for hundreds of miles along the Rio Grande. My story begins with that period.

That was in the days when there were few barbed-wire fences in the western country, when the range was still open, when the term "rancher" did not include the owners of half-acre tracts, the breeders of chickens or rabbits. In those days one could ride a thousand miles or more and never leave the range, or encounter any obstruction, save those put there by nature to block the way.

When I say that the country was still unfenced I am not forgetting that the X I T Ranch in the Panhandle of Texas had crisscrossed much of its three-million-acre domain with barbed wire. That, however, was virtually the only exception, and since it applied to less than I per cent of the acreage contained in Arizona, New Mexico, and Texas, it left over 99 per cent of the range free and unfenced. And as a matter of historical fact, the X I T fences were down as often as they were up—thanks to the never-ending feud between the Eastern and English owners and the cowboys and ranchers of Texas and New Mexico.

It was a tough life, but not too strenuous, or so filled with hardships, as to have a brutalizing effect upon those who lived it in the open. We were not petted or pampered, and it was expected that every man should take care of himself. The one who could not measure up to the rough standards soon fell out of line; it was not an existence designed for mollycoddles. And although many of the "men" that rode the range were beardless youths, they proved just as self-sufficient and reliant as the old-timers who had grown gray in the saddle.

Hours were long, the work hard, the pleasures few and far between. Looking back upon those times, I find that the good things we enjoyed were largely of our own making. We did not know the artificial stimulus of ready-made diversion, such as theaters, movies, dances, radio entertainments, automobile tours, and all the other time-killing devices modern youth has flung at its head. In fact, most of that sort of entertainment had not yet been invented. When we desired frolic and diversion we had to create our own fun—there were no knobs to be turned, no tickets to be bought. Of course, our ideas of relaxation might not have met the present-day standards; I fear that sometimes we did behave somewhat unrestrainedly.

That makes me think of a little episode which took place in Ciudad Porfirio Diaz, where the unpleasant experience of seeing the inside of a Mexican jail marked the end of my riding for the El Paso meat packer.

In company with some half-dozen other riders I had celebrated the gathering of the clan in most of the *cantinas* in what was then known as Ciudad Porfirio Diaz, now called Piedras Negras, on the Mexican side of the Rio

Grande opposite the little Texas town of Eagle Pass. All of us had brought a fine, full-grown thirst for cold beer along, and soon we began to feel quite happy. The memory of hot, dusty, scorching days along the nearly dry Rio Grande passed into oblivion; the world was a soft-glowing, hazy-tinted place, whose immediate boundaries were the cool adobe walls of the *cantina*. Good will toward men filled and completely permeated our beings; no wonder we desired to share this pleasant mood with others.

Our endeavors to be good companions may have been too strenuous for the taste of the *cantinero* and his native customers; in any event our friendly overtures met only a cool reception, which prompted us to still greater efforts.

Possibly those earnest attempts proved a bit frightening to the proprietor and other guests of the *cantina*, for instead of appreciating our well-meant invitations to join in the celebration, made emphatic by shots of our six-shooters into the ceiling, our Mexican host and his compatriots remained aloof. Perhaps a messenger was sent posthaste to the *comandante* with tidings of an American invasion. Anyhow, of a sudden we were honored by a troop of Mexican cavalry encircling the *cantina*.

Did I say "honored"? That is a mistake, for this was *not* a guard of honor. Nor had the soldiers come to help us pour libations to Gambrinus. No, the sergeant in command asked us kindly to accompany him to headquarters, and while we declined at first, eventually we realized that it would be the right thing to accept the hospitable invitation.

As it was but a short distance from the *cantina* to our destination (no two points in Ciudad Porfirio Diaz can ever be very far apart!), and as the horses appeared to have grown in stature so as to make getting into the saddles a bit awkward, we walked. Our mounts were led by some troopers, while others of the soldiers gave us a helping hand, boosting not so much our spirits as our sagging bodies.

Very likely it was only a colonel who eventually interviewed us, but he may have been a general. Mexico, not only then but at all times, has had many generals; in any event, it would be more diplomtic to address even a mere *capitán* as *"Mi general"* than to commit the unpardonable offense of demoting (by inference) an officer in command of Republican forces by giving an improper salutation. Of course, our meeting with the military ruler of the city did not take place immediately. No, nothing ever happens as quickly as that in Mexico!

Upon our arrival at the *cárcel* we were led into a spacious, cool room. It was large, providing accommodation not only for all of us, but for some eight or ten Mexicans, a dozen narrow cots, several benches, tables, stools, a large earthen water jar, bone dry and without dipper or bail, bundles of straw matting, a heterogeneous lot of personal effects, evidently the property of our roommates, two mangy cur dogs, some chickens tied with strings to the table legs, and, a crowning joy, two guitars.

Extra-heavy adobe walls, an unusually high ceiling, and the absence of windows accounted for the pleasant coolness of this quarter. The only opening was the door, facing the inner court, or patio. It stood wide open, thus providing plenty of ventilation and fresh air. However, two soldiers were on guard, and they pointed out to us that it would be wisest not to create illusions in our minds that the friendly open door might be synonymous with unhindered egress. Knowing something about Mexican rurales and the *ley de fuga*, we heeded the admonition and kept to the shady interior of our quarter as if ringed in by a magic circle.

Nevertheless, we had no intention of allowing the change of scene to disrupt the happy fiesta too suddenly, so we persuaded two of our newly found Mexican friends to play their guitars in impromptu accompaniment to our songs. Some of the ballads were cowboy laments, sad, unintelligible, endless, and not suited to the ears of re-fined persons; others were the Mexican folk songs popular along the border, such as "*La Golondrina,*" "*La Paloma,*" and "*Donde Estás Corazón.*"

While the stimulant of *cerveza* cold from the tap was lacking, we did not acquit ourselves poorly on that account. In fact, we sang so feelingly and persistently that soon we were joined by the men already held in the *cárcel* when we came to swell the population of the jail. To the strains of the guitars we lifted our voices in ringing song, assuredly not giving a finished choral effect, but making generous use of barbershop chords. Loud and lusty welled the notes until finally the guards "begged" us to desist. To preserve the *entente cordiale,* we acquiesced in their demands, being rather weary by that time, and quite willing to rest awhile.

Since we had neglected to make arrangements for sup-per, nobody took the trouble to feed us. Even drinking water was at a premium in that institution, and we dis-covered that we wanted a great deal of the cooling mois-ture before the evening and night were over.

The guards seemed in doubt whether or not we should be entitled to use the highly odorous toilet facilities, evi-dently holding to the theory that as foreigners, and gringos at that, we had no claim to those privileges. It required a great deal of conversation and a special order from the noncommissioned officer on duty before we were allowed to satisfy the demands of nature. Even then we were not permitted to go without an escort, and only one of us at a time could pay a visit to the place provided by the military authorities, but surely never approved by any sanitary board.

By morning the confinement did not appear so much of a joke or cause for hilarity as it must have seemed during the previous afternoon and evening. Our little band was rather impatient to be gone; any other place would have looked better than the apparently steadily smaller-growing quarters facing the inner court of the jail. After another lengthy argument we were granted the special concession to send for coffee and *pan dulce*, paying several times the legitimate charge besides adding a generous tip.

An interminable wait ensued. Ages later, a slovenly fellow brought some stale sweet rolls and a liquid that he misnamed coffee, without sugar or milk. He carried it in an earthenware vessel, and in lieu of cups and saucers, furnished us with some grimy glasses. The thick, muddy coffee was bitter and sharp, but very hot, and it helped clear the cobwebs from our befuddled brains. We thought that soon after the sumptuous repast we should be brought to face the *comandante,* but several more hours elapsed before our group entered the audience hall.

The guns had been taken away from us when we "checked in." That was fortunate, for if we had retained possession of the artillery, bloodshed might have resulted. None of us had yet reached the age of discretion, or possessed any excessive quantity of restraint or patience. We had already arrived at the stage of making plans to overpower one or two of the guards and had debated on how best to relieve them of their arms when a sentry arrived and told us to follow him. He took us across the patio into another wing of the building and a surprisingly clean room, where we found ourselves facing the *comandante,* a heavy-set, very swarthy, and still unshaven officer.

Our determined looks and obviously impatient attitudes may have prompted him to make the examination or interview as short as possible. He told us in a few words that we had been "asked" to quarter in the *cárcel* overnight for our own protection. Of course, his only desire had been to act in our interest—he felt certain we would understand the concern for our well-being. Would we please tell him that we had not missed any comforts while in his care? At a signal from him, two of the soldiers returned our cartridge belts, holsters, and guns, making us feel more fully dressed and normal when we had buckled on those outward signs of free men.

Our horses had been placed with the mounts of the cavalrymen, and when we strolled to the stables to saddle up we found that the beasts had been well provided for. It took us but a few moments to get ready for departure, and, accompanied by ten men and a sergeant of the troop, we rode to the international bridge over the Rio Grande. The halfway mark across the stream divides the two republics—south of it lies Mexico, north is the territory of the United States. At that point the escort halted horses; with happy grins and bidding each other *vaya con Dios* and *hasta luego*, the cowpunchers and soldiers parted.

It was thus the *comandante* wound up the little international affair—leaving everybody happy and preventing serious trouble for all.

That was my last meeting with the gang with whom I had shared hard work and still more strenuous fun. Soon after this little episode I got to El Paso, headquarters of the outfit for which I worked, drew my accumulated pay, and quit. Mr. Nation, the boss, probably was used to such leave-takings, and did not ask why I desired to give up the job, or about my future plans. A puncher or fence rider or herder drawing his pay and quitting was nothing exciting. It would have been more unusual if that had not happened.

El Paso, more than forty years ago, was a great deal different from the modern city of today. It was a wild and wooly mining and cow town, no place for greenhorns, amateur gamblers, or similar innocents abroad. If anything in the way of free and unrestricted liberty or pleasure or license happened to be missing, the town across the river, Ciudad Juarez, could, and did, supply the want.

Booze flowed freely; generally speaking, gambling was not considered a vice, but a recognized institution; the red-light district existed as an acknowledged civic division; life was not deemed particularly important or held to be of excessive value. No concrete highways bisected the city and extended beyond its confines into the desert. There were no filling stations in arrogant possession of the best corner lots. The automobile had not yet begun to defile God's pure, fresh air with carbon monoxide fumes. Hitching racks decorated the front space of private dwellings, stores, banks, saloons, post office, and shops. Men rode into town aboard more or less "broken" broncos or on the high seats of big freight wagons. Sometimes one would see a dashing outfit—a fine team of nervous pintos prancing in front of a mountain buckboard loaded with a huge bedroll, camping paraphernalia, perhaps some mining tools, and, generally, a saddle tied atop the whole load. Every wheeled vehicle of that description carried water casks; most of them had grub boxes bolted to the rear end.

El Paso stands at the crossing of several of the oldest highways established by white men on this continent. It was visited by some of the earliest Spanish explorers: Cabeza de Vaca about 1532, Onate on his trip from

Mexico in 1598, and Mendoza in 1684, all came to the pass city. For long years it remained an unimportant village with a mere handful of inhabitants. Look up the statistics and you'll find that some sixty years ago, in 1880, the population was recorded as numbering only 736. By the end of the nineteenth century, however, it had started to rise, and continued to gain in population and importance. While the census of 1900 gave the population as a little short of sixteen thousand, ten years later El Paso boasted a citizenry of almost forty thousand. That figure was doubled by 1920, marking an enormous increase in just two decades. But the city had only just begun to find its stride, for in the census of 1930 the enumeration of inhabitants totaled 102,421, a truly astonishing gain in the barren desert country, formerly the abode only of wild life and Indians.

Today, El Paso is the biggest city between San Antonio and Los Angeles, an important trade center, doing a substantial business in copper, silver, lead, livestock, wool, hides, and many other commodities. Fort Bliss, adjacent to the city, is one of Uncle Sam's largest army posts. The tourists have discovered El Paso, although that is considered by some a doubtful blessing. During prohibition days, when many were suffering the pangs of the Noble Experiment, it was the mecca of thousands of thirsty ones who slaked their desire for something stronger than buttermilk in Ciudad Juarez.

Pancho Villa, of unsavory renown, made things interesting for the El Pasoans when he staged his battles for Juarez virtually in the front yard of the city. Incidentally, more than half of the population of El Paso is Mexican— the 1930 census gives their number as nearly sixty thousand.

Since the repeal of the dry amendment, Juarez has lost

much of the attraction it exerted previously, although tourists and others still go sight-seeing to attend the bull-fights, cockfights, and gaming rooms. Many gape at the "quaintnesses" of the public market or stare in an ill-bred manner at the natives, usually making derogatory re-marks about the different mode of life or the particular customs of the Mexicans.

My pay drawn, I wanted to taste the joys of freedom from long, hard, working hours that had been the routine while riding the range. But realization took away the charm that glittered in the anticipation, and I soon tired of wandering up one street and down another. I had rented a small room which, of course, was used only for sleeping. Having become accustomed to the sweep of illimitable expanses of prairie, it felt like being in jail to have to remain indoors for more time than was absolutely necessary. Therefore I took in the sights, such as they were, made frequent excursions to Juarez, watched with disgust a much-advertised bullfight, sat in the Plaza and listened to the Mexican band concert, slipped into the gambling halls and pitied the poor fools who lost piles of hard-earned money in a short time, joined the Salvation Army band in singing hymns, ate *chile con carne* and *frijoles* bought from a street vendor hawking his wares at a corner, and with each new day worked up a more consistently unbearable case of boredom.

There were several small restaurants in El Paso at that time, operated by Chinese, and in one of them I took my meals. The proprietor sold meal tickets and I invested in a pasteboard, entitling me to twenty-one meals—three full meals a day for a week. The regular price of the meals was fifteen cents each, but by buying a ticket I saved fifteen cents, obtaining a week's meals for three dollars. And those meals were man-sized feeds. They included soup, meat, vegetables, dessert, coffee, and all the bread and butter one wanted. Breakfast meant bacon or ham and eggs, a stack of flapjacks, butter, syrup, toast, coffee, tea or milk. A choice of several entrees permitted the selection of a preference, even to "flish on Flidays." Roast pork, roast beef, and veal were the regular standbys; lamb stew or mutton was held in general disfavor. Chicken appeared on the bill of fare quite frequently. The "vittles" had to be good, because the customers, including miners, freighters, cowpunchers, surveyors, railroad men and other hardy characters, expressed themselves freely and fluently if any place failed to provide the right sort of grub.

For a change I would visit Eggers' saloon, where good beer and fine sandwiches could be had. There a motley crowd of ranchers, miners, cowpunchers and others would gather, as well as many businessmen of the town. A certain atmosphere pervaded the air, bespeaking friendliness and good cheer. The drinking in that place was moderate, the food of excellent quality. Old-timers will remember the little, half-concealed entrance in one corner of what in later years has been transformed into a brilliantly lighted movie house, flanked by a large department store and hotel building.

In Henry Beach's Mexican curio store I purchased a pair of beautifully made Mexican spurs—hand-wrought steel with exquisitely inlaid silverwork. The price was fifty-seven dollars, but the fact that this sum represented nearly two months pay could not keep me from acquiring the beauties. Of course I already owned a pair of good, hand-forged spurs, but this other pair simply obsessed me from the moment I spied them resting upon a piece of wine-colored velvet in the show window of the shop.

For two days I exercised every bit of my will power and

resisted the temptation, but my first walk each morning was past the shop, to ascertain that none had found the treasure and made off with what I had come to consider my own particular property. On the morning of the third day I visited the store before the place opened. When the door was unlocked, I entered the shop and demanded the spurs, simultaneously pulling out of my pocket the money to pay for them. I had inquired as to their sales price when I first saw them, so I did not have to find out just how much they were to cost. Extravagant, wasn't it? But didn't somebody at some time say something about selling half your loaf of bread to buy hyacinths?

I put them on, then strolled to breakfast, the clank and jingle of the newly acquired *espuelas* the sweetest music in my ears! Proud? Why, I would not have swapped that pair of spurs for a dozen cows!

Loafing is much more tiresome and wearying than hard work, and unrestrained leisure palls quickly. The pleasure of being one's own boss, with nothing to do, soon becomes vapid; mind and body crave occupation and exercise. This I learned after less than three weeks of unrestricted laziness. I got so restless and fidgety that nothing would do but I had to go to the feed stables and corrals where freighters left their wagons, punchers put up their horses, and ranchers and stockmen were wont to gather.

There I listened to ranch gossip, news of the range, reports of roundups, cattle movements, steer loadings, and other bits of information pertaining to the life in the open. I asked a number of men about employment, but it was nearly a week later before one bowlegged fellow told me that possibly I might get a job in Carrizozo, New Mexico. He had heard that a rancher there wanted a few extra hands to help round up horses and cattle in the Capitan Range.

Chapter 2

WE RIDE TO NEW MEXICO

My horse had been enjoying a fine rest during the time I lazied about the city. Of course, every day I took him for a ride, but the rest of the time he spent dreaming in the corral, palling with chance friends just come from the range, and "eating his head off" in the barn at night. Now he, as much as I, was ready for work. Thus, bright and early on the morning after I heard the news that meant the possibility of another job, we started away.

Back of the saddle I carried a light blanket roll holding some extra socks, a change of underwear, my "other" shirt, shaving kit, toothbrush and comb, and a box of .45 caliber cartridges. The outside of the roll was protected by a slicker, part of every range rider's outfit. My clothing conformed to the typical getup of the puncher; high-heeled boots, Levi Strauss overalls, chaps, flannel shirt, vest, and tall-crowned Stetson hat. A cartridge belt, well filled with forty-fives, and the Colt in its holster, completed the ensemble. Without gun and long-shanked spurs I would have felt undressed, habit becomes so firmly fixed.

Seven days were required, riding leisurely from morn-

ing till evening, to complete the trip to Carrizozo, a distance now covered by the automobile in a few hours. But
Jack and I had a better time of it than the speedster of
today, rushing through the country at fifty or sixty miles
an hour. We saw things and enjoyed thrills that must
forever remain foreign to the hurrying motorist behind
the wheel of his car. There were many miles when we
had the whole world to ourselves. Peace and quiet and
beauty all about us—nothing to mar the perfection of that
portion of God's world where the Creator lavished in His
most generous mood. That may sound strange to the ears
of the traveler accustomed to viewing the "barren desert"
from Pullman windows, or from a rushing motorcar.
Nevertheless, it's true; the great Southwest of our United
States comprises a region of more varied beauty and
scenic grandeur and inimatable and unique "settings"
than any other portion of the earth.

I know whereof I speak, for I spent many years wandering over this world of ours. England, Holland, Germany,
France, the Riviera, are not strange places to me; I traversed Switzerland and Italy. I am familiar with the rugged
beauties of the Scotch Highlands, and with the attractions
of the Selkirk Range and the Fraser Canyon country.

Four years of my life were passed in the Far East and
Malaysia; Egypt saw me, the Suez Canal, and various other
parts of northern Africa. Extended trips took me to the
Azores, the Canaries, and into explorations of some three
thousand miles of the West African coast countries.

I sojourned in Central America, and during two years
lived in Cuba, visiting virtually every city, town, and
village of the republic, from Pinar del Rio to Oriente, and
including the Isle of Pines. Every one of the forty-eight
states of our Union, as well as the District of Columbia,
have been traveled and viewed by me, and I know Canada

from British Columbia and the shores of the Pacific to the Atlantic. Twice I availed myself of opportunities to visit the Hawaiian Islands, and many trips were made by me into various parts of Mexico.

Let California's native sons and daughters sing paeans to their state, and Florida brag about palms and sunshine and climate. Let North Carolina boast of the wonders of the Blue Ridge Mountains, Michigan and Wisconsin praise their lakes, New Hampshire eulogize the White Mountains, and every other state laud the advantages or beauties of its own domain: I still persist in doing homage to the glories of the Southwest.

Others, better qualified than I, have tried to paint word pictures of my beloved Southwest; each and all failed in the attempt. Neither words nor pictures, no matter how skilfully woven together, can make one understand or see the incomparable splendor of the Great American Desert. The mind cannot visualize the glorious upheaval of the canyon country of the Colorado and the San Juan, the stupendous spectacle of the gash we know as the Grand Canyon, the breath-taking sweep of the sage-covered mesa lands, the inspiring parade of mighty trees on the Kaibab Plateau, or the wind-and-water-eroded sandstone formation.

There, the ever-changing lights and shadows are the despair of anyone who attempts to perpetuate them in colors upon canvas or describe them on paper. How can one explain the brilliant sunrises, the riotous sunsets, the ever-changing play of massed clouds, the magnificence of vivid rainbows against a background of jet-black or dark purplish-blue ranges or yawning, cavernous canyons?

No language can describe adequately the taste of the air, as exhilarating as champagne, the clarity of the dust-free ether that brings out in sharp relief every object within many miles, the unsullied atmosphere, free from smoke, smells, uncontaminated by humans, serene in its freedom from industrial contacts. Only the palette and paintbrush of the Almighty, the power of Omnipotence and the wisdom of the Supreme Architect could produce those wonders that will forever belittle even the mightiest efforts of the human race to depict or imitate.

On our ride we passed through Alamogordo, where one strikes out into the pine-clad mountains of Cloudcroft. We also came through Three Rivers, where in later years Albert B. Fall, Secretary of the Interior in President Harding's cabinet, established the headquarters of his large ranch.

Travel was light on the road we followed northward. Occasionally we would meet freighters or cowboys, and several times we enjoyed the company of riders going for a distance in our direction.

Aloof Indians, members of the Mescalero Apaches, passed on pinto ponies without giving us a glance. They belonged to the tribe that was known for its savagery and cruelty, and during many years were a much-feared scourge of the country. However, they were peaceful now, and no longer constituted a menace.

Thus traveling in a leisurely manner, upon the seventh day after leaving El Paso, Jack and I approached the town we had come to find.

Carrizozo proved to be a small place, in no way different from scores of other towns of the Southwest of that period. A scattering of adobe houses, some few frame buildings, a large general store, the Carrizozo Trading Company, a bank, post office, several saloons and gambling places, the depot with the freight house adjoining, loading pens and corrals for livestock, a lumberyard, feed stable, and a small hotel, which differed from the other dwellings not in general outward appearance but in size only, made up the physical aspect of the town.

Alongside the railroad station building a well spouted mineral water. According to local information it possessed all the constituent parts of one of the world's most famous spas, the one in Carlsbad. It was claimed that the analysis of the Carrizozo water proved an exact duplication of the European watering place's springs. Both were said to contain the same ingredients, and the respective percentage of salts, sulphur, and mineral contents were declared to be identical. Nothing was told about the *odor* of the Carlsbad water, but the local product smelled strongly of overripe eggs or putrefaction in the nth degree.

Not wanting to appear narrow-minded or unappreciative of God's gifts, I tasted the water, my nose closed tightly between the thumb and finger of the hand not holding the cup. I am not, by nature or inclination, a doubting Thomas, and I was, therefore, quite willing to admit that water smelling and tasting so powerfully must or ought to have some strong influence. However, I cannot say whether any such influence would be exerted for good or for evil. I was *more* than satisfied with just sampling it. Still, it is possible that there are many people who hanker for that sort of thing. Those who do probably come to relish the mineral water of Carrizozo and other springs like it; I can imagine that the habit might get an unbreakable hold on a person. Once addicted to that particular kind of water, it is easy to understand how all other springs and wells must taste insipid and flat.

Jack, evidently belonging to an orthodox strain of horses, refused to follow my example. He sniffed at the water, but declined to drink. This despite the fact that he was thirsty, for soon afterward he drank long and heartily from the trough in the stable corral. Maybe the finer or more sensitive animal instincts told him things that were hidden from me. In any event I consoled myself with the theory that failure to take advantage of the opportunity constituted Jack's loss, not mine.

It was late afternoon when we rambled into Carrizozo. Inquiry from some gentlemen of leisure near the station brought the information that the ranch of my boss-to-be was but a short distance from town. After watering Jack at the stable, we continued our trek and arrived at the ranch about suppertime. There was no design or premeditation in this—it simply happened—but it would have been altogether strange and possibly unprecedented if we had reached there at any hour except just at mealtime! In my years of experience in the southwestern range and ranch country I never knew personally, or heard indirectly, of the arrival of punchers at any ranch except at about the time for the dinner bell to ring.

Conditions change; many of the good old institutions have been uprooted by the march of time. But I am telling of the days that did not know of hobo-tourists in antiquated cars of uncertain vintage, of dude ranches, concrete highways, and tens of thousands of deaths annually from motorcar accidents, of radios, talkies, and the many other "blessings" that complicate our present mode of life. Then, riding the "grub line" was still an honored custom and the prerogative of the rider temporarily without a job. Any cow hand, puncher, rider, was welcome to food for himself and feed for his mount, always with the tacit understanding that the privilege would not be abused.

As we rode into the large yard of the McDonald ranch, a green oasis by virtue of the fine group of cottonwood trees encircling it, I met several punchers going toward the bunkhouse. One stopped long enough to tell me to

put my horse in the corral and come over to the bunkhouse to wash and get ready for supper. Then he re-
joined his companions. He took it for granted that I was
hungry; his invitation came as unconsciously as his breath.
None made any pretexts in those days: here was a man,
dusty and tired from a long ride, so what more natural
than to ask him to share the meal?

Soon Jack was made comfortable. Wise old fellow, he
knew, intuitively, that our destination had been reached
and that this was not just another one-night stop. After
being unsaddled, watered at the trough, and turned
loose in the corral, he first indulged in a luxurious roll
in the soft earth, pulverized by the pounding of thousands of hoofs. Slowly he rose to his feet, shook himself
thoroughly, then approached the group of horses already
in the corral in a leisurely and dignified manner. He was
tired and hungry, which gave him an excuse to skip lightly
over the matter of presentation and introduction; he satisfied himself with merely going through the motions, so to
speak. At one side of the enclosure Jack discovered a long
crib filled with sweet-smelling prairie hay, and in just a
moment or two he was munching away very contentedly.

The horse taken care of, I walked over to the bunkhouse.

Beside the door stood a low bench with pails of water,
several tin washbasins, and some pieces of soap in up-
turned can lids; from nails in the wall dangled two large
towels of the endless, roller variety. I classified their color
as dark white; there was evidence that both had been
quite popular, and it was difficult to find a patch large
enough to dry hands and face after performing the ritual
of washing.

It was a wonder that I live to tell of these things for I
must have been exposed to many millions of germs from

day to day, what with using community towels and public drinking cups. Being blissfully ignorant of the fact probably kept me from falling victim to the lurking dangers. Or was it the outdoor life, with a generous exposure to the sun's rays, that immunized us? For the cowpunchers were not afflicted in any physical manner, rather the contrary: all boasted of splendid health, good digestion, freedom from ailments, sound sleep and steady nerves.

At the bunkhouse all ears were tuned up, listening for the supper bell. We did not have to wait long, for presently the cook's helper, a Mexican youth, began hammering an old iron wagonwheel rim that hung suspended between a frame of upright and crossed poles. That produced a sound more nearly resembling a fire alarm than a gentle mess call, but no other noise could have served the purpose more admirably. We trooped over to the cook shack to seat ourselves about the long table. Plates, cups, and knives and forks had already been laid; teaspoons stood in the center of the table in a large glass jar originally meant to hold sugar. There were also oil and vinegar cruets, several bottles of catchup, two enormous sugar bowls, salt and pepper shakers, yes, even a thick whisky glass filled with toothpicks. How the boys on this ranch were pampered!

The legends surrounding the figure of Paul Bunyan tell of the fabulous repasts consumed by the loggers of that famous woodsman. Well, maybe so, and maybe not. To me it seemed as if the meals served by the cook on that Carrizozo ranch could hold their own with the best that were ever reported. There was not only abundance but also quality. Too, we enjoyed fine variety insofar as it was possible to effect dietary changes in a country many miles removed from the principal sources of supplies. In my time I have had meals in many cow camps, ranch cookhouses, and from chuck wagons, but none of them offered better fare or more variety than did the ranch where I found myself after I landed in Carrizozo.

Generally supper constituted the big meal of the day. Dinner, at noon, did not, as a rule, see many of the boys around the table. Most of them were far away from the ranch at that hour and they did not return until late in the afternoon. By evening, however, the "hands" were assembled in force, and the maestro of the kitchen played to a full audience.

Not only on the McDonald ranch, but on every ranch I ever visited, meat and beans were the most often served staple items of food. To them should be added bread, generally in the form of hot bread, baked for the particular meal either in the stove or in one of the heavy, cast-iron "Dutch" ovens. Too, there was always coffee, but never fresh milk! The range might be crowded with thousands upon thousands of cows, many of them with calves and consequently giving milk, but the lacteal fluid that we used in our coffee came from a tin can.

Eggs were an almost unknown luxury on the cattle and horse ranches of the southwestern range lands. Speaking generally, it would be safe to bet that nine times out of ten a cowpuncher's first order upon entering a restaurant would be "ham and aiggs," something he probably could not indulge in again until his next trip to town.

Breakfast did not include grapefruit or toast; those predilections of a more effete East had not influenced the still-rugged West. Before starting on a day's work that might easily include ten to twelve hours of hard riding, the puncher would fortify the inner man by eating a substantial breakfast of meat, potatoes, flapjacks drowned in syrup, some slices of bread and butter and jam, and by drinking an indefinite number of cups of coffee. In lieu of flapjacks, the men would as often as not sop up syrup with chunks of bread. Inelegant, it's true, but this provided a fine substitute for after-dinner dishes and satisfied the natural craving for sweets.

In the matter of desserts every ranch cook was severely handicapped, seldom being able to obtain eggs, fresh milk, or cream, those three ingredients essential to many of the more intricate preparations with which good housewives wind up their dinners. Nevertheless, most of the cooks that I knew could (and did) make such desserts as puddings in various forms, sweet rolls, pies filled with cooked, dried fruits (prunes, raisins, desiccated apples and pears), or a sort of plain tart filled with jam. That, however was the exception rather than the rule; ordinarily, the meal was considered complete without any dessert.

Of course, all this was in the long ago. The Hollywood cowboy, the imitation wrangler singing hillbilly songs and playing a mandolin, and the "dudes" of both sexes had not yet put in an appearance; it all happened before the flowering of guest ranches featuring electric refrigeration, outdoor swimming pools, and cocktail bars.

After supper we sauntered back to the bunkhouse. Before going inside I took another look at Jack, who was too busy with his own affairs to waste any attention upon me. So I joined the men and presently found an opening permitting me to sound out the foreman about the possibilities of a job with his outfit. Not that I came right out with the question, for that would have been too crude. No, I began by telling him of the trip from El Paso to Carrizozo. He was interested to hear of the water supply at various places, the condition of the range, how the stock looked, what and whom I had met and seen along the route. He complimented me upon Jack, "reckoning" that he was a good horse. When I volunteered the information that I had been riding for old man Nation, he warmed up; he happened to be personally acquainted with my former boss.

"Will you be riding far?" came the guarded inquiry. I admitted, without envincing too much enthusiasm, that it would suit my purposes very well to remain for a while, to *rest* my horse, provided I could find something to do "somewhere in this neighborhood." After a short pause, when he was apparently lost in thought and meditation, he gave voice to his "belief" that perhaps the old man might take on an extra hand to help the boys for a few days.

"I'll let you know in the morning," closed that part of our conversation.

Not one word had been said about credentials, recommendations, pay, former jobs, union affiliations, or any other matter that would be discussed between worker and employer nowadays. He had watched me riding in and from that short observation was satisfied that I knew the work so far as horses were concerned. My information that I had been holding a job under old man Nation, and the description of my ride from El Paso to the McDonald ranch in stockmen's terms, simply confirmed his already-formed opinion. Where I was born, which school, if any, I had attended, other qualifications I might possess, yes, even my name and origin, did not interest him. Nobody ever asked questions of a strictly private nature; most men would resent such prying in an unpleasant manner; too, there were many who could not afford to have others become unduly inquisitive about their personal history.

I have known many men by their first name only, and during our associations they were Jim, or Bill, or Fred to me, and by the same sign they knew me as Joe, or "Red," never learning or caring to know my family name. They would spend several months with an outfit and then drift along. When they were ready to leave, the foreman simply computed their "time" and paid them off in cash, or had the boss draw a check. It was nothing unusual to hear the boss or the foreman say: "Now let's see, it was about March when you started with us, wasn't it, Fred?" and to receive the confirmation or a correction from the one interrogated. Then came the computation of the pay, from which would be deducted any advances made. There was no weekly or fortnightly or monthly settlement. Payday came when the puncher saddled his horse and hit the trail for some other place. Any money he might have drawn before then and charged against his account would be deducted from the total due him at the time of reckoning.

An unusually obnoxious, harsh-voiced alarm clock roused me from sound slumber. It was not more than half past three o'clock, still completely dark, and decidedly chilly. My bunk did not know that such things as Beautyrest mattresses or inner-coil springs existed. It was just a space in which to sleep. A couple of folded quilts, through long usage padded down to the thickness of the felt in one's hat, took the place of springs and mattress. To offset that, the boards underneath the quilts had to be imagined resilient—they were *soft* pine! However, a tired body, weary muscles, healthy nerves, and a well-filled stomach, plus youth that makes light of discomfort, had granted to that narrow, hard bunk all the attributes of the downy couch of luxury, and to me restful, regenerating sleep.

All about me in the darkness were to be heard the stretchings of bodies, the cracking of muscles, prodigious yawns, and the many other queer noises that accompany the waking moments of the human animal. Someone struck a match and put light to the wick of an old battered kerosene lamp whose rays caused the obscurity to take on a still deeper hue. Gradually, however, everybody slipped from between the blankets and began dressing. The absence of pajamas, shower baths, and valet service facilitated the process. Like most of the other men, I slept in my underwear; some of the men had not even removed their overalls but had been satisfied merely to open the button at the waistband. To slip into boots, buckle on spurs, put on the flannel shirt, and to splash some icy water over face and hands constituted the toilet and dressing.

From the cookshack shone the lights of several lamps, inviting all hands to breakfast. But before going there, every man got some oats from a large bin in the stable, halfway filling a nose bag, and put this on the horse he meant to ride that day. Invariably a puncher would attend to his horse before thinking of his own needs.

Drones have no place in the life on a cattle ranch, so when everybody got up, I, too, arose and joined the men in their chores. While we were dressing, the foreman asked me in a casual manner whether I would like to "lend a hand" that day, which question I answered in a cheerful affirmative. He then suggested that I let my own horse rest and take, instead, one of the ranch horses, designating a certain roan gelding as a good mount for me. So I took two nose bags, one for the roan and the other for Jack. After breakfasting in a manner that would have amazed persons not accustomed to range life, we repaired to the corrals and removed the now empty nose bags, watered the horses, completed our dressing by donning chaps and guns, saddled up, and within a few minutes started out.

Still a half hour before five o'clock, our little group of

six or seven men left the ranch. Dawn had commenced to dispel the grayness of the last remaining remnants of night, a thin wedge of anemic daylight protruded over the eastern horizon. The air was crystalline, sharp, biting. Faces and hands tingled under the numbing impact of the rarefied air, chilled in that high altitude during the night hours. The horses were full of pep, prancing and champing against the bits. They would become much more manageable before returning to the home corral! Then Aurora emerged victorious once again, resistlessly pursuing her heavenly course and definitely routing the forces of night. Her golden arrows shot through space, coloring the universe with flame; everywhere was brightness, cheer, light. Glorious, sunlit day had arrived.

Almost simultaneously with the coming of warm sunlight, the earlier numbness dropped from us like the old skin from a snake. No longer cold, we became cheerful, yes, happy to the point of boisterousness. Our tongues felt unleashed, our thinking machines functioned, jokes flew back and forth, we were high-spirited, gallant adventurers with not a care in the world. Our work was but fun, hardships and dangers to come of no importance whatever, the present the most desirable existence ever known to man.

This is not intended to be an exhaustive or complete history of cowboy life and therefore a recital of the less-important details pertaining to the work performed by us from day to day is omitted. The routine did not vary greatly, our daily tasks were of an almost uniform sameness. We rode over a great expanse of country, including level plains, broken canyon terrain, the hills of the Capitan Range, and the malpais, a long, wide stretch of jagged, sharp-edged, dangerous lava rocks. Only in a few places can one cross that terrible piece of badlands, and it is next to impossible to drive out stock that strays into the maze and gets lost in the infernal breaks.

The boss and foreman had made their plans to shift some cattle from one section of the range to another. That sounds fairly easy, something like transferring docile cows from one pasture into the adjoining one, but on the Western ranges, with wild stock as principal actors, the change from the accustomed grazing grounds to new pastures develops into a job requiring plenty of stamina and patience from horses and riders. Range cattle, habituated to their particular stamping grounds, do not relish being dislodged. They have decided feelings in the matter and seldom fail to show their displeasure over the eviction in many ways.

The usual procedure follows this routine:

The cowboys, after locating the cattle, spread out fanwise and start to drive the small bunches and single animals toward a predetermined point, there to form one large group. Thus concentrated, the herd is moved in a body toward the new feeding grounds. To this well-intentioned program some peevish old cow may object and at the first opportunity make a wild dash, breaking away from the nucleus of the herd, her only impulse to remain on the old range. The cowboy chases after her, again putting Bossy upon the right course. While he is busy doing that, some young steers may have taken a notion to deploy to the opposite side, and they, in turn, must be driven back. In the course of ten miles or less, a cowboy may actually cover twenty miles or more by zigzagging back and forth. That is especially strenuous in hilly or broken country, and hard on the horses.

Slowly, but inevitably, the cattle are pushed farther and farther away from the old range, and with the steadily increasing distance they become more manageable and tractable. The riders, forming a semicircle, shaped like the spokes of a wheel, draw ever closer together, toward the hub as it were. As the circle contracts, they are able to assist each other more effectively in keeping the bunch together and in moving it in the desired direction.

It is relatively infrequent that any serious accidents happen in this kind of work. A horse may stumble in loose rock, or step into a prairie-dog hole, or slither over shale or other slippery, flat pieces of stone, but grave mishaps form the exceptions. Of course, horses do break legs and riders suffer fractures or other accidents, but considering the nature of the work, the ratio of injuries sustained is very small. Too, despite the many charges and counter-charges amid the sea of waving horns, it is extremely rare that either cowboy or horse are gored. Equally scarce are snake bites, although several varieties of rattlers infest the country. In a number of years passed in the south-western states, I never heard of a man's death due to snake bite, and of only a few cases, relatively speaking, of authentic bites. There has always been much more potential danger in the commonly accepted "cure" for snake bites, good old John Barleycorn, than in the poison sacs of Mr. and Mrs. Diamondback or Sidewinder.

The extra work on the McDonald ranch, to which I owed my job, came to an end after about three weeks; once more I was "at liberty." Incidentally, my boss, Mr. William C. McDonald, later became the first governor of New Mexico by popular election, running on the Democratic ticket. Previously, before New Mexico achieved statehood, the territory's governors were appointees of the President. And while on the subject of state affairs, a few paragraphs of interest are added about New Mexico. To many Americans this state has remained, even in these days of rapid and easy travel, terra incognita.

Chapter 3

HISTORY AND GEOGRAPHY

We are prone to commence our American history with the *Mayflower* and the coming of the Pilgrims to Plymouth Rock. We forget, or are ignorant of the fact, that almost a hundred years before that event on the bleak New England coast, Spanish priests and explorers were already at work in what we now know as New Mexico and Arizona. Nearly a century before Jamestown, one Spanish adventurer, Alvar Nunez Cabeza de Vaca, who was shipwrecked on the Florida coast, wandered into New Mexico. Some years after (1538), Fray Marcos de Niza came far enough north to get a distant view of the walls of the pueblo of Zuni, one of the legendary Seven Cities of Cibola.

Excepting Florida, New Mexico is the oldest state name in the United States. It was first mentioned in 1583 in a narrative of the Spanish discoverer Antonio de Espejo. For hundreds of years the term New Mexico embraced a tremendously large territory, taking in all parts of the continent north of Old Mexico and situated between the Pacific Ocean and the Mississippi River!

Florida, at that time, meant the country beyond the

Mississippi, eastward. One hundred and sixteen years after Espejo first brought the name New Mexico to Europe, on Sauerman's map of North America (published in Bremen in 1699), New Mexico extends from the Gulf of California to the Mississippi, Florida ending at that river. Santa Fe is indicated on the map as the most important place in the New World if we judge by the heavy type used for printing the name. Actually, Santa Fe has remained the seat of the New Mexico government for more than three hundred years. It is the oldest of all the capitals of the states of the Union, far ahead in years over Boston, its nearest rival in age.

However, Santa Fe was not the first capital in New Mexico. Nearly a quarter of a century before the Pilgrims landed on Plymouth Rock, Don Juan de Onate, who may be considered the real conqueror of New Mexico, led the first Spanish settlers into the territory and established the first capital of the new province at San Gabriel, on the Rio Grande, at the mouth of the Chama, northwest of the present Santa Fe. He came at the head of a great wagon train, with several hundred colonists, large herds of sheep, cattle, horses, pigs, and other domestic animals. The beautiful Espanola Valley became their home—there they established themselves, forming the first permanent settlement of whites in the territory. That was in 1598. The capital remained at San Gabriel for over a decade.

Boston, Smithfield, or York may satisfy our Anglo-Saxon taste for town names, but the sturdy newcomers from Hispania had different notions. Nothing so prosaic as a one- or two-syllable word to designate an outpost of the far-flung Spanish empire. Consequently, at the christening, it was *La Villa Real de la Santa Fe de San Francisco de Assisi* (The Royal City of the Holy Faith of St. Francis of Assisi) that became the high-sounding name of the capital founded sometime between 1610 and 1612 by the third governor of New Mexico under the Spanish crown, Don Pedro de Peralta. Since that time, for nearly three and one-half centuries, Santa Fe has remained New Mexico's seat of government under the flags of Spain, Mexico, the Confederacy, and the United States.

Ten priests, Franciscan friars, were with Onate and his band when they established themselves in New Mexico, and without delay they began the work of Christianizing the Indians. About twenty years later, in 1621, Father Alonzo Benavides and twenty-six new friars arrived to augment the original group of missionaries. From that time dates the great era of church building and the expansion of missions in New Mexico, antedating the celebrated California missions by one hundred and fifty years.

Some of the missions built during that period are now total ruins while others are standing and in use to this day. Among the latter is famous Mission San Miguel de Santa Fe, whose foundations were laid in 1621. It is claimed that San Miguel is the oldest mission in the United States. It is an eloquent witness of history, rich in tradition, and has mellowed through more than three centuries. The colorful romance of the conquistadores was played around its walls; many tragic events took place within the range of its silver-tongued bells. The prayers of the faithful still rise from between its heavy walls of sun-baked adobe and native plaster.

History records that the labors of the Spanish priests did not produce the desired results, for in the summer of 1680 the rebellious Pueblo Indians joined forces and in a surprise uprising took the Spaniards unaware. Reinforcements for the Spanish garrison had been requested from Mexico, but they failed to arrive. Food was scarce and when, after the siege had lasted a few days, the Indians succeeded in cutting off the water supply of the city, the position of the whites became critical. There were but few settlers, scattered over a wide area. Communication was almost completely disrupted. Those considerations, and the fact that the Indians were daily gaining in numbers, prompted the Spaniards to make one final onslaught on their besiegers. They drove them back, but had to abandon the city. The fugitives made their escape down the Rio Grande, fleeing toward the more densely settled sections of Mexico.

Those missionaries hapless enough to fall into the hands of the enraged Indians became martyrs to their faith. Churches and missions were destroyed, and in a twinkling the patient work that had taken the best part of a century was wiped out. Christianity went into the discard; medicine men and the tribal religion once again held sway.

For a dozen years subsequent to the revolt, the Indians kept the mastery of the captured city and repulsed the various attempts by the Spaniards to reconquer New Mexico. During the time of the Indian occupancy of Santa Fe the province had been governed, nominally, from El Paso del Norte. It was not until after Don Diego de Vargas, in 1692, was made captain general and governor of New Mexico, that the reconquest of the province met with success.

The Stars and Stripes were raised over Santa Fe when General Stephen Watts Kearny and his troops took possession of the city in 1846. The place had been abandoned by Governor Manuel Armijo— this was at the time of the Mexican War. Santa Fe was occupied by Confederates shortly after the outbreak of the Civil War when General H. H. Sibley and his Texans defeated Union soldiers at the battle of Valverde and gained the upper hand in New Mexico as far as the old capital. However, the stay of the Confederates in Santa Fe was of short duration. Union forces, augmented by volunteers from Colorado, battled the Confederates in Glorieta Pass and after two days of fighting won a decisive victory. The Texans retreated from New Mexico and since then there has not been a change in the political status of Santa Fe.

But while there is no question about New Mexico being one of our United States, it would not be hard to conjure up the days of the dons when reading the names of counties, cities, towns, rivers, mountain ranges, and other geographical divisions. Listen to them: Valencia, San Juan, Bernalillo, Rio Arriba, Colorado, Pajarito, Trujillo, Las Vegas, Portales, Villanueva, Gallinas, Rancho del Rio Grande, San Cristoval, Sangre de Cristo, Hondo, Las Cruces, and hundreds of other designations that are pure Spanish. The city directories of such places as Albuquerque, Raton, and Gallup contain many Spanish listings, while in scores upon scores of smaller towns the entire population is of Spanish or Mexican origin and the prevailing language is the Mexican version of the old Spanish mother tongue.

It is a long span from the time of the expeditions of Francisco Vásquez de Coronado, who came from Spain to Mexico in 1535 and in 1539 was appointed governor of Nueva Galicia, then embracing all of New Mexico and extending indefinitely northward. Cabeza de Vaca had reported about the Seven Cities of Cibola where, he claimed, gold waś used for street paving. Friar Marcos de Niza corroborated those fantastic fables, and Coronado began to investigate. He crossed and recrossed this area in several expeditions, and in the winter of 1541 established a camp just north of Albuquerque. One of his trips took him as far as the plains of Kansas; all these tremendous efforts and privations in the elusive quest for the golden-paved Cibola. More than four hundred years have passed since then—Santa Fe, above all, still mirrors some of the glamorous past.

True, it is modernized. There are neon signs and gas stations, concrete sidewalks and streets, modern hotels, and a commercialized Indian "handmade" industry. Pottery making and weaving still retain some individuality, but Navajo silver jewelry is turned out as if by an assembly line, horribly stereotyped.

The Indians bring into the stores of Santa Fe traders large quantities of pottery; the two most popular kinds are produced in the Santa Clara and San Ildefonso pueblos. The Santa Clara variety is particularly striking, being entirely black, and possessing a beautiful gloss or sheen.

Weaving is practiced by the inhabitants of the various near-by Indian towns and to a considerable extent in Santa Fe itself. The principal output is of the so-called Chimayo type, produced on perpendicular looms. The first weavers using the Chimayo loom were members of the above-mentioned band of settlers under Onate who brought with them that particular style of weaving. They, in turn, had imported the knowledge of the craft from Europe, by way of the Spanish colonies in Mexico. The Pueblo Indians adopted this style and use it to this day.

However, the loom was known to prehistoric peoples. A product of it, a scarf woven from dog hair, has been found in the ruins of an ancient pueblo and is now in the possession of the Laboratory of Anthropology at Santa Fe. It is estimated that this scarf was woven nearly two thousand years ago.

Just a few miles from Santa Fe are the famous Tiffany

turquoise mines, formerly one of the principal sources of the much-valued stone. Turquoise (French for Turkish stone), is supposed to have been so named because it was first introduced into Europe by way of Turkey. The southwestern portion of the United States furnishes large quantities of this lovely semiprecious gem stone; turquoise of fine quality is produced in mines in Arizona, Colorado, the Los Cerrillos Mountains in New Mexico, and in Nevada.

Most of the southwestern Indians have a pronounced regard for turquoise; the Navajos, especially, value it highly and make lavish use of it in their handmade silver ornaments.

Although greatly reduced in area by the formation of the various states that now make up the vast domain formerly included in and known under the name of New Mexico, the state still ranks with the largest in the United States, more than 120,000 square miles being contained within its boundaries. It is nearly square in outline, measuring, roughly, 350 miles from east to west, or from south to north. It is the next to the youngest of the forty-eight states, barely ahead of Arizona, the baby: the proclamation admitting New Mexico to statehood was signed by President Taft on January 6, 1912.

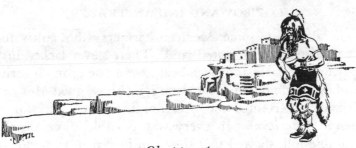

Chapter 4

ALBUQUERQUE

When my job on the McDonald ranch came to an end, and without any immediate prospects for finding similar employment in or near Carrizozo, I decided to visit Albuquerque and thus carry out a plan I had been cherishing for some time. Jack, after his long rest, was more than willing to hit the trail, and one fine, bright morning found us on our way.

To avoid the lava beds (malpais) we followed the Southern Pacific's line of rails northward until we had cleared those terrible obstacles. Then we pointed our course in a westerly direction, following dim trails through the Sierra Oscura, until eventually we reached the Rio Grande. Thence we had no trouble finding or keeping to the trail; we could not lose our way because we simply followed the river's course upward to reach our goal.

However, where it had taken but seven days to cover the distance between El Paso and Carrizozo, this ride consumed nine days. True, we did not hurry; traveling along the banks of the river was agreeable. At the coming of each night we managed to find shelter and sustenance, generally with some Mexican farmers who cultivated small patches of irrigated land. There never lacked lush pasture for Jack, and since beans were one of my favorite dishes, I did not have to go hungry. Those good Mexican friends entertained me heartily; their best was for *el Senor Americano*. In every way possible those simple, humble folk showed that they considered it an honor to have me as their guest. What more natural than that Jack and I proceeded leisurely?

It was impossible not to notice one obvious fact: the general excellence of the house and other property of the village priest, *el cura*, in the small settlements through which we traveled. Invariably he lived in the best-looking place of the *pueblocito*, surrounded by flowers, a garden, fruit and shade trees. His livestock was sleek and fat, his barn chock-full of fodder, grain, and other supplies. The *cura* himself was never anything but rotund, the shining face and whole outward appearance bespeaking satisfaction with life and loudly proclaiming good food, rich wine, and utter contentment. Gilbert and Sullivan may have sung about the unhappy lot of the policeman, but in justice they could not have bemoaned the fate of the Mexican village priest.

There comes a time when people go to sleep, when villages, towns, and cities wrap themselves in slumber. The hurry and the bustle ceases, and even the marts of trade and the great white way become silent. However, that does not apply to a Mexican settlement, be it merely a group of farmhouses, a village, town, or city.

In the small places where we stopped the stillness of the dark was broken at frequent intervals, but Jack and I became used to the disturbances. I slept despite the yelping of the dogs that would growl and bark upon the slightest provocation—or none at all, despite the intermittent braying of burros that apparently never closed their eyes. Energetic cocks crowed at all hours of the night instead of confining their alarms to the break of dawn, as they are supposed to do.

In the larger places one could expect quiet-shattering *serenatas* from lovesick swains, impassionately telling their ladyloves and the world at large about the pains in their hearts. Or it was the brave music of a group just returning from the *cantina*, the musicians playing guitars, bass drums, horns, and other instruments. Fortunately, however, the saxophone, that ultimate horror, had not yet been generally adopted.

The ceaseless racket would have alarmed the custodians of the public order had the disturbances taken place anywhere else, but in the pueblo they were part and parcel of the nocturnal routine. The inhabitants were immune—accustomed to the never-ending noises, they did not even hear the noises when their attention was called to them.

To the general clamor must be added a mention of the eternal ringing of brassy, harsh-sounding church bells. They would raise their strident voices not only to call the faithful to mass, but at intervals would chime throughout the entire day and night. I never learned the purpose of the bell clanging during the hours of darkness, but there it was, perhaps the relic of some ancient ritual.

Early in the forenoon of the ninth day after leaving the McDonald ranch, we rode into Albuquerque. Jack was put in Springer's feed barn and corral, while I found for myself modest quarters in an unostentatious little hotel.

Albuquerque! In the year 1706 it was officially founded and named in honor of Alfonso, Duke of Alburquerque, who at that time was viceroy of New Mexico. Later the first "r" was to be dropped in the spelling of the town's name.

Parts of Albuquerque looked to me as though they had remained unchanged over the years; the old Spanish church of San Felipe, dating back to 1658, stood, and still stands today. The dusty, unpaved streets were bordered by adobe houses; goats, pigs, and dogs paraded about; patient little burros stood docilely, now and then wiggling their abnormally large ears. Chickens scratched busily, and partly clothed or entirely naked children played in the warm dust and sand. A sleepy atmosphere pervaded the whole scene.

"In no way different from a thousand other small Mexican pueblos." Such was my first impression upon coming into town and entering what may be, today, one of the exclusive sections of the suburbs.

Gradually the street became more modern; better-built houses appeared, even sidewalks. The houses, including stores, saloons, banks, hotels, restaurants, and other structures were mostly of one-story construction; a few had risen to more pretentious proportions, boasting two stories. Often a false front created the illusion of height. As yet there were no signs of concrete paving or macadamized surfacing. Horsemen could be seen riding everywhere; wheeled vehicles, from the light fancy town buggy to the ponderous eight-mule freight wagon with trailer, stirred up clouds of fine dust that hung in the still air, loath to settle back into the rutted roadbed.

Southwestern folklore asserts that most pioneer and frontier towns had their beginning with a saloon as nucleus. That was to supply the "necessities" of life. Later would follow trading posts, grocery stores, markets, and suchlike to take care of the demand for *luxuries*. If that legend rested upon the solid foundation of truth, Albuquerque could look forward to a bright future: it was plentifully supplied with drink dispensaries. In several blocks along the main thoroughfare, the present Central Avenue, were more saloons and gambling places than commercial establishments. True, to make the picture complete, some pawnshops and cheap restaurants had wedged in, but the principal space was given over to liquor and gambling.

Those gambling places exerted a strange fascination over me; I never tired of watching the drama enacted in them nightly. Yes, I even wagered a few dollars on roulette and came out winner to the tune of forty-odd dollars. However, in me the gambling instinct, so far as games of chance were concerned, must have been atrophied. I could not work up any consistent enthusiasm or get excited over the spinning of the ivory ball. And yet I never failed to thrill to the performance of the dealers and players, so intent upon every move of the ball or the turn of each card.

There were many who did not feel as I did, and consequently the gaming tables never lacked patronage. In a country and at a time when life meant one continuous gamble, gaming formed an integral part of existence itself and was not looked upon as something extraneous.

Every game of chance flourished, including poker, monte, twenty-one, roulette, dice, faro, keno, and others. All of them were "strictly on the level," but that did not prevent the house or the bank from winning consistently. The percentage, of course, was always in favor of the bank or dealers, and that alone would have been sufficient to insure a handsome profit for the operators.

Occasionally, somebody made a big winning. Possibly it was engineered for advertising purposes; invariably the news circulated promptly and widely. It lent weight to the foolish assumption that anyone might become rich almost overnight and, in addition, was a splendid method of *proving* the honesty of the game. Such "killings" never failed as sucker bait, tables were always crowded, and many who desired to joust with Dame Fortune had to wait for a vacant seat.

It was not considered good form, or "sporting," to walk off with a big winning. The etiquette of the place and time demanded that the winner stay in the game or risk being considered a poor sport or a piker. Also, it was the accepted custom that the winner share his good luck by treating the house, which meant all guests present. The bank, needless to say, never suffered from those nice scruples! It had a much tougher hide and could not be put out of countenance while raking in the accumulated earnings of the deluded fools who staked their hard-earned all on the turn of a card or the vagaries of the bouncing little ivory ball.

Maybe in itself the gain or loss did not make so much difference. To the miners, the cowpunchers, herders, lumberjacks, freighters, and others of that rough and ready crowd, gambling was part of life as they knew it, and they derived their principal enjoyment from the thrill of the game, regardless of outcome. They came to town knowing full well that their pay or gold would be gone before they left. Money was meant to be spent for booze, gambling, and the society of women with convenient ideas of morals. Most of those hardy characters could figure out to a nicety just how much of a "spree" their accumulated hoard would allow, and they did not miss the estimate often or by large margins.

Had one attempted to point out the futility or foolishness of their delights and pastimes, he would not have found willing ears or sympathetic understanding. Sky pilots, preachers, reformers, "well-intentioned" people or, for that matter, all individuals or groups interfering in any manner with their pursuit of pleasure, were most unwelcome. The votaries of wine, women, and gaming would have resented in a most discouraging manner any efforts to stop their indulgence in the various forms of relaxation that common usage seemed to approve, if it did not openly and actively encourage them.

Appraising the comparative evils of bad whisky and gambling, most employers preferred that the men get rid of their money in the more painless manner at the gaming table. That procedure accomplished the separation of the fool and his money quicker than the saloon, and, furthermore, did not incapacitate the man for work. He might have a bad headache and grouchy disposition over his losses, but if his troubles did not arise from poisonous whisky fumes, the man could return to his duties so much quicker. Also (an important consideration!), excepting in rare occurrences, gaming failed to result in those boisterous brawls, shooting and knifing affairs, and fistic battles that were so frequently the outcome of protracted sessions in the bars.

In the southwestern towns like El Paso, Albuquerque, Santa Fe, and Gallup, the customers of the saloons and gambling houses presented a picturesque sight. The vigorous outdoor men, ranchers, freighters, cowboys, prospectors, miners and others, toughened by their strenuous vocations, lean, tanned, alert, contrasted strikingly with the beefy, paunchy bartenders, the pasty-faced "bankers," and the weasellike musicians, pimps, and other hangers-on of the night life. Their distinctive garb, including ten-gallon hats, silver-studded belts, boots and jingling spurs, chaps, low-slung gun belts and holsters, and their sun-faded kerchiefs, might appear almost theatrical to the tenderfoot just arrived from the East. The dealers behind the bank, arrayed in spotless linen and broadcloth, deceptively dandified, usually wearing diamond rings and stickpins, presented the extreme opposite.

Mexicans, swarthy faces under broad-brimmed sombreros, colorful serapes draped over left shoulders, immense-roweled spurs clanking with each step, mingled with Indians from a dozen different tribes, a sprinkling of Chinamen and (but this very rarely) some colored men. Negroes were rather scarce in the southwestern territories at that time; whites associating with them made themselves guilty of a breach of the social proprieties. At the bars or in the gambling rooms, Mexicans and Chinese were admitted upon terms of equality with the white patrons, but Negroes did not enjoy the same privileges. Some bars refused service to colored customers at any price, and in other places excessive charges were imposed to discourage their patronage.

I heard a story of a colored man asking for a drink of whisky in a saloon. He tendered a five-dollar gold piece in payment, which the bartender dropped into the till, remarking: "That's right!" Unabashed, the colored customer pulled out a ten-dollar coin and slapped it on the bar with the invitation to the barkeep: "Give me another one, and have one yourself!"

No man ever asked a bartender for a glass of water, except as a "chaser," or insulted him by ordering coffee and doughnuts! The patrons were served by men, not frizzy and marcelled waitresses. No padded or upholstered stools prevented free and easy access to the bar. Debutantes and bridge-playing matrons did not grace the inside of the saloons. The swinging doors effectively barred the gentler sex, except those ladies commonly distinguished as such between quotation marks. And even those had to use the side door, known as the family entrance.

Straight whisky and beer were the common drinks,

cocktails and other mixed drinks rather out of the ordinary. Most bars charged fifteen cents a drink for whisky. It was the bartender's custom to offer the guest a token, good for a second drink, instead of giving him change for a quarter, thus making each drink cost twelve and a half cents. Beer and ale could be had in wide variety, including Pabst, Schlitz, Anheuser Busch and other Eastern beers, imported ales, and, of course, the product of the local brewery. In the majority of saloons, the floor was sprinkled thickly with sawdust; large, shiny brass spittoons, placed at strategic points, decorated the front of the bar from which hung, fastened by metal clips, and spaced at convenient intervals, napkins for public use. The proprietors certainly did everything to provide all the comforts and conveniences imaginable for their patrons!

Money was counted in two bits, four bits, and six bits instead of being called twenty-five, fifty, and seventy-five cents. Very few banknotes or "greenbacks" were in circulation. Throughout the Southwest and in the Pacific Coast States, the usual medium of exchange was the hard coin, with silver predominating. Golden "eagles" rang on counters and bars, the free American people not yet having been deprived of the right to own and use golden coins minted from the yellow metal produced in the mines of their own country.

Albuquerque was then a town of just a few thousand people, but it had already risen to the importance of a great distributing point for the surrounding country for a radius of hundreds of miles. It had, and still has, extensive lumber interests, and through the years has maintained a brisk trade in wool, hides, and livestock. Now, of course, it is a *modern* town, conscious of Civic Virtue. It boasts a fine university, several excellent hotels, large mercantile institutions, a chamber of commerce, country club, strong banks, newspapers, Rotarians, Lions, Masonic and other fraternal organizations, golf links, Legion posts, and everything else that makes for the progressive, up-to-date American community. And today, on the roads over which in other times the patient ox teams of the Mexican farmers and overland freighters plodded their weary and hazardous way, falls the shadow of the luxurious air liner that makes regular stops on the ideally situated Albuquerque airport.

During the course of years the city has become the mecca of unfortunates afflicted with the dread white plague, tuberculosis, until now it shelters a large colony of those health seekers "chasing the cure." In the callous-sounding vernacular they are dubbed "lungers." The elevation of five thousand feet provides a rare, dry air which, in combination with all-year-round sunshine (New Mexico is known as the Sunshine State) is miraculously effective in many cases. I have known strong men and robust women, radiating splendid vitality, who years before had been sent to the desert as incurable, left hopeless, pronounced ready to die, or told not to expect to live another six months. In the bracing atmosphere of Albuquerque they regained health and happiness, and with a merry twinkle in their eyes, or a contented chuckle, enjoyed telling in a good-humored manner how wrong their doctor's diagnosis had proved.

(It is only fair to state that many other places are as good as Albuquerque in providing health-giving climatic conditions for tubercular patients. Also, New Mexico has no monopoly on dry air and sunshine.)

Every man in the Southwest, or at least that portion of the male element whose occupation involved outdoor life, moved about armed with a six-shooter, in natural conformity with the rights granted in the second amendment to the Constitution. Automatic pistols, repeating rifles, and machine guns were unknown; as yet prohibition beer barons, gangland leaders, vice lords, rum racketeers, dope smugglers and kidnappers had not made their need felt for super-modern firearms. The Colt six-shooter dominated the scene.

Gradually it became the custom to park one's artillery with a friendly bartender or with the keeper of the corral or livery stable where the horses and wagons were put up. The guns were called for at the time of taking the last drink or when making ready to leave town. Eventually, that practice fell into disuse when the habit of carrying firearms also became obsolete.

The money that I had won by a lucky guess of the right number enabled me to live handsomely for some little time. My own wants were modest and inexpensively satisfied, and Jack's board bill was a matter of fifty cents a day. To keep him from forgetting his duties and routine, I took him out of the corral every day, exercising him and myself with a good workout along the Rio Grande and up into the Bernalillo sandhills. After those constitutionals he and I felt better and relished our meals much more than if our days had been passed in utter idleness.

Chapter 5

A NEW HAND FOR THE TRIANGLE BAR TRIANGLE

Between days spent in seeing the sights of the town, talking with cowpunchers and freighters just off the range, exercising the horse, and passing the evenings until an advanced hour as an interested bystander at the games (I rarely participated in a whirl of the wheel), two weeks or more went by almost unnoticed. By then the attractions of the town had palled and I was eager to get back to the open country. With that thought uppermost in my mind, I made special efforts to find somebody willing to give me a job. I fraternized with the men from out of town, listened to gossip pertaining to ranches and range, made inquiries at the corrals and feeding pens, talked with stablemen, and loitered in the saddle and harness shops, notably Korber's store, where ranchers might be encountered.

My persistence bore fruit: one morning, while assisting several punchers engaged in getting a bunch of unbroken horses into a corral, I learned that their employer might take on an extra hand, two of his men intending to quit the outfit since they planned to return to Texas. That bit of news induced me to wait at the corral, making myself useful to the men, picking up more information from them about the location of the ranch, the owner, the nature of the work, and other items of interest to me.

The boss arrived. He was Richard Wetherill, from Chaco Canyon in northwestern New Mexico, a man well known throughout not only that section of the country, but also in Utah, Colorado, and Arizona. Of medium height, clear-skinned, quick and energetic, his keen, blue eyes seemed to drill through a man. Fine horses were his particular hobby and he delighted in horse trading.

Wetherill talked with the foreman for some time before I found a chance to tell him about my desire to take a job with his outfit. However, once we got to conversing, he decided the question in a couple of minutes.

"Can you work horses?" he questioned. Upon my affirmative answer, he wanted to know whether I had a complete outfit, horse, saddle, and other necessary pieces of equipment. It seemed to astonish him to hear that although I had already spent several weeks in town, I still possessed all my personal effects, horse and equipment. Various items from the outfits of too many men find their way into pawnshops, or else they are left as pledges for unpaid saloon or boardinghouse bills.

Later, I learned that Wetherill never smoked or drank liquor in any form, and that he had been reared in the Quaker religion. Anyhow, after just a few questions, he told me to stay with his men and to help with the work. He suggested that I make myself at home in their camp about a mile from town, on the bank of the Rio Grande, where the saddle horses and wagon mules were pastured.

I was hired! No fussy inquiries, no investigation of my record, no demand for a pedigree—simply the question: Can you do the work, and the general sizing-up as to the apparent fitness and ability for the job at hand. On my part I did not ask: How many hours do I work each day? What is my salary? Do I get Sundays and holidays off? Where will I live? Do you furnish room and board? And possibly a dozen other questions. That was not the way men were hired forty-five years ago, at least not for range work. The boss depended upon the men being able to do the work and left it to the foreman to handle all details pertaining to assignment of particular duties and similar matters.

Wages were pretty well standardized at from thirty to forty dollars a month, with food and shelter provided. In my own case I was put on the pay roll at thirty dollars a month, although I was not curious to learn the exact figure and did not know it for some six months or longer. After working for Wetherill nearly a year, my wages were raised to thirty-five dollars monthly. I had not made a demand for an increase, and for some months was without knowledge of the fact that *an* extra five dollars was being credited to my account each month.

Having settled with my Albuquerque landlady, I took faithful old Jack from the feed stable. With one of Wetherill's men we rode to the camp established by the riverbank, where we found several freight wagons drawn up, an outdoor kitchen in full operation, and three men loafing in the fragrant grass. The Wetherill men, or the Triangle Bar Triangle outfit as they were known from one of the brands registered in the boss's name, told me that their work was almost exclusively with horses. Wetherill "ran" only a small bunch of cattle, but owned many horses, the number varying from time to time between five and six hundred to well over a thousand head. Just then they had brought in a bunch of Indian ponies to be auctioned off in Albuquerque, and nearly three-fourths of the number they had driven to town had already passed to new ownership.

My informers stated that Wetherill was constantly trading for, or buying outright, Indian ponies, both broken and unbroken stock, and that he had found good outlets and a steady demand for his horses. Periodically, he would send large numbers to Albuquerque and other points, to be sold at auction. In the preceding year his riders had taken a bunch of horses as far as Goodnight, Oklahoma, a drive of several weeks' duration. Regular buyers, among them livestock dealers from Joplin, Missouri, were in the habit of coming to the ranch twice or three times yearly, making their selections right on the range and, assisted by their own wranglers, herding their purchases to the nearest railroad point for shipment to the Midwestern states.

Only no cowman or horse rancher ever referred to the overland transportation of his livestock as "herding." It was, invariably, "driving." Herding had a hateful association with sheep, an obnoxious subject to the men engaged in the horse and cattle business.

The Wetherill ranch was located in Chaco Canyon, approximately 150 miles northwest from Albuquerque. An average of ten days travel was required to reach it unless seasonal disturbances, breakdowns, accidents, or unforseen delays increased the time to two weeks or even longer. At that particular season, under favorable road, grazing and water conditions, it was expected the trip would be made within the ten-day limit. My informants added some other bits of general advice relating to the nature of the country to be traversed between Albuquerque and the Chaco region, regarding trail lore, warnings about tricky crossings, the location of hidden springs, and then enlarged upon the ornery habits of certain of the wagon mules. They impressed upon my memory some pointers on how to keep to the right road by watching for prominent landmarks and other natural guides, which they described fully.

Those various items of information reached me piece-meal, and not all at once, as if read out of a guidebook. For example, one of the riders expressed the hope that they would find the Puerco dry upon the return trip. This referred to the Rio Puerco, which had to be forded at the small Mexican settlement of Cabezon.

That, in turn, prompted another of the men to explain, for my benefit, how the Puerco had been running pretty high when they forded it on their way to Albuquerque, and he spoke of the difficulties one might expect at that particular crossing.

Upon the casual query whether Wetherill used the same brand, namely the Triangle Bar Triangle, for cattle as well as horses, there came the answer that enlightened me as to the predominance of the horses on the ranch, and the estimate that not more than a couple of hundred head of cattle were under Wetherill's brand.

Similarly, the other details pertaining to ranch and range and trail pieced themselves together, until I had a fairly comprehensive picture of the entire setup. All of it was, of course, but a thumbnail sketch compared with the fuller and all-embracing knowledge that came as a result of several years spent with Wetherill's outfit.

Whoever reaches Chaco Canyon will have some experience with the desert. Pueblo Bonito lies in the center of an area a hundred miles square, without a regularly flowing stream of any sort. It is surrounded by the mystery of the wastelands. Regardless of the point of approach, the bare, arid plains must be crossed. Nowadays, with trading posts established at more frequent intervals, improved roads, steel and concrete bridges taking the place of dangerous fords, and the substitution of automobiles and trucks for jaded horses and mules, it is a fairly easy journey that can be accomplished in as many hours, or less, as it formerly required days. In our time, we toiled across on horseback or by wagon, and it was a trip for seasoned campaigners of the trail only.

That night, after Wetherill hired me, I slept in the camp by the river. Speaking more correctly, I managed to get some sleep when, toward morning, I gave up slapping at the myriads of mosquitoes that wanted to sample the supply of fresh blood brought by the newcomer. They were tireless in their efforts to sate their bloodthirsty appetites; those pests never gave up trying for a new hold from shortly after sunset until daybreak. During the day they disappeared, and only occasionally would one bother man or beast, but with the coming of darkness they attacked in force.

Early in the morning the cook was stirring. In a short time the air carried tantalizing scents of fresh coffee and frying bacon. Before the cook had a chance to sing out "Come and get it!" the hungry gang was assembled. After breakfast we saddled our horses that had been hobbled during the night. They had remained close to camp since feed and water were plentiful. Then we rode into town to look after the horses still left in the auction lot. Feeding them was an easy matter of breaking open and scattering some baled hay along the corral wall. The watering trough at one end of the enclosure, emptied by the horses during the night, was filled again by simply turning the faucet of the pipe line running from a large galvanized iron tank.

Toward noon the boss came to the corral and brought the news that he had concluded a deal for all but five of the unsold horses; that those few remaining ones were to be driven back to the ranch. He directed us to get the camp, wagons, and animals in shape for leaving the following morning. The wagons were to be loaded that same afternoon, in readiness for the return trip.

These orders moved us into quick action. One of the men rode to the camp, leaving proper instructions there, one in another direction to round up the wagon mules and extra horses that had been grazing at some distance from the camp. The second man had been told to take the mules to a blacksmith shop, there to have their shoes looked over. A third man and I took charge of the horses in the corral.

The purchaser of the broncos came with two cowpunchers. With their help it was an easy matter to separate the bunch, keeping the five unsold animals in the corral. The others were driven off by the buyer and his men. Later we joined the man who had driven the mules to the blacksmith shop and helped him with the refractory animals. Having enjoyed a fine vacation in the meadows deep with grass and alfalfa, the mules had grown playful. It took a good deal of persuasion to calm them sufficiently for them to submit to the less interesting matter of getting their hoofs and shoes prepared for the hard work of pulling a heavy load over tough roads.

An extra team, which had been kept in camp for that purpose, drew the empty wagons into town. They were pulled alongside the loading platforms of the wholesaler's warehouse and soon the stowing of freight began under the careful supervision of the boss himself.

There were boxes with canned goods, baking powder, hams and bacon wrapped in burlap, coffee, matches, notions, sacks and barrels of flour, sugar and salt, bales of collar pads, horse collars, blocks of stock salt, baled hay, some large cases containing Pendleton robes, quilts, and other dry goods, iron drums filled with kerosene, smaller bundles and cardboard boxes with purchases made by Mrs. Wetherill—in short, a heterogeneous collection of all sorts of articles and merchandise. To properly distribute such freight on wagons and trailers was quite an art and required almost as much careful planning as loading a ship. In some respects it was even more difficult than loading a vessel because the wagons did not afford much protection to the goods since they were exposed on every side, and even at the bottom, to the changes of road and weather conditions.

Part of the load in every haul had to be especially protected against dust and sand; another lot would require particular safeguards against crushing or chafing; and certainly almost all must have protection against rain, mud, or other moisture, and be kept safe from the danger of wetting when crossing rivers and streams. Oil, paint, turpentine, kerosene, and similar odorous or leakable items had to be stowed in a manner to prevent damage to flour or other susceptible goods.

Another point requiring careful consideration was the distribution of the load according to weight. The heaviest pieces must always ride as far forward as possible. It was considered poor stowage and the sign of an inexperienced freighter to permit heavy articles to bear down the rear end; a good teamster would never allow such practice. From this it can be seen that the correct loading of a large freight wagon and trailer, carrying a combined cargo of approximately eight thousand pounds, was an accomplishment gained only through long experience. Wetherill proved that he was more than equal to his job.

The cook wagon, too, was pressed into the freight service, although it did not carry quite as heavy a load as the other wagons. Part of its space was reserved for the cooking oufit. It also carried the bedrolls of the riders and several sacks of oats and corn that were to be fed to the teams and horses on the trip. In addition it had to provide room for nose bags, rawhide hobbles, large tarpaulins, and various other miscellaneous items that might be wanted on the trip. Every stick of wood we saw by the roadside was pitched onto the tail end of Cookie's wagon, to be used for firewood. That was a wise precaution—there were many places along the trail entirely without fuel of any sort.

Two large water kegs were lashed to the sides of the cook wagon, resting on platforms built against the outside of the wagon box and flush with the level of the wagon bed. They were to provide drinking water for men and beasts in those camps where water was not obtainable or where it was found to be so saturated with alkali as to make it unfit to drink. Wherever good, pure, sweet water was available, those kegs were refilled.

At the rear end of the trailer attached to the wagon carrying the cook's outfit was fastened a large box, stoutly built of thick boards and reinforced at all corners with iron bands, containing provisions, the grub box or chuck box. It was stocked generously with the staple food items needed on a trip such as ours: coffee, sugar, flour, baking powder, bacon, lard, dried beans, rice, canned milk, raisins, canned tomatoes, spices, and so forth. Built into the box was a partition making a compartment for cups, plates, knives, forks, and spoons. No arrangement existed for serving hors d'oeuvres, salads, soups, or desserts. So far as we were concerned, napkins, salad forks, and finger bowls were only dictionary terms, but the postprandial smoke was an established and rigidly observed custom.

During the last day in Albuquerque, before starting upon the trip to Chaco Canyon, I learned that the Wetherill ranch location was referred to as Pueblo Bonito. "Beautiful Town"—what an unusual name for a horse ranch, I mused. Not until some time later did I discover the true meaning of those words.

Not sharing the boss's aversion to beer and wine, I joined the other men for a "last" drink in The White Elephant, one of the principal saloons of the town. Each "last" drink turned out to be the penultimate in a series of tall beers, coming rather more quickly and persistently than I relished, until finally our foreman decided we had better "be goin'."

Hearing those words, the bartender grew softhearted. With a generous expression he invited all hands to have another one—"on the house, boys!" So we planted our feet once more on the brass rail and with becoming solemnity performed the rite of imbibing the parting drink, donated by the owner of the establishment. Then there was handshaking with the unemotional barkeeper, a waving of hands to acquaintances and friends, shouting and laughing, and we passed through the swinging doors into the street.

Chapter 6

FREIGHTING TO CHACO CANYON

The mules as well as the saddle horses and the five unsold broncos were kept in the corral during the last night in town to avoid losing any time the following morning in hunting for stock that might have strayed.

Quite some time had yet to elapse before dawn brought the light of day; objects in the large lot where the loaded wagons had been drawn up were still blurred and indistinct, and the air possessed a sharp nip when we rolled from between the blankets and prepared to feed the stock. The mules had been impatient for their breakfast for a good while. They had circled our tarpaulin-covered beds, all but stepping on us while we tried to tell ourselves that many minutes of precious sleep remained before we should have to leave the snug warmth of the blankets. After the liberal potions in The White Elephant we felt no inclinations to be early risers, but the foreman, hardened to such experiences, coldheartedly roused us with his "Time to git up, boys!"

Nose bags were filled with a mixture of oats and corn and hung over the heads of the mules and saddle horses. Even the unbroken broncs thrust their nozzles toward

the armful of bags that we distributed, eager for a taste of
the luscious grain. However, since they would have nothing to do except trot along, unburdened by saddle or
collar, they did not share in the feed. They had to fill their
bellies at the cribs with the leavings of hay fed to them
the previous evening. One or another of them would try
to nibble at the outside of the bag hung over the head of a
horse or mule without meeting much satisfaction: usually
the bothered one retaliated by whirling about and kicking
at the intruder.

The stock having been looked after, we rolled up our
beds, fastening the unwieldy rolls with large leather
straps. Then we took them to the cook wagon, there to
hoist them atop the load. Followed a quick toilet, a simple
washing of face and hands, and we, too, were ready for
breakfast. A few minutes only were required in which to
gulp down a couple of tin cupfuls of scalding hot coffee
and to eat some mush with canned milk, fried bacon, hot
bread and jam, luxuries made possible by our being in
town. Almost at once we again turned our attention to
the stock, now finished with the contents of the nose
bags. However, instead of removing the bags, we left
them over the noses of the animals and while they were
thus dressed up, put on harness and saddles. Then, at
the last moment, they were relieved of the bags and those
replaced with bridles and headstalls. Since there was a
watering trough in the corral, we did not need to take
the beasts to water; presumably they had drunk their fill
during the night and in the early morning.

There were three wagons, each with a trailer, and twenty mules had to be put in their respective places, two wagons being drawn by six mules each, and the third one
having a team of eight mules.

Presently the three wagons and their teams were pro-

perly hitched up and the saddle horses ready. Now the
corral gates swung wide and we started. Off for Pueblo
Bonito! Good-by, Albuquerque! Down Third Street,
past several blocks lined on both sides with houses of ill
fame, through the very heart of the Tenderloin of the
town. The creaking of harness and the squeaking of
wagon beds, brake poles, and the noise of the animals,
drivers, and riders, failed to disturb the gentle slumber of
the lights of love. None of them raised a shade or peeked
from behind the closely drawn curtains. Their days did
not begin until well toward evening. About the time
when decent, law-abiding citizens (as often as not among
their staunchest customers!) brought their workday to a
close, those purveyors of pleasure would just start to feel
fully awake and make ready for another evening and night
of excitement.

Some early workers were about, men driving stock to
pastures, a half dozen Mexicans plodding down the road
to their labors, a sleepy-eyed policeman sauntering his
beat, obviously glad to note the approach of his relief.
Otherwise there were no signs of activity as our wagon
train left town. A scattering of houses and we were in
the outskirts; but a short distance more and we traveled
in open country, having the world all to ourselves.

To drive the extra horses was my particular charge.
In addition, I could assist in any way I cared to with the
multiple chores coincident with the taking of a freight
train across the country. Feeding and watering a large
number of animals, harnessing and unharnessing, hitching
up and unhitching them, means a considerable job. An
extra helper is always sure of a warm welcome from the
teamsters. More work was brought about through the not
infrequent occurrence of horses or mules straying and
wandering off during the night. Although hobbled, they

would, at times, cover long distances and had to be hunted far and wide in the morning before they were found and returned to camp. To facilitate that part of the daily routine, it was the practice to keep one horse tied to one of the wagons, a so-called night horse. This one was fed hay and grain; every evening a different horse was picked for that duty, thus giving all horses a chance to graze, and, also, to prevent tying up the same animal night after night. Naturally, only a trained saddle horse would be "kept up"; an unbroken animal could not be depended upon.

When there were a number of horses in the caravan, it was customary for riders to change mounts and take fresh saddle horses each day. The fact that some animals were still unbroken and not used to the work required of them did not matter. The supposition was that there could not be a better opportunity to train them than on a drive, and this idea worked out in actual application. Thus, upon almost any morning, one might witness some frantic performance when an unbroken horse was initiated into the duties of driving its free-running mates.

First, there was the job of saddling the beast, not exactly a simple undertaking, then to keep it from pitching and bucking itself and the rider into the orderly line of team animals or against the wagons. With a peculiar streak of perversity the bronco might pick the still-glowing coals of the campfire as the spot to stage the buck and wing dance, seemingly impervious to the heat. Or he might decide to waltz through the arrangement of water buckets, grub box, feed bags, stacked harness, or anything else that is not supposed to be disturbed.

Since an unbroken horse does not know what a bridle means and is unused to having a rider guide it, no bridles or bits are used on raw stock. Instead of annoying the animal with the unaccustomed feel of the bit in its mouth, the rider employs a hackamore, which resembles a halter and has reins or ropes on both sides of the horse's neck.

After the first wild bucking spell, pitching and tearing about and "sunfishing," the horse learns by degrees that he is being guided, and, as a rule, by the end of the first day he has grasped the rudiments of his duties. Of course, to train a cow pony into being "a real horse," and make him perfect in the many phases of work required of him, means not days but weeks and months of patient labor.

Only a short distance from town we reached the ford where we had to cross the Rio Grande. This was accomplished without difficulty, the river being nearly dry. Three or four narrow little streams, all shallow ones, had to be forded, but the lead mules did not hesitate a moment to enter them. Ordinarily, mules are rather shy of water and generally quite careful to test their footing before venturing into streams. The fact that our teams kept going without being urged was the best indication of the safety of the ford. After gaining the opposite shore, however, we encountered trouble because almost from the river's edge we struck sandy hills. A long range of dunes presented a formidable barrier to our progress. In the absence of any other road that we could have taken there was no alternative: we had to drive through the sandy waste to reach the heights of the mesa, a distance of perhaps two miles or more.

The freighters urged the teams to draw their heavy loads as far upon the bank as was possible, then called a stop. At that point the trailer of the first wagon was unfastened and while one of the men attended to that, the teamster of the second wagon unhitched his team of mules. Keeping the "string" intact, he led them to the head of the first wagon's team. There, all were combined into a fourteen-mule team by fastening the second team to the long chain by which the first wagon's lead team was pulling its load. The task at hand required the strength of both teams; even when pulled by the fourteen animals the single wagon could be moved a short distance only before it was necessary to "spell" the mules. They were allowed to stop and catch their breath, then once again leaned against their collars and pulled the wagon for some yards.

The sand, dry as powder and fine like flour, would pack around the wheel rims, burying them to the spokes, as if determined to keep the hold forever. It appeared as if there were no solid bottom to the treacherous and ever-changing ruts, hardly discernible against the side of the slope.

After many stops and starts, the first wagon finally got safely over the sands. It was pulled well beyond the end of the dune, onto the harder ground which marked the beginning of the tableland. There the long string of mules was unhitched, turned about, and driven downhill, there to duplicate the feat with the first wagon's trailer. That vehicle, not being quite so heavy and carrying less freight, could be hauled up the heartbreaking slant of the hill at a somewhat faster pace than the cumbersome lead wagon. Nevertheless, it too required plenty of stops and breathing spells for men and beasts. The trailer atop the rise, it was coupled up with the first lead wagon, then men and animals returned downhill to assist in the job of bringing up the second and third wagons with their respective trailers.

Under the terrific strain of the repeated operations trace chains might break and whiffletrees pull apart. When that happened, they had to be mended with spare chain links and repaired with lengths of baling wire. Several times it happened that pieces of harness split, mules got tangled up in the long line of chain or stepped over their traces and began kicking up a general row, collar pads slipped from under the collars and required readjustment—in short, it was a strenuous performance for both men and animals. Long before the last wagon and trailer had been put over the crest of the sandy hill, everybody was drenched with sweat, tired, worn out. The day was nearly gone; to take the loads across the sandy waste had required hour after hour of extremely exhausting work, and at eventide, after all our exertions, we were still within walking distance of Albuquerque, which we had left so sprightly at sunrise!

The spare horses had enjoyed the grazing at the river's edge while the teams and the men struggled to get through and past the sands. There was little danger of any of them straying far, what with plenty of fresh, green feed and water directly under their noses. Knowing this, I had left my charges to their own devices and helped the teamsters. However, once the teams were again ready for the road, I rode downhill and rounded up the horses, driving them up over the ridge and toward the wagons.

That day we did not drive more than another mile or so before it was time to make camp, and presently all about us were mules luxuriously relishing a long roll in the grass, shaking themselves, and almost upsetting the whole camp in their eagerness to get their feed bags. True, they had been watered and fed during the noon hour, when men and beasts took a rest of about an hour and the cook prepared a hasty lunch, but they knew that now their day's work was done and that they had earned a good supper.

In stage productions of musical comedies, such as *Rio Rita*, or *The Rose of the Rancho*, and in many talking picture films, one can see how romantically the cowboys and freighters loaf about their campfires, strumming guitars, twanging banjos and mandolins, and singing songs with a great deal of the old barber shop harmony. On stage and screen that sounds and looks fine, but in the years while I lived in the range country nothing like that ever occurred to enrich my experiences. I never saw a guitar in any trail camp, and though possessed of a good pair of ears, never heard the soft modulations of touching cowboy ballads at the end of twelve hours or more of strenuous activities.

The riders and freighters with whom I associated must have been deficient in those more aesthetic accomplishments. After a hard day's work they did not relax and make merry with song and dance, not they. Instead, they would find themselves as comfortable a place as the campground permitted and there make their beds. First, they would pick up and throw to one side small rocks and stones and other knobby protuberances, level the ground as much as possible, pull up bunches of wiry grass, kick out of the way pieces of dry sagebrush, scrape out a hollow to accommodate the hip, and then carefully spread the tarpaulin over the space so prepared.

The "tarp" not only formed the bottom of the bed but extended full length over the top of the blankets as well, keeping out dew, rain, snow, dust, and sand. It was a large piece of heavy canvas, sufficiently wide to protect the sides too, thus keeping the bedding itself dry and clean. Of course, after a roundup, or upon the return from a long freight trip, blankets required shaking and airing and straightening, but, on the whole, a properly arranged bedroll kept its contents in order and free from moisture or soiling without requiring daily attention. A rolled-up slicker, or shirt, made a good pillow, and Mother Earth

in any emergency, but of all those that I came to know, Sanders was within the small group of the top-ranking ones.

Five days after leaving Albuquerque we reached the ford of the Rio Puerco. On the other side of the deep gulch that formed the river bed was Cabezon, a small Mexican town. It had been planned that we were to drive some two or three miles beyond that settlement before making camp for the night, partly to have better grazing grounds for the animals, but mainly to be so much farther away from the town and some of the light-fingered gentry residing there. With those thoughts urging us to haste, we did everything to accomplish the crossing of the Puerco as quickly as possible.

As it happened the river was low and the ford itself fairly well packed and free from quicksand or other obstacles. However, the road leading down to the river was very steep and slanted unevenly, tilting the heavy wagons and their high loads at a dangerous angle. As at the fording of the Rio Grande, the trailers were unfastened, but at the Puerco it was not necessary to double up the teams. The first team got its own lead wagon safely through the river and out upon the top of the opposite bank, then returned for the trailer and pulled it through the ford and back into position behind the wagon already across.

The mules hesitated before entering the river, so I fastened one extreme of my lariat to the tip of the wagon tongue, took a couple of turns around the saddle horn with the other end of the rope, and led the way through the river, my horse straining against the pull of the *reata*. This bit of encouragement persuaded the mules to follow the lead of the horse, and while the actual assistance of my rope was not much, the moral support of having a horse leading them was of considerable help to the mules, and, therefore, to the driver. Of course, at bad crossings, or when mired, several punchers, if available, would simultaneously pull with their horses and ropes and often succeed in freeing teams and wagons from the sticky mess of mud and sucking quicksand.

At subsequent crossings, the Rio Puerco showed a different visage, and I learned in later times to accord more respect to that innocent-appearing stream. But at that particular moment, the fording gave us no trouble, and soon the three wagons and trailers, and the extra stock, were on the far side of the river; presently we were passing by the outskirts of Cabezon.

About an hour after the last wagon had effected the safe crossing of the Puerco, we made camp, and our bedding down for the night differed in only one respect from the camps of the preceding nights: we took turns at night guard. Not to be on the lookout for savage Indians or wild animals—no, we merely wanted to make secure against unwelcome visits from our Mexican neighbors in the village.

During fully two days before reaching the Puerco, we had seen Cabezon Peak, one of the outstanding landmarks of the region, appearing like carved ebony, forbiddingly raising its sheer heights from the broad valley of the Rio Puerco. In solitary grandeur it stands; mountain ranges surround it on every side. Its wide-spreading base, the plain, is broken by deep canyons, cut through successive layers of lava streams that cooled aeons ago, topping strata of sandstone and clay. The rains, floods, and swirling sandstorms of untold ages caused many queer erosions, forming all sorts of fantastic shapes.

Cabezon Peak is the halfway mark between Albuquerque and Chaco Canyon, and from now on we would have to watch our mules to keep them from straying during the nights. These smart animals knew that they were approaching the end of the journey and might decide to start hobbling toward the ranch instead of feeding their hungry stomachs after the day's work was done.

Another disturbing possibility to be guarded against, once Cabezon had been passed, was the inclination of some of the Navajo Indians to "prompt" and encourage the livestock to wander off. The absence of the horses or mules in the morning would furnish them with a perfectly valid excuse for offering their services, to assist in hunting the lost. I had had no personal experience of that little trick the wily savages liked to play, but the others in our group were well aware of it. All had become acquainted with occurrences of that nature, or knew of happenings when some Navajo would appear in camp at about breakfast time, his emotions completely hidden under a stolid poker face. With deep understanding, he would listen to the cursing of the freighter who could not find his teams, then indicate in an offhand manner that for a consideration he could be persuaded to join the hunt.

After striking a mutually satisfactory bargain, Poor Lo would mount his pony and gallop away. Barely gone, he would reappear, driving before him the missing mules and horses. The suspiciously short absence made it obvious that the animals had been concealed cleverly by him during the night or early-morning hours; it would have been impossible to locate the strays so quickly without previous knowledge of their hiding place. Just a polite little holdup. It was to prevent some such possibility, and to frustrate any attempt at pilferage, that we mounted guard during our camp at Rio Puerco, near Cabezon.

The town of Cabezon, hardly more than three miles

from our campground, was then entirely Mexican in population. At one time, and that was not so very long before we camped there, it had been considered one of the "bad" towns of the Southwest. Even in our day, but slightly removed from the unregenerate period, it behooved one to visit the place with circumspection and to be on the alert.

The *cantina*, where an oily proprietor dispensed *aguardiente*, tequila, cognac, vino, mescal, and other potent drinks, wore a disturbingly sinister aspect even in the bright glare of day. In the evenings, illuminated by some smoky petroleum lamps and crowded with swarthy customers, most of them conspicuously and heavily armed, it made one look for a strategically placed table or seat to provide either cover or means of quick exit, if needed. The truculent fellows who frequented that inviting joint carried a chip as large as a log on their shoulders and they made it plain that they would welcome anyone to knock it off.

Americans were looked upon as intruders, as particularly undesirable companions. The very atmosphere breathed the tacit declaration that gringos had better beware, that they were allowed to be present on sufferance only.

Fights, brawls, knife plays, and shootings did not disturb the tranquility of the town—they belonged to the routine that made up the daily or nightly life of the settlement. The sheriff and other peace officers used to give Cabezon a wide berth; after all, should it matter if some drunken greaser cut up or shot another? Let them kill themselves, good riddance! That expressed the prevailing opinion. Even cowpunchers bent on a spree, not afraid of the devil himself, would remember enough of the admonition that discretion beats valor to tread

softly when in that little rip-roaring town on the banks
of the Puerco.

It was difficult for me to account for the hostile attitude
displayed by the Mexicans of Cabezon, so utterly at
variance from the friendly spirit, camaraderie, and unfailing amiability generally found in the Latin-Indian
people. Here, open antagonism and ill-concealed bitter-
ness had taken the place of the happy courtesy, the unstinted hospitality and good-fellowship I had come to
associate with Mexicans. Eventually, I learned that their
hardened attitude was, to a large extent, the result of
persecutions, insults to their nationality, exploitations
by powerful individuals, land grabs which caused them
to lose their little homes and *ranchitos*, deprivations of
open range for their stock, and other injustices. In a
supposedly free country, granting equality, they were
forced into economic peonage and could fight back in
only one way, they seemed to think. Sanders, aware of the
situation, asked everybody to stay close to the wagons.

We experienced nothing untoward while encamped
near Cabezon and early the next morning we continued
our journey, traveling steadily in a northwesterly direction. The "road" to Chaco Canyon was merely an Indian
wagon trail, consisting of two parallel wheel ruts, crazily
winding in and out of the sagebrush-covered valleys and
mesas. At times the track was "as straight as a string," but
mostly it followed serpentine convolutions. There were
places where the furrows had worn so deep as to scrape
the axles of the wagons; several times we were forced to
take axes and shovels and break into the concrete-like
adobe in order to enable the wheels to leave the sunken
track. Thus, where the ruts had worn too deep for the
wagons, or failed to provide adequate footing for the
mules, a new track was made paralleling the old one by

simply swinging out of the road and driving alongside it until it was safe to return to the original roadway.

In some stretches this practice had been followed so often that, up to a width of hundreds of feet, there were deeply hollowed tracks that had become gullies. In those spots, as far as the eye could see, the down-reaching furrows ran in long parallel rows resembling the teeth of a gigantic comb turned edge upward. That was especially the case in those parts of the road which followed the original Santa Fe-California trail, first broken by the ox teams and covered wagons of the forty-niners. There the ruts were eroded to a depth of from six to ten feet, running side by side over a width of fully two hundred feet or more and forming a dangerous obstacle to stock and riders.

Occasionally it happened that a cow or calf died directly in the road, or that a horse fell in the trail, broke a leg, and had to be destroyed where it had stumbled. Then again, heavy rains would form deep, sticky puddles; rocks might slide from a higher bank or hillside onto the wagon track. Those obstacles were not removed but were allowed to remain; it was easier to drive around them than to clear the road or to drain off the water. Under those conditions, it was small wonder that straight lines of road were the exception; the trail, as a rule, wove snakily in and out, its zigzagging curves frequently the result of some temporary obstructions. And like sheep following their leader, the next one to come over the road would keep to the newly made track, even if the hindering obstacle no longer existed. The swing around a slippery, muddy place was followed faithfully by everyone long after the moisture had dried and the roadway become passable.

The Indians, who used the wagon trail more than anyone else, were not concerned over tilting roadbeds. They had supreme confidence in themselves and their ponies; surely a wagon ought to be able to travel over the same trails as a saddle horse! They knew where they were going and attempted to follow a straight line, without regard for topographical hindrances or without taking any thought to alleviate next-to-impossible grades. Loose sand, glassy lava beds, deep arroyos, steep mesas, unbridged canyons, treacherous fords, quicksand, the scarcity of water or the absence of grass for grazing, the lack of shelter, fuel, or protection, all of that meant nothing to them.

Undoubtedly they did not put it in those same words, but, nevertheless, they were fully aware of the fact that a straight line is the shortest distance between two points; unconsciously, they applied that knowledge to their freighting and driving. Only positively insurmountable obstacles, such as unscalable cliffs, sheer canyon walls, or streams too deep for fording, could swerve them from their original direction and persuade them to detour.

Between Albuquerque and Cabezon we had seen several large herds of sheep and goats, the property of Mexican *rancheros* and tended by Mexican herders. After leaving the Puerco we did not encounter any more Mexicans, but every now and again would see some Indian herds, invariably in charge of Indian boys or girls. With each day the range became more majestic, the spaces more illimitable. Our little wagon train shrank to microscopic proportions in the vast domain through which we traveled. In every direction, and as far as the eye could see, were mountains piled on top of mountains. The immense mesas, those boundless tablelands, dwarfed us. They form a characteristic part of the great central plateau from which rise the chains of the Rocky Mountains and the

Sierra Madre, the mother range that extends from Alaska to Patagonia. Our small party was but a speck in that vast sea of olive-green sagebrush, not of any more significance than a rowboat in the middle of the ocean.

Although moving toward the heart of the Navajo Indian country, entire days passed without bringing to sight even a solitary representative of those aboriginal American nomads. Nor did we see any of their habitations, except a few abandoned hogans whose original earth covering had washed away and exposed the skeleton of the framework. Of course, we might possibly have passed quite closely by Navajo encampments without noticing them; hogans, as a rule, blend into the background of their surroundings to such an extent as to make them virtually invisible. The materials from which they are contructed and their moundlike design combine protective coloring, and their inconspicuous shape does not contrast or mar the harmony of the setting.

Numerous extinct volcanoes dot the ranges. In ages long gone by they were active, pouring forth the hot lava which cooled and now covers the tops of mesas, isolated peaks, and, as in Lincoln County and along the line of the Santa Fe Railroad near Grants, extensive surfaces of valley lands. Frequently the mesas are cut by deep canyons, probably formed by immense masses of water rush ing down the slopes when the world was young and not as dry as it is today. Erosion, working patiently and untiringly through millions of years, has been a master sculptor and carved out bizarre designs of weird and unearthly shapes and proportions.

Many times the road passed by prairie-dog villages. Often these spots, completely undermined by the burrows of those little animals, are quite extensive in area. Quick, shrill yips were the warning signals given by the fat brownish dogs as they rushed to the very edge of their burrow holes. At the last moment they would disappear as if whisked away by magic, but almost immediately their heads would again pop out of the holes to observe the progress of rider or team. Or the watchful sentries sometimes descried a more real and deathly danger above, likely to swoop downward upon silent wings and with the speed of lightning; a hawk or an eagle, banking in majestic circles against the incomparable blue of the sky.

Those dog villages are exceedingly dangerous to riders who may find themselves into them before seeing the hazardous openings. They are doubly perilous after nightfall or during stormy weather. Cow ponies, as a rule, are careful not to become entangled in the burrow-pitted mazes, instinctively sensing the menace. Those smart horses know that they are likely to stumble and break legs or necks should they step into one of the deep openings.

Burrowing owls, small brownish birds, so common in the Southwest, do not share the aversion manifested by the ponies. They like to make their homes in deserted prairie-dog burrows, converting them into ideal traps for the mice and insects upon which they feed. Rattle-snakes, too, find the cavities ready-made dens and hiding places.

Ever since Cabezon had been left behind, we had been drawing nearer to the immense Chaco Mesa, and now the wagons were rolling over the far-flung tableland. This marked the homestretch to the Wetherill ranch; the mule teams began to strike out with more enthusiasm and required no urging. We enjoyed an almost unlimited view, the high altitude and rarefied air combining to give us marvelous visibility. In the far distances loomed range after range of lofty mountains, some of them, like the La

Plata Range, snow-capped. They appeared near, but it is a commonplace to be deceived as to distances. The high elevation and the clear, unsmudged ether of those mountainous tablelands bring faraway objects so close as to make them quite distinct. One may travel for days toward some landmark, peak, or range and apparently, at the end of each day, be as far from the goal as at the beginning of the ride.

Particularly at sunset the coloring of our surroundings became exquisite. The changing lights played upon the yellow sands, the red sandstone, and the various greens of the vegetation, producing every known shade of color from inky purple to bright silver. Especially beautiful were the indescribable fantasies of lights and shadows after a shower, or when the curtain of night was drawn over a background of sheer mountain.

No vexatious occurrences had marred the trip, we felt assured of reaching our destination in less than average time. The weather remained uniformly fair and mild, the fordings of the Rio Puerco and Rio Grande had taken the minimum of time, the heartbreaking pull to the ridge of the Bernalillo sandhills was accomplished more speedily than usual. Largely due to those favorable circumstances, we were approaching Chaco Canyon nearly two days earlier than we had expected to reach there and everybody was happy over the fine trip.

The boss, accompanied by Mrs. Wetherill and a young child, passed us shortly after we were established in the Cabezon night camp. He held the ribbons over a good-looking team of matched pintos, hitched to a specially built mountain buckboard, and could cover the entire distance from Albuquerque to the home ranch in two days driving. That performance represented, even in those days, an extraordinary feat. It required not only exceptionally fine horses but also a superior sort of driver, one able to get the utmost out of his team without permanently harming the animals or taking reckless driving chances. When he stopped for a short chat we had told him to expect us on the twelfth day out of Albuquerque, but now it appeared certain that we would pull into the ranch not later than the evening of the tenth day.

Dusk mantled the sleepy earth when our teams made their way down the last slope into Chaco Canyon, and by the time we came within less than four miles of the ranch, it was quite dark. Due to the absence of light and the deep shadows cast by the canyon walls, I was not able to see the immediate approach to the ranch, or to get the lay of the land that same evening. However, on the following day I returned on a ride over the territory that we had covered after nightfall.

The mules had been driven an extra-long distance on that last day, but despite their weariness it would not have been advisable to make camp so close to the ranch. The nearness of the corrals and water troughs, which they were eager to reach, might have induced the animals to hobble toward home; those considerations forced us to continue our travels through the palpable obscurity. After an hour's drive down the canyon, whose walls were shrouded in pitch-black shadows, we saw the glimmer of a light: the Wetherill ranch was before us.

Here the animals were on their home grounds; without light or other guidance the lead team swung through tall gates into a large yard, pulling up well ahead to make room for the wagons that followed. From the corrals in the deep end of the lot, under the sheer cliffs of the canyon and from the stables at the left, flanking one entire side of the huge enclosure, sounded welcoming stampings and neighings, answered by our teams and saddle horses.

Several men emerged from the bunkhouse carrying lighted lanterns. They assisted in unharnessing the mules
and looking after the teams and horses. Wetherill, who
had reached home four days ahead of us, appeared from
his house to greet everybody and to cast a critical eye
over stock and wagons. Evidently satisfied with the condition of both, he complimented us upon our quick
trip.

Then, after the animals were taken care of for the
night, the tired humans found food and shelter for themselves. I put my bedroll in an empty room adjoining the
feed bins while the others of our caravan sought the places
they had occupied before they made the trip. The married couple was quartered in a small room next to the
blacksmith shop.

While we had been busy getting the stock fed and
watered, and finding our respective quarters, the ranch
cook prepared a supper. Before long we were seated about
the table; for the first time since leaving Albuquerque,
we did not eat our meal alfresco. There was a big platter
heaped with thick, juicy steaks, a bowl filled with boiled
potatoes, the ubiquitous Mexican pink beans, a stack of
freshly sliced homemade bread, butter, and a large pot
full of steaming-hot coffee. The extra wait and unusually
late hour had sharpened our already good appetites, with
the result that the visible food supply was annihilated in
short order. However, the cook had plenty for all and did
not object to second and third helpings. Presently, all
were satisfied, happy and contented. Then, supper over,
we made our way by lantern light to the "office," a sort of
general assembly room in the boss's house where everybody was wont to gather in the evening or upon special
occasions.

Up to the moment of reaching the office, Wetherill's

place had not presented an aspect different from that of any other ranch with which I was acquainted. While putting up the horses and moving in the gloomy darkness, I had been able, despite the poor light shed by stable lanterns, to gain the impression of the same general arrangement of corrals, feed stores, bunkhouse, blacksmith shop, cookshack, and stables as could be found on other ranches, but there the resemblance ceased. For upon entering the room referred to as the office, I was as if struck suddenly, completely overcome with the wonder of it.

From the nearly total darkness that reigned outside, I passed into a brilliantly lighted interior that had none of the features usually associated with an office. Instead, it appeared as if an Indian museum had been combined with a collector's den. The room itself was rather large, rectangular in shape, and low-ceilinged. Heavy timbers, exposed overhead, supported the roof and ceiling, the latter formed of smooth, slender stems of cedar and pinon, not thicker than one's small finger, laid closely side by side. The sturdy beams of cedar, pinon, and pine had been salvaged from excavations of the Pueblo Bonito ruins. The slim wands that formed the unique ceiling also came from the rooms uncovered in the prehistoric apartment building.

The walls of the office, formed of heavy, sun-baked adobe bricks, smooth-plastered on the inside, were virtually hidden under a large assortment of specimens of Indian handicraft and the pelts of wild animals. There were priceless "Chief" blankets; fine old bayetas; marvelously woven antique Navajo rugs, showing the original native dyes; squaw dresses; Hopi belts; Katchina dolls; dance masks; gourd rattles; mountain lion and fox pelts; Indian drums; water-color reproductions of Navajo sand paintings; turquoise-inlaid ornaments; ancient Pueblo pottery; Mexican ollas; silver-mounted headstalls; buckskin-braided lariats; medicine baskets; Hopi plaques, bows and arrows in fringed quivers; soft leather saddle bags beautifully decorated with beadwork, made by Ute Indians; and a great variety of other interesting things that dazzled and dazed the beholder. The floor was thickly and entirely covered with exceptionally fine Navajo rugs that did not leave bare so much as a handbreadth of space.

The vivid, yes, barbaric colors of the blankets and rugs blended into a harmonious whole. Nothing could have been more fitting than this bewildering arrangement of Indian handicraft coupled with the mementos of the past, as exemplified in the various articles excavated in the ancient ruins. Many centuries ago those utensils had been fashioned and used by the inhabitants then living in this region; here, in Wetherill's ranch home, the white man employed them again after they had slumbered under the debris for ages.

Although it was my good fortune to live on the Wetherill ranch for nearly three years and to spend many evenings in the office, I never failed to be thrilled by the splendidly barbaric magnificence of the aspect upon opening the door and entering into that bright wonderland. Too, during those years I had numerous opportunities to observe in others the very same reactions to the completely unexpected and therefore so much more overpowering spectacle.

The rare visitors that came to the ranch invariably gasped their astonishment at the almost perfect theatrical effect of the setting. And Wetherill was, undoubtedly, a showman at heart for somehow or other he managed to nearly always stage the first entries in the evening, when the canyon was wrapped in purplish shadows or when a brilliant desert moon created weird images among the ghostly remnants of the ruins. Then, when his guests were under the mystic influence of the outdoors, he brought them into the office, the brightly lit lamps placed advantageously and so arranged as not to cast shadows. The exclamations of the stunned beholders must have been very pleasant to his ears, as one could see from the happy and satisfied smile that would cross his face.

I recall but one occasion other than on principal holidays when all hands assembled in the office during the day, and that happened upon a time when some Navajo Indians had a grievance to air and exhibited a sullen mood. There had been a dispute over some debts and about the manner employed by the boss to effect a settlement. It had its inception when Wetherill sent out some of the boys to round up a number of horses belonging to one of the complainants, who was indebted to him for goods bought in the trading post and who had persistently avoided making payment one season after another.

The roundedup ponies had been branded with the Wetherill iron, and sold to Eastern horse buyers that chanced to be in Pueblo Bonito. With a number of others, they were driven to the railroad, and while thus being moved across country, a member of the owner's family saw and recognized the horses and informed the Indian accordingly. That man lost no time in gathering together some twenty friends and relatives, and, accompanied by them, had come to the ranch to protest the transaction.

They had arrived during the preceding evening, and until a late hour Wetherill talked with the man who felt himself injured. As a matter of fact, the credit allowed him for the horses was fair and just; he was receiving full market value for the stock, but because the horses had been rounded up without his knowledge or participation, he felt entitled to nurse a grievance. Evidently he meant to make the most of the opportunity, seeing before him a welcome chance to drive a hard bargain, and in order to gain both moral and physical support for his arguments, he had brought his band of sympathizers.

All were armed, and as the arguments dragged on interminably, degenerating into a vicious circle that seemed to admit no break or change of sentiment or position, the tone of the claimant became more and more threatening. The speaker's harangue, at first a scowling complaint, changed by degrees into a menacing denunciation and the situation was developing an ugly aspect when Wetherill closed the session, announcing that he was tired and going to bed. The office, where this had taken place, was thus cleared, for the time being, of the mob of Indians. After they were gone, the boss instructed us not to leave the ranch in the morning on our daily round of chores, but to remain close at hand, and to notify the blacksmith, the cook, and several freighters to be ready for any call and all eventualities.

Early the next morning, the boys held a council of war and it was decided to assemble in the blacksmith shop, the building nearest to the boss's house, and from there to drift toward the office in an unostentatious manner. Waiting until the Indians were again gathered in the office, we, too, joined the meeting. We arrived singly and in groups of two or three until eleven of us were massed between the door and the group of Indians.

To do this had taken over an hour and the clock's hands were pointing toward noon. None of the boys had said anything; we simply walked into the office in a nonchalant manner and placed ourselves in strategic positions. It was only a short while after all of us had arrived when Wetherill began to wind up the arguments. He told the unwelcome callers that he could not change what was an accomplished fact and reiterated his willingness to listen to any reasonable proposals if his own solution of the matter was not entirely satisfactory. His firmness of tone and gesture, and the presence of nearly the entire ranch force, heavily armed, must have given sufficient weight to his words to persuade the Indians to see the affair in a different light.

There was some more perfunctory grumbling, the aggrieved party holding out for minor face-saving concessions in the way of donations of food and feed for the horses, but presently the proceedings were brought to a mutually satisfactory conclusion. Unquestionably, Wetherill's way of handling the situation proved both effective and eminently diplomatic. The Indians left the ranch convinced of having had the best of the deal, proud in the knowledge of a demonstrated ability to hold their own against the white man, and, most important of all, still friendly.

However, I am getting ahead of my story, and before relating any other experiences with the natives or Mexicans or others with whom I came in contact during those years in the desert country, it is well to say something about the locale—Chaco Canyon and Pueblo Bonito. It will be easier to follow the story if I insert, at this point, a few details pertaining to the stage upon which the scenes were played.

Chaco Canyon is situated in northwestern New Mexico, near the southern rim of the great San Juan drainage basin. In an air line it is about one hundred miles from the state capital, Santa Fe. To reach the closest railroad point, Thoreau, on the Santa Fe line, one has to travel nearly seventy miles in a southwesterly direction. Going

almost due north, it is equally distant to the Denver &
Rio Grande Railroad at Farmington, located on the Ani-
mas River where that stream is about to enter the San
Juan, a short distance south of the Colorado state boundary. Approximately 150 miles of hard, wearisome trails
formed the link between the canyon and Albuquerque,
the principal source of our supplies at the time of my stay
in Pueblo Bonito.

While there are some fertile patches of country, notably in certain canyons and protected valleys, virtually
the whole Chaco Canyon district is little better than
desert. Many parts of it are absolutely barren wastes of
sand and rock. The total area is almost entirely devoid of
springs. It has no permanent streams, is subject to severe
sandstorms, and the temperature ranges from one extreme
to the other: blistering heat in summer, and sharp, biting
cold in winter. Even in summer the nights are uniformly
cool, yes, chilly, and one can do very well with woolen
blankets and other bed coverings. The rare air of the
high mesa lands does not know fogs; rains are scarce,
except for the cloudburst-like downpours during the late
summer. Those storms, however, last for a short while
only.

Chaco Canyon is never more than a mile wide, generally much narrower. Its channel is eroded through the
sandstone cap that originally covered the entire region to
a depth of more than two hundred feet. The walls vary in
height up to two hundred feet to a mere ten or twelve
feet where the sifting sands have swirled dunes of foothill
dimensions directly against the escarpments of the bluff
cliffs. The level floor of the canyon is rich black soil and
brown loam, with some adobe, highly fertile when watered, and cut by an arroyo from twenty to nearly forty feet
deep. Except in the rainy season when black cloudbursts

flood the mesas, hills, and slopes, and drain into the arroyo, this ditch is always dry and carpeted with a deep layer of finely sifted desert sand.

Vegetation is sparse throughout the district. Trees are a rarity except for the scrub pines and cedars growing on the higher mesas. Sagebrush is everywhere, as is cactus, various species of grasses, Spanish bayonet, and the ubiquitous amole whose roots form a splendid substitute for soap, hence the more common name of soapweed or soap plant. During late spring, when the winter's snows have melted and the sun's rays get stronger, the desert takes on a bright flagging of wild flowers. Then the range blossoms out and fresh grass forms a green carpet. This picture changes when the burning shafts of real summer sunshine turn the spring beauty into scorched land and dried-up brown drabness. However, some time later, the desert again becomes green and lovely when the torrential rains of the wet season wash away the parched and dusty aspects left by the summer's heat. The different kinds of cacti produce some marvelously beautiful blossoms, and nothing can be more striking or sweeter smelling than the clean freshness of full-leaved sagebrush after the heavenly shower bath of a thunderstorm.

Late summer and fall are exquisite and represent the ideal period of the seasons. Real cold and winter weather often do not set in until well after Thanksgiving Day. Then storms proclaim Jack Frost's ascendancy, and over snow-blanketed mountains, mesas and canyons, winter holds sway, thus completing the cycle.

Chapter 7

PUEBLO BONITO, THE STUPENDOUS

The principal objects of interest in Chaco Canyon are the ruins of the prehistoric buildings erected by the community dwellers, especially those of Chettro Kettle, Pueblo Bonito, and Pueblo Alto. I first saw Pueblo Bonito on the morning after my arrival in Chaco Canyon and even a short, superficial inspection convinced me that here was a truly remarkable monument to human endeavor. During the months and years that I spent in the canyon I became more and more enthralled with the wonder of those impressive ruins, and my admiration grew accordingly. Many a day was devoted to little private tours of exploration and excavation, and I felt amply rewarded when my labors uncovered some heretofore unseen object, even if it happened to be only a fragment. In the course of time I made myself familiar with the history of the ruins and I shall give, as briefly as possible, some of the most important facts and data pertaining to the Chacones and their communal edifices.

My arrival in Pueblo Bonito coincided with the time when the Hyde Exploring Expedition was bringing to an end the large-scale excavations that were the first of several similar undertakings. Their activities provided ample opportunities to gain firsthand knowledge of the subject. Later efforts to solve the riddle of the Chacones, many years after my sojourn in that enchanted canyon, were undertaken by the Archaeological Society, by the National Geographic Society, by New Mexico, Utah, and Arizona universities, and by other institutions. Each one secured valuable data and gained new information of far-reaching historical import. A number of famous scientists have written their reports and findings; these can be found in every reference library.

Lieutenant James H. Simpson gave to the world the first account of the Chaco ruins in any official report; he was the first to use the spelling "Chaco."

It was August, 1849, that he accompanied Governor John M. Washington on an expedition to the Navajo country, starting from Jemez and, by way of the Nacamiento, striking west to the head of Chaco Canyon. The troops that formed the body of the expedition undoubtedly committed acts of vandalism when they pulled the huge timbers and beams from the ruins and used the wood secured in that fashion for their campfires. However, in a treeless country it was perhaps to be expected that the soldiery would not be restrained by aesthetic considerations; field service is not conducive to foster appreciation of historical or artistic monuments, but of necessity must give way to the pursuit of strictly utilitarian purposes. In any event, while from an archaeological point of view much damage was done, a great deal of the possible extent of vandalism was prevented simply because in the course of centuries time had built a protective wall against just such marauders: an accumulation of sand had drifted high over the ruins, safeguarding them and leaving only a minor portion of the mighty buildings exposed.

In his report to Washington, Lieutenant Simpson estimated that in the construction of Chettro Kettle, by no means the largest of the community buildings, not less than thirty million pieces of stone had been quarried, transported, shaped, and laid in the walls. We know now that he might more accurately have made his estimate fifty million, since a much greater portion of the town was buried than he supposed. In addition to this, thousands of locks, poles, and slabs had to be cut in distant forests, transported by man power, prepared with stone tools, and built into the structures. All of the Chaco ruins are noteworthy for massive architecture and, particularly, for excellent masonry.

Entering Chaco Canyon from the eastern end, Chettro Kettle, the Rain Pueblo, is the first of the three large community buildings to come to the view of the traveler. The splendid town, covering a site of about six acres, with fine curving façade, inner towers, an immense sanctuary within its court, and a half-dozen adjacent structures, must have been one of the most striking buildings in ancient North America. On the northern sky line, a mile away, looms Pueblo Alto, traditionally the house of the Great Chief. Beholding it, one recalls the noted places of antiquity in the Old World. Between Chettro Kettle and Pueblo Alto spreads the magnificent pile of Pueblo Bonito—a truly impressive ruin with a vast sweep of curving wall over 800 feet in length, still standing almost fifty feet high in places, and embodying virtually every style of masonry known to and employed by the Chacones.

The season for excavation in the Chaco is from spring to fall. During much of this period the heat is scorching. Dust storms and high winds that carry with them pieces of rock as large as walnuts are frequent and become nearly intolerable at times. Undaunted by those handicaps, the

Hyde Expedition carried on its work under the scientific supervision of Professor Frederic W. Putnam, of Harvard University. A large amount of archaeologically valuable material rewarded the efforts of the explorers; it can be seen in the American Museum of Natural History in New York. Some of the objects are among the most precious treasures of American archaeology; Mr. George Pepper, Field Director of the Hyde Exploring Expedition in the excavation of Pueblo Bonito, has decribed in detail a number of the surprising finds that were unearthed in the ruins.

To form a better idea of the tremendous size of Pueblo Bonito one must consider that upwards of *five hundred* rooms were excavated by the Hyde Exploring Expedition. Most of them were refilled, the idea being that thus the structures would be better preserved and kept from the ravages of erosion and other destructive forces. The excavators and explorers, having satisfied their curiosity, emulated nature's example by refilling the rooms they had laid bare, using the same protecting substance the elements had piled up in the course of nearly ten centuries.

Thirty-two kivas, circular council chambers or sancturies, were uncovered in the course of the excavations, all in the interior of the enormous building. These prehistoric kivas were, normally, circular subterranean rooms, the roof being flush with the ground. Ordinarily, the entrance was gained by a ladder leading down through a combination hatchway and smoke vent in the roof. Invariably there was a fire pit in the floor, and a benchlike stone seat circled the entire inner wall.

Careful measurements were taken of all excavations, and numerous photographs and artists' sketches recorded every phase of the gigantic undertaking.

The Chacones, as the inhabitants of these community dwellings have been named, did not excel as architects and builders only; they were also experts in the minor arts and handicrafts. Their pottery forms a typical group. It is distinctive, and different from the kinds found in all other pueblo excavations. The builders of those monumental works were adept at farming, too. It must have taken not merely intensive, but actually *scientific* cultivation of the canyon floor, and a high standard of husbandry for preserving the fruits of the soil, to feed the large population of the town's buildings.

One of the many mysteries of the Chaco is the fact that, although searched for persistently, the cemeteries of the large ruins have never been found. Careful examinations of the rubbish heaps of Pueblo Bonito, Chettro Kettle, and the other great community buildings disclosed that they contained no graves whatever. Some bodies were taken from the excavated rooms, possibly the remains of sick or disabled persons who could not be moved and had to be left to their fate when the great exodus that depopulated the dwellings took place. Of the many hundreds that must have died during the time the buildings were occupied, none was found. Likewise, science has not yet learned a satisfactory answer to the question: What happened to the surviving Chaco dwellers who migrated else where?

The Chaco Canyon area, in respect of human associations, is without a parallel. Uninterrupted quiet brooded here for ages. This hush was broken by the voices of humanity for some centuries, followed by a silence more poignant than that of the waste which remained forever uninhabited. Here, puny man erected monuments to his vast endeavors, but made no visible lasting impression on the country—the desert remains unconquered.

Scientists, with their special ways of ascertaining time and periods, tell us that Pueblo Bonito, the colossal community building, was under construction in the year A.D., 919, and that the settlement reached its heyday in 1067.

At that period, in other parts of the world, the compass had been perfected; Irnerius had given impetus to the resurrection of Justinian's law texts that had lain dormant for more than five centuries; the Greek Church separated from the Latin Church; the madness that ultimately gave birth to the Crusades was germinating; the kings and emperors of the Saxon house ruled over sections of what is now known as Germany and France, and laid the foundations of the German monarchy and assumed the bombastic title of the Holy Roman Emperor of the German nation; Danes and Northmen warred in England and ravaged that country; the Danish invaders of England established their supremacy when Cnut (Canute) became king of the country and reigned as such from 1016 to 1035; in France the clergy succeeded in securing the adoption of the Truce of God which permitted and left only eighty days in a year available for actual warfare; Spain witnessed the brilliance of the Moorish civilization, and Cordova, one of the most populous cities was recognized as a seat of science and arts.

Those two world-revolutionizing discoveries, the gun and printing press, still slumbered in the womb of time; hundreds of years were yet to pass before their invention, but already the Chacones had fitted together the pieces of masonry that became Chettro Kettle, Pueblo Bonito, and Pueblo Alto. Since then a thousand years have rolled by. During the millenium the Chacones are turned to dust, and even *that* last reminder of their brief appearance on the earthly stage is missing and cannot be found.

The Chacones lived, loved, and died, as all of us do and shall. They had their problems, their joys and pains, their rise and decline. Their lives paralleled ours, describing the same curve that begins with the cradle and ends with the grave.

Sitting upon the ruins of their proud edifices, a long procession of peoples passes before the mind's eye. One seems to see to the beginning of time and to watch the evolution of mankind. Through the dim ages there shape themselves the single figures, swelling gradually to clans and tribes and nations. Thousands of years are bridged in an instant, one lives with the Sumerians, the precursors of Babylonians, the Persians of antiquity, and the successive occupants of the Mesopotamian and Nile lands. Assyrians crowd Phoenicians who, in turn, are followed by Carthaginians, Medes, peoples of India, Celts, Britons, Greeks, Romans, and Teutons.

All of them, untold millions, lived and died, and no other fate is in store for us. They had their family life, they struggled for existence, for shelter and food and wealth and position. They labored and toiled and slaved. Some achieved high positions—none gained independence. That state has never yet been reached; we still lean upon each other and cannot exist singly or by ourselves alone. Fundamentally, all our forefathers on earth passed through the same cycle of existence that is present-day man's lot. And the sum total of their combined or individual efforts, both physical and mental is pitifully small, yes, almost negligible. Shamefacedly, one must admit that the staggering amount of every type of energy expended through billions of human beings over a period of many thousands of years has produced, comparatively, the same result as the labor of the mountain that brought forth a mouse. Ruins, more than anything else, prove the utter futility of human labors. No other example shows more clearly that even the mightiest works of men are predestined to come to the same end. Paradoxically, there is only one thing that defies time and corruption, and is everlasting: Change!

Thoughts like those come unbidden while one gazes at the tremendous pile of masonry that once housed the busy and industrious tribes which made Chaco Canyon ring to human speech. It is not difficult to visualize their daily tasks; seemingly, the ruins become alive and swarm with hundreds of small people. Then, suddenly, there is the stillness of death; the sounds cease; no longer can the scurrying of bare and sandaled feet be heard; there are no fires, no, not even a wisp of smoke. Chaco Canyon has again been claimed by the silence of the desert, to remain sleeping for nearly ten centuries.

It gives one a peculiar feeling to think that, between five and six hundred years before the discovery of America by Columbus, there were busy people erecting in the heart of the desert, in our own United States of America, skyscraper apartment houses. History takes on an entirely different expression when considered in that light. Columbus' unknown continent proves to have been the home of races that even modern science finds hard to classify. And although at the close of the fifteenth century Columbus and other discoverers and conquistadores after him found the peoples of Mexico, of Cuba, Central America, Peru and other places, five centuries more had to come and go before the glory that was Pueblo Bonito dazzled and bewildered the archaeologists.

Of course, even a thousand-year interval is regarded lightly by archaeologists, and while the life of the Chacones remains an unsolved mystery, they were by no means the first humans to occupy that particular region.

Possibly *ten thousand* years ago, many centuries before the era of the community dwellers, prehistoric men hunted the mammoth elephant and left the skeletons of the shaggy beasts, pierced by stone-pointed javelins and other weapons, in the New Mexico plains. That was the age when the Great Lakes were basins filled with ice a mile deep and the whole continent a vast expanse of Siberia-like tundra as far south as New Mexico.

During the period of the Hyde Exploring Expedition, Pueblo Bonito, (whose official post office name was Putnam, in honor of Professor Putnam, of Harvard), became the headquarters of an extensive trading enterprise. Supplies were needed for the maintenance of the large number of Indian and Mexican laborers employed in the actual work of excavating, and for the members of the expedition. Taking care of this need formed the nucleus of the trading business that was to flourish under Richard Wetherill's management for years. The natural outgrowth of handling supplies for one's own commissary was to engage in trading with the Indians, stock buying, stock selling, and stock raising.

Great lines of freight wagons moved between the Pueblo Bonito headquarters and the various centers of supplies, principally Albuquerque, Gallup, and Thoreau, stations on the Santa Fe railroad, and Aztec and Farmington in the San Juan River country to the north. Many things, such as fruits and vegetables, feed, hay, lumber, and other items came from the Mormon settlements in the north. Beside the main depot at Pueblo Bonito, Wetherill operated trading posts in Farmington, Thoreau, Tiz-Na-Tzin, Ojo Alamo, Largo, Raton Springs and at the Escavada Wash. For the exclusive use of the expedition, a harness shop was established in Farmington.

In addition to an exceedingly active retail trading business, the commercial activities of the Hyde Exploring Expedition included wholesale dealing in Indian traders' supplies, Navajo rugs, Indian silverware and curios, wool, hides, pelts, sheep, cattle, horses, and mules. The heavy freight wagons carried loads of wool, hides, and other products of the country to the railroad towns, bringing on their return trips flour, coffee, sugar, calico, robes, hardware, and the thousand and one items of goods usually found in general merchandise stores and particularly in Indian trading posts. Many wagonloads of excavated treasures had to be transported over the rough trails, in itself an undertaking of magnitude, and doubly hazardous on account of the fragile nature of the articles that were shipped without benefit of springs and shock absorbers.

Whether history repeats itself I do not know, but I hold it to be rather doubtful. However, for a brief span of years, Chaco Canyon was once more bustling with activity. The quiet slumber under the turquoise-blue desert skies that had lasted for centuries was disrupted by the swarming horde of workers, Indians, Mexicans, freighters, scientists, cowboys, adventurers, investigators, visiting ranchers; a truly heterogeneous lot. The canyon rang to the shouts of the teamsters; the crack of their long whips reverberated from the cliffs. Cowpunchers and Indians staged races to determine the fleetness of their ponies. The shrill encouragement of the onlookers seemed strangely out of place, disturbing the brooding calm of the mighty ruins.

For some years after the Hyde Exploring Expedition concluded its labors, Richard Wetherill and his family remained in Pueblo Bonito, but the panic of 1907 inflicted losses from which he never recovered, financially speaking. And in 1908 a Navajo Indian shot and killed this man who had befriended the red men for more than a generation—who had fed them when hungry, who had tended their sick and disabled, who had helped bring them into this world and who often performed the last service for their dead—who was, in his heart, as much an original American as the Indians themselves!

After the tragedy, Mrs. Wetherill and her children moved away. Taking with them their Indian treasures, household goods, horses and cattle, they established a new ranch in northeastern Arizona.

Since then the canyon has serenely returned to its interrupted hibernation, wrapped in the mystery of folded sleep. The ranch buildings have disappeared; long ago, the post office was discontinued; several excavating expeditions have come and gone; the ruins still lie where the first white men found them, apparently the same as they were before the frantic diggings attempted to wrest their secrets from them: the unchanging desert holds its own, unmastered, unconquerable!

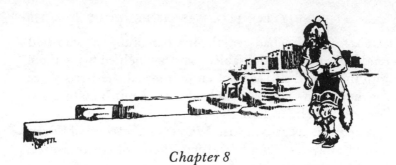

Chapter 8

THE TRIANGLE BAR TRIANGLE

Life on the Triangle Bar Triangle ranch was decidedly more interesting and diversified than the routine existence of ordinary cattle or horse outfits. Wetherill's varied interests developed a multiplicity of duties that prevented a tiresome monotony in the repetition of daily chores. We were not just cow hands, or fence riders, but Jacks-of-all-trades. My principal job was to share with several other "boys" the handling of large herds of horses, to "break" broncos, and to maintain in good order the fences and windmills of our pasture. Incidentally, that pasture was a sizeable lot, measuring fully three miles in width and eight miles in length, thus containing twenty-four square miles of ground. In other words, a playground for the horses embracing over fifteen thousand acres.

To ride the boundaries of that enclosure was a good day's work. One of the hands had to do so each day, rain or shine, summer or winter. The southern limits of this extensive tract were the steep walls of Chaco Canyon. Those sheer cliffs, rising perpendicularly from the canyon floor to the top of the mesa, unscalable and equally difficult to descend, provided a more effective barrier than man-made fences or other obstacles. The northern boundary was a wide, sandy wash. There barbed-wire fences had been built to keep the stock from straying. The eastern and western ends were marked by broken cliffs, in part sufficiently rough and craggy to prevent escape of the horses, and in other sections made impassable through stone barricades built by Indians, augmented by stretches of barbed-wire fences.

Several windmills had been erected in this pasture, pumping water from shallow wells into long troughs of galvanized sheet iron. Pumps and troughs required constant attention. The first needed periodic oiling and adjustment of vanes; the troughs had to be cleaned out and kept fresh and sweet. Pipes would clog if not watched carefully; now and then it happened that the horses would break fittings in their mad rush and scramble for water. The man who was on duty "riding" the mesa left the ranch carrying with him hammer, staples for nailing down loose pieces or broken lengths of fence wire, pliers and wire cutters, a medium-size monkey wrench and, at times, a compact outfit of block and tackle for tightening up sagging wires. His saddle pockets held so many tools and other pieces of hardware as to resemble a perambulating plumber's outfit. Cans of oil, rags for wiping, pump packing material, extra bolts and washers, and other necessary supplies were kept in covered and padlocked boxes at each windmill.

In addition to attending to his mechanical duties, the mesa rider would observe the disposition and temporary grazing habits of the scattered groups of horses. That enabled him to inform the boss just where the different bands could be encountered should Wetherill wish to have certain portions of the big herds rounded up and brought to the ranch corrals. Ordinarily, the horses would be seen in segregated, small groups under the leadership of a stallion, or in charge of some wise old mare. Those individual bands would keep pretty much to themselves, grazing and bedding down in their chosen locations, and from week to week shifting but slightly while the feed remained good. They would march to the watering troughs once or twice a day, breaking into a trot upon approaching the windmills, then return slowly to their grazing grounds after having quenched their thirst.

During mating season this quiet life was disrupted to a greater or lesser extent by the advances of the young bachelor stallions. They attempted to wrest control of the harems from the established leaders, or, if unsuccessful in that, tried to break away with some of the mares and fillies to form separate bands of their own. The shrill neighing that accompanied the rushing charges and countercharges, and the squealing of the fighting stallions left the mares unperturbed. Let the males scratch, bite, and kick each other; they kept a watchful eye on the colts that stared in wide-eyed wonder at the commotion and did not always get out of the way quick enough in the melee of blind fighting.

Eventually, the battles were decided; old stallions had, in most cases, maintained their rights and trotted off proudly with their bands. Others, however, tasted defeat and were forced to give away to younger blood. Once the changes had taken place and conditions on the mesa and among the horses became stabilized again, the mesa rider could answer without hesitation such questions as: "Where did you see old Scarface today?" or "Are the palominos still at the upper end of the mesa?" or "Did you count the colts in White Stocking's herd?"

A precipitous trail, not more than eight feet wide at its

broadest part, had been cut into the wall of the canyon approximately a mile below the ranch. Over this narrow passageway the horses were driven to the mesa pasture, and down again to the corrals when wanted. Almost daily a part of the stock was rounded up and brought to the ranch, there to undergo the various stages of taming, or "breaking," as the process is termed in the vernacular of the range. "Broncobusting" was a regular portion of our routine, all hands, except the blacksmith and cook, taking part in the job of "gentling" the wild range horses. Generally, two or three lessons were considered sufficient to turn a bronco into a gentle saddle pony, but this was measured by *cowpuncher standards* that considered any horse "gentle" and "saddle broke" when it could be ridden at all. He might not yet be "bridle-wise," but that did not prevent him from being classed with the docile horses. The finer points of making a dependable cow pony out of unbroken stock required a great deal of patience and time, much more than was wasted upon ordinary broomtails.

The prolonged and trying efforts necessary to transform a bronc into a horse which the cowpuncher could use for range work were not spent upon stock that was presently to be sold; that sort of training was not required of horses which in all probability, and before long, would be hitched to a light delivery wagon or put to similar service in Middle Western towns.

In the case of likely-looking ponies that the punchers desired for their own mounts, however, no exertion was too strenuous or wearisome to achieve perfection. Cowboys would spend many months of patient labor in order to teach their pets all the tricks required of a top cow pony, and in time they could boast proudly that "this here horse knows more about the work than I do."

Particular care was taken with horses that had to be trained for women riders, or were intended to perform on the polo field. Or the boss might decide to "break" a stout four-year-old for harness, to become a recruit for his various teams that he used when driving light buggies or the sturdier mountain buckboard.

Every man had his "string" of horses, which nobody else used. Of course, the stock belonged to the rancher, and the right to use the particular horses ceased to be valid when the cowboy quit the outfit, but during his stay on the ranch, the puncher was to every intent and purpose the proprietor of his string. The boss, himself, would respect that status and not sell, or otherwise dispose of the horses that formed part of the strings of the punchers. In addition to the horses that the ranch furnished each man for his work, most punchers had horses actually their own, just as I had brought my personal mount with me upon joining the outfit. Feed and pasturage for those privately owned horses was furnished free, no matter how much or how little the puncher used his own pony.

Generally, those private mounts were excellent horses and outstanding in some particular qualities. All of them were especially well trained and knew their masters like a good dog knows his owner-friend. They would come when called, or upon hearing a peculiar whistle or other signal. None required tying—they stood without hitching, anywhere, and under all conditions. They were speedy and possessed great endurance, were quick as a cat, never gun-shy, and able to turn "on a dime." They were good climbers, not afraid to enter water, smart in many ways, such as discerning quicksand and other dangers, and could take care of themselves even in poor feeding country. That sort of horse was never tough-mouthed; each one was perfectly trained to "neck-reining." Naturally, such a horse was not for sale—as soon ask a cowpuncher to sell his brother!

On many ranches could be seen old horses that had served out their usefulness under the saddle, peacefully grazing now in some pasture, pensioned off, so to speak, until their natural end should take them to some horse heaven.

From Missouri Wetherill had brought three fine jacks for stud service. They were mated with Indian mares and in due season a number of mule colts augmented the mesa herds. Being out of pony mothers, those frisky fellows were not especially large, but Wetherill reasoned that the combination of good Missouri stock and proven Indian toughness and endurance ought to produce a strain particularly adapted to southwestern conditions. Anyhow, he had more orders for "Indian" mules than he could fill.

There was a never-ending change in the number of horses that roamed the mesa, as we called our big pasture. Wetherill was always buying and selling, replenishing the herds through trades or outright purchases from the Indians, and selling the accumulated stock to horse buyers or at auction. The auctions meant drives over trails to Albuquerque, Santa Fe, El Paso, into the Panhandle of Texas and, at least upon one occasion, all the way to Goodnight, Oklahoma. Several hundred head of horses would be assembled, all properly and plainly branded, and then started on the trail. A grub wagon would accompany the drive. The foreman in charge of the outfit carried a bill of sale, making him the legal owner of the horses, and upon the return from the trip he accounted for the receipts, less incidental expenses incurred during the long trek.

On cattle ranches it happened frequently that a man was sent to Omaha or Kansas City or Chicago with a trainload of beeves, carrying full authority to sell the stock and collect the money for it, without having been bonded or assuring the real owner any other security or guarantee than his word. In the years I spent on the range it never came to my knowledge that any man ever betrayed such confidence or failed to make the proper accounting, or neglected to discharge in the most honorable manner the trust reposed in him. Hijacking and embezzlement did not thrive in the cow country.

Upon several occasions we rounded up bands of wild burros. Those funny-looking longears we drove to Pagosa Springs, Colorado, there selling them for two dollars each to miners. The hardy little beasts were easily trained and put to work carrying loads of ore from the mines to the smelter. The mines, being located in virtually inaccessible places, could not be reached by wagon or other contrivance. The employment of burros solved the problem; sure-footedly they carried their burdens, walking with mincing steps over trails bordering precipices that might have caused a mountain goat to hesitate.

There were opportunities to make a trip to the railroad other than going with a bunch of horses to be auctioned. When a man arrived at the decision that he must have a fling at the pleasures which were dangled before his imagination by the glittering towns, he had the privilege of turning teamster for a trip or two. Sometimes he would go by himself, at other times in company with a wagon train. I recall distinctly one trip I made to Albuquerque, unaccompanied. It cured me of the desire to repeat the experience.

In order to make the trip "pay," that is, avoid hauling empty wagons, I was carrying eleven bags of wool on the lead wagon but only the grub box, my bedding roll, and some hay and grain for the mules on the trailer. I had a span of six mules, good, tough animals who, with their long-gaited walk, could cover a great deal of ground in a day's drive. For the return trip I was to collect a load of miscellaneous freight from three of the wholesale houses with whom the boss was in the habit of dealing. It was September; the heavy rains of late summer were over, leaving the range fresh and green and all holes or other depressions in the rocks filled with water. Days and nights sparkled—it was an ideal time for making an overland trip.

We left Pueblo Bonito one morning about six o'clock. It was my intention to put as many miles as possible between the ranch and the first evening's camp. That was to discourage the mules from attempting to return to their beloved stables and corrals. Nothing happened to mar the day's drive, and we had covered a long distance when I decided to make an unusually lush section of mesa land the resting place for the night. So I let the mules pull the wagons toward a clump of cedars and stopped.

First I had to unharness the team, then take them to drink at a near-by water hole in the rocks. Willingly the six animals returned to camp and stood with eagerly lifted nozzles about the wagon, impatiently watching me apportion their feed of mixed oats and corn into the nose bags. While they were munching their supper, I slipped from one to the other, fastening the rawhide hobbles to their forelegs, to which procedure they submitted with accustomed docility. Then I gathered dry sagebrush for a fire and soon had a small blaze started. The grub box yielded food already prepared, donated by the cook to save the chore of cooking meals for at least the first day or two, depending upon the appetite.

The only thing to do was to boil water for coffee, and that did not take long. But before putting the finishing touches to my own meal, I removed the emptied nose bags from the mules, thus enabling them to hobble off and begin grazing. Then, ground coffee was added to the furiously boiling water and allowed to steep for a while before it was considered ready for drinking.

After the dishes were washed in some water heated for that purpose, and the bedroll spread in a space free from rocks and stubbly growth, I visited the mules that had strolled away some short distance. All seemed to be well: they were grazing contentedly, the grass was abundant, and water plentiful in the troughlike depressions in the sandstone. No signs indicated the presence of any other living being within a radius of miles, no reflected gleam of fire marked Indian camp sites. To all outward appearances we were alone in the sea of sagebrush. Overhead the stars put on a display of pyrotechnics that shamed all the glitter of diamonds ever exhibited in Tiffany's. With sundown, a chilly little breeze had sprung up which, in the high, rare atmosphere, presaged clearly the coming of fall and winter. One more look about the camp and toward the animals, grazing closely enough to be discernible in the mantling darkness, and I made my simple preparations for going to sleep. Then, between the blankets of the bedroll, I drifted off immediately into a sound slumber.

Before daylight, the thumping of the hobbled feet of the mules wakened me; they had just returned from the water hole and were almost stepping upon me in their eagerness to get close to the wagon that held the grain. In a matter of minutes I was dressed and filling the nose bags. This time I slipped a short piece of rope around the neck of each animal, tying the mules to the wagon to prevent their straying after breakfast. Then I prepared the morning coffee, a simple procedure. While the coffee steeped, I took off the hobbles and harnessed the mules. Then I breakfasted, cleaned and packed away the dishes and supplies, rolled up my blanket roll, and got the empty nose bags from the mules. Everything was stowed in good order and nothing remained except to put the headstalls on the mules and line up the team before the wagons. Then we started on the second day of our trip.

As on the first day, we covered a fair distance before we made our evening camp. I had purposely cut short the noon stop in order to reach a certain spring and campground with an abundance of grass. The routine of establishing ourselves did not differ from the procedure of the preceding night, and nothing unusual happened between dark and daylight. Early upon the third day after leaving Pueblo Bonito we continued on our way, but that day was not to pass so uneventfully as had the other two.

Well along in the afternoon we came to a piece of road winding about the base of a dome-shaped hill. Following the contours of the hill, the roadbed, or, more accurately speaking, the wagon ruts that formed the trail, slanted outward and downward. Instead of being banked as are modern roads and race tracks, to overcome the centrifugal attraction, the opposite slant of that hillside actually assisted the force of gravity. My load of wool was properly put on the wagon and securely lashed with tie ropes; nevertheless, in exactly the most awkward place, the lead wagon began a slow motion of turning over on its right side. I had barely time to jump away and to hold tightly onto the six reins, thereby preventing the scared mules from stampeding and tearing up harness, wagon, and load.

The pressure of the combined weight of the wool bags proved too great for the ropes. They snapped, and, free from restraint, the bags rolled down the incline, coming to rest in a tumbled heap some fifteen or twenty feet from the overturned wagon. The trailer remained upright. The only damage I could discern upon hasty inspection was a bent connecting iron that could be straightened and put back into shape. But now to work—to get out of this mess.

First I unharnessed the team and tied the animals to some near-by pinon trees, then uncoupled the trailer from the lead wagon. The broken pieces of lash rope had to be untied and spliced. After that came the problem of righting the wagon and putting it back on its four wheels. All my efforts proved unavailing: I could not budge the bulky mass. I might have been able to do so on level ground, but to lift the wagon with its heavy bed and wheels uphill without the help of a jack or other mechanical contrivance was impossible for me. "Sheer strength and awkwardness" would not do the trick, although I possessed more than my fair share of both. After several attempts that tried muscles and lungs to the bursting point, I desisted. Instead, I improvised a sort of long hauling rope by doubling the tie ropes, looping them about the upper portion of the wagon bed and around the center of the box and below the running gear. To that I hitched two of the mules and, holding them to a steady, slow pull, soon had the wagon back on its four wheels. Before starting the pull I had set the brake, to prevent the wagon from rolling forward or backward.

All of this sounds much easier and quicker than it could be done. After the wagon turned over, I had to get the mules unhitched and keep them from tangling the harness. My efforts to right the wagon by sheer strength alone took some time. The matter of disconnecting the trailer required nearly half an hour of strenuous work as the bent piece of iron that held the two wagons together had twisted in such a manner as to make it into an almost solid link. For a long time it resisted my efforts to straighten it. Every operation, described in just a few words, took planning and time to execute, with the result that nearly two hours passed before the wagon had again been placed in its proper position. By that time it was beginning to get dusk, so, rather than attempt the loading of the wagon that evening, I let the wool lie where the bags had rolled and made camp then and there. The wish being father of the thought, I hoped that some other freighter or cowpuncher might come along, or that some Indians would pass by, any of whom could be induced to lend a hand in reloading the wool.

The mules were taken care of as on other evenings, and the grub box found an enthusiastic admirer of the good things to eat. The hard work had put a keen edge on my appetite, and supper became a real feast. To repay myself for the strenuous efforts, I even opened a can of tomatoes— a generous sprinkling of sugar converted the contents into a luscious dessert. And so, with my bags of wool scattered on the ground and the wagon somewhat scratched up and battered, I laid me down to sleep, praying that by morning assistance might be at hand to help put the heavy load back upon the wgaon.

This expectation did not materialize: dawn failed to bring the desired aid. There was no choice, except to face the task of reloading the wool unaided, a job I tackled as soon as breakfast was over. Before it was completed I was bathed in perspiration and shaking from muscular exhaustion. It proved a tough proposition to roll the bags one by one close to the wagon, the ground being loose and uneven and sloping upward. Every inch of the distance had to be fought for, almost as players battle for yards on the gridiron.

I had to dig in with my heels, then push with all my might to move the weight of the bag, gaining a foot or two with each effort. The bags were about seven feet long, over two feet in diameter, and packed with an average of about three hundred pounds of wool. They resembled pieces of heavy logs, but their smooth sides offered no hold for the fingers. I could not drag them to the wagon by the teams as that would have burst the sacking and torn the bags apart, scattering the wool. The mules were no help to me, I had to do the job myself. How the animals must have chortled in unholy glee to see the master tug and strain, pitting his puny man-strength against the inert mass of heavy wool.

After getting the bags to the wagon, I upended them, then tipped them over the side and straightened them out afterward. That was not so hard to do with the first few bags because those merely filled the bottom part of the wagon bed. It turned into a much more difficult job with the other bags that had to be hoisted correspondingly higher as the load resumed its original shape. To prevent a repetition of the accident, I piled the upper layer of bags 'way over to the near side of the wagon, thus relieving the lower side of most of the weight, very much in the manner sailors will hang over the side of a dangerously tilted boat to prevent capsizing.

At the end of a heartbreaking struggle I finally got the wagon loaded and provisionally secured the bags by ropes that held the odd-looking stowage. The trailer had been fastened to the lead wagon, the brake pulls adjusted, the mules were standing ready to start once again. One more look to see that nothing was left behind, and I gave the signal to start. It was almost noon—the upset had lost at least half a day.

Well away from the sloping curve, I halted the team and put my load in proper order. I had cut a young pinon tree and used the trimmed stem to twist the ropes that held the bags onto the wagon. The ropes cut deeply into the wool bags and left concave marks in the wood of the wagonbox, but the twisting lashed the load so firmly to the wagon as to virtually make one homogeneous mass of both. Nothing short of a cyclone, it seemed, would be able to tear them apart, and, indeed, I had no further trouble from shifting loads during the rest of the way to Albuquerque.

Two days over a week after leaving the ranch, I guided the team toward the livery stable and corral where the animals were to rest for the next two or three days. The trailer was uncoupled and four of the mules turned into the corral. The lead wagon, with its load of wool, pulled by just two of the mules, was taken to the storehouse of one of the wholesale firms. There, with the help of some men employed in the warehouse, the wool was unloaded promptly, weighed, and a receipt made out for the total. I turned in my order for the miscellaneous cargo of goods that was to be taken back to Chaco Canyon, got some feed for the mules, then returned to the stable. My own effects, such as grub box, bedding roll, gun, harness, whip, ropes, and other paraphernalia, including two large tarpaulins, were locked in a storeroom used for that purpose. Only then could I consider myself free to take in the sights and enjoy my stay in the big city.

The first pleasure was to get a shave, haircut, and bath, and to change into clean clothing. Meanwhile, an industrious Mexican *muchacho* worked over the boots, attempting to restore the pristine gloss and beauty they had brought with them from the Texas maker. However, like maidenly virtue that, once lost, cannot be regained, the scars of the range, the scratches from brush and cacti, the grinding marks of rock and sand, are not to be erased from the soft calfskin. Polishing may give it cleanliness, but it cannot hide the signs of service; these are engraved to stay and refuse to be ironed out or smoothed away. Presently, fresh and clean, shaved and shined, I emerged from the rejuvenating establishment, face all aglow from the generous use of hot water and plenty of soap, hair slicked down with sweet-smelling barbershop lotion, boots glossy, hat brushed and once again showing its original color instead of a layer of sand and dust. Now for a long drink of cool beer!

Albuquerque, like almost every other town of its size, boasted a German brewery. Is there any place on this earth where the votaries of Gambrinus have failed to establish a dispensary of the fluid particularly dedicated to the old German deity? The Albuquerque product proved good, and there was no lack of places where one could satisfy the desire for a drink of nicely cooled beer, or, for that matter, humor the craving for anythng else in alcholic beverages, both foreign and domestic.

Followed then a good meal in the restaurant adjoining the old Sturges Hotel. After the more or less unrestrained manner of the ranch, and the absolute nonobservance of the conventions while on the road, it was both a bit awkward and at the same time gratifying and distinctly enjoyable to sit at a restaurant table and be attended by an alert waiter. The pleasure of having the choice of selection, the service, the napery, the sparkle of glasses, dishes, and silver, the presence of many others, all combined to produce a warm feeling of well-being and good fellowship.

Albuquerque offered quite a variety of cookery, combining good old-fashioned American dishes with ranch-style menus, and, in addition, a large selection of Italian and Mexican concoctions. The latter particularly distinguished themselves through sharp seasonings, what with generous dashes of ground chili, plentiful additions of hot peppers, ground onions, and garlic. Just as in El Paso and Juarez, street vendors hawked hot tamales, chile con carne, enchiladas, and frijoles Mexican style. They did not lack customers once the sun had disappeared and the desert air became chilled to the freezing point in the late hours of the darkness.

The saloons stocked sideboards with all sorts of appetizers, the so-called "free lunch." However, in none of the southwestern towns was the spread as varied or generous as in the beer parlors of the Eastern coast cities, or in the steam beer dispensing places along the water front of San Francisco. Restaurants and saloons were still distinct and had not become one, except in rare instances. And since the Eighteenth Amendment had not yet been written into the Constitution of the United States, there was no excuse for blind pigs, "clubs," soft drink parlors with a back room, bathtub gin, blindness from denatured alcohol, or other phenomena that were to become part of the American scene in later years. True, there were "dry" sections, and local option was enforced in other areas, but I do not know of any place in the Southwest of those days where a man could not satisfy his desires for beer and hard liquor without running afoul of the law.

Besides the orders for the dealer with whom I had left the load of wool, I had taken several commissions to two other wholesale houses. There were no efficiency experts to tell the owners of those various establishments how to run their businesses, consequently I was not informed that the orders delivered by me in the forenoon would be ready for shipment within an hour and seventeen minutes, or be dispatched by Air Express. Instead of that disposition-ruining hurry and heedless rush, a quieter atmosphere pervaded the business houses. The genial managers, more often than not, were ranchers and stockmen themselves, vitally interested in range life and stock. They could spare sufficient time to invite me into their offices for a neighborly visit and an exchange of local gossip.

They wanted to know about the condition of range and stock, and about the water supply and the hay crop. Had I been to the Mormon farms on the San Juan of late? What did I think of the crops there? How was old Bill, Chetworth's foreman, getting along—the broken leg he had suffered while riding the range, was it mending properly? And was it true that Mrs. Goodnight had another baby? There had been some rumors of fights between cowpunchers and Mora's sheepherders, and some shooting, what about that? Two troops of the Fifth Cavalry had been sent from Fort Wingate to the Navajo reservation to quell a disturbance—was it really a serious outbreak, or just part of the military maneuvers for training purposes? And our own ranch family at Chaco Canyon—how was everybody and everything? When did Old Man Wetherill intend to come to Albuquerque? Would we have as many horses to ship this season as in the preceding one?

Many of those questions were prompted by friendly, neighborly interest. Others were phrased in a manner to gain valuable information for those sharp-witted merchants who had no Dun & Bradstreet to report on ranchers and stockmen living perhaps a hundred and fifty miles from the nearest town, and whose financial responsibility from season to season was affected by wind and weather, water and grass, crops, the increases or decreases in their livestock holdings, and other circumstances and conditions. And not only did the merchants and dealers keep close check upon these matters, but the local bankers as well—even more so. Without the information garnered in this informal but nevertheless surprisingly accurate fashion, they would have been unable to determine the credit risks involved in applications for loans, financial and material assistance between shipping seasons, harvests, and other matters. And they did not gather merely those facts and figures that would or could be assembled on a balance sheet, but the family news as well, thus keeping fully acquainted with the personal lives and intimate problems of the far-flung circle of "neighbors." The men were not Mr. Jones or Mr. Smith to each other, but Tom, or Frank, or Bill, whatever their appellations might be.

That same evening I spent in one of the "gambling-hells." Yes, I even sat at the roulette table and managed to lose and win a few dollars. Now and again a waiter would come and ask in a quiet voice what he might bring: the drinks proffered were "on the house." After an hour or so of that pastime, I cashed my chips and sauntered about from table to table, enjoying watching the various games and the reaction of the players. Only the poker players maintained a ritualistic decorum; at the other tables the gambling fraternity would whoop and shout and swear or rejoice over the turn of a card or the roll of the dice. The roulette wheel had its own code of behavior—not quite so restrained as that of the poker players, yet not as noisy as that of the followers of twenty-one, chuck-luck, dice, and other games.

The players would make their own peculiar demonstrations over the vagaries of fortune, the noisiest generally being the cowpunchers and lumberjacks. Miners and prospectors were, as a rule, a quieter group. Possibly their calling made them more serious-minded, I don't know. The Mexicans did not show their emotions as freely or openly as did the Americans; usually, their rejoicings found quiet outlet in flashing smiles, or some simple, short ejaculation. They would take their losses quietly, with hardly a murmur of disappointment. Indians and Chinamen managed to hide just about every bit of feeling—they sported true poker faces.

Despite the gambling halls, saloons, and red light district, Albuquerque was not going to the dogs in those days. If there was suffering or want, nothing gave outward testimonial of it. The city did not appear to have slums; I do not think it ever harbored anything resembling them in its entire history.

The wide-open policy was to be amended and curbed in years to come, but a look at the city of today proves that the free and easy times were not a deterrent to the lusty development of all civic enterprises, or a stunting influence on growth of a vigorous inland center. Far from that, it became amazingly healthy. Today the town is more important than ever, and from the days of unrestrained ardor it has preserved a virility of spirit that is evident on all sides and in every municipal action.

In my heart is a warm spot of affection for the glamorous old town. The mellowing years have not diminished the glow, rather the contrary. It makes me feel proud and happy when there is an opportunity to declare: I knew Albuquerque when—

During the afternoon of the third day in town, I loaded up. For the return trip, both the trailer and the lead wagon had to carry freight. In addition to the various articles of merchandise, I carried feed for the teams and, of course, a carefully replenished grub box. After the entire load was properly stowed aboard the wagons, I drove them into the corral of the livery stable. To discourage pilfering, I made my bed under one of them, and as it was my plan to get away to a good start the next morning, I did not linger in the saloons that night. Instead, I repaired to the corral early in the evening and crawled between the blankets before nine o'clock.

About daybreak, the mules wakened me. I got up, dressed, gave them their grain, and then got my own breakfast at a near-by restaurant that kept open from quite early in the morning until late at night. That saved time and was more pleasant than making a fire to cook over in the center of the corral. The mules had their breakfast in cribs—after this feed they would eat their corn and oats out of nose bags until we reached the stables of the ranch in Chaco Canyon.

Quickly the teams were hitched to the wagons and, as the first rays of the sun peeped over the Sandia Mountains, one of the men employed by the livery barn threw wide the gates of the corral to permit our passage to the street. Having enjoyed a good rest and being full of good feed, the mules leaned against the collars with a will, stepping out briskly, and after a short time we came to the ford of the Rio Grande.

Upon my first crossing of the river with the Wetherill freight teams, it had been almost dry. This time, however, the late summer rains had brought a considerable flow of water from the mountains and while not very deep, the bed of the river was entirely covered, presenting the appearance of a swollen python slowly undulating its brown length between the low banks. Not to take unnecessary chances on washed-out places in the ford, I disconnected the trailer from the lead wagon and made two trips of the fording. It would have been possible to take both wagons at one time, but caution comes with experience in crossing western streams. The opposite side of the river gained, I let the teams rest for a lengthy period, feeding them their noonday ration of grain.

The whole afternoon was consumed in reaching the ridge of the mesa after passing through a heartbreaking stretch of loose sand on an uphill pull.

Nothing worth recording took place between the Rio Grande and Cabezon. There the floods had worked a similar transformation as with the river above Albuquerque.

At times the Rio Puerco mirrors the indescribable blue of the desert skies and reflects the snowy whiteness of the fleecy clouds. Again, it may flow almost black, threatening, sinister. At all seasons it holds much of the unknown and is to be approached with great care. When wearing most innocent looks, it may prove suddenly an ambush of treacherous quicksand or spring the surprise of unexpected depths. Too, it is dangerous on account of changing beds. Heavy floodwaters during the rainy season may wash out the fording place to a depth of five or six feet, or even more, thus changing completely a crossing that was but recently perfectly good and easily passable. There is an ever-present chance of wagon wheels sinking hub-deep into liquefied mud or burying themselves in quicksand.

To avoid the annoyance of petty thieving and other troubles so often coincident with a stopover at Cabezon, we made the last camp some three or four miles before coming to the river. Thus we reached the ford while it was still early in the morning and just after the mules had got warmed up to their day's task. As I had done at the Rio Grande, so I did here at the Puerco: I effected the fording in two trips, first taking the lead wagon across, then returning with the mules to get the trailer. A lucky precaution, for the fording turned out to be quite slimy and sticky. It was about all the mules could do to pull the wagon through the river. We had a bit easier time with the trailer, it not being loaded so heavily as the first wagon, and it was of lighter construction, too.

Mules, harness, wagons, and driver were generously splashed with the gooey reddish adobe mud churned up from the river bottom. The peculiar pigmentation of that earth leaves virtually indelible stains upon clothing, leather, and wood. After a thorough splashing with that sticky mass, harness and boots acquire a color never dreamed of by the tanner, the harness maker or shoe-store owner. Scraping, washing, soaping, or oiling will not eradicate the rustlike stains; they penetrate the very fibers of the leather. And how beautifully that same 'dobe mud changes the glory of a nutria-grey ten-gallon Stetson hat!

Safely through the always uncertain fording of the Rio Puerco, I thought all troubles at an end; such is the optimism of youth. It would have been better had I kept in mind the German saying: *Man soll den Tag nicht vor dem Abend loben!* (Don't praise the day before evening.) While the overturning of the wool load on the trip to town would have been enough hardship to satisfy one for an entire tour, I had yet some other surprises awaiting me that proved equally difficult to bear. The first one came upon the morning after we crossed the Rio Puerco.

Camp had been made in the late afternoon in a likely spot blessed with grass and water in abundance. The mules had been fed their grain rations, then hobbled to allow them to graze. I heard them in the middle of the night, and could observe them within a short distance from camp. At about four o'clock in the morning I awakened, but could not see anything of the animals.

That did not particularly disturb me, I imagined them hidden from sight behind one or other of the rolling hills studding the terrain.

As was my custom when on the road, I started the camp-fire, blowing upon and fanning the embers left from the previous evening till I had them whipped into a blaze. I put on water to boil for coffee, then filled the nose bags with the proper rations of grain. Ordinarily, the rattle of hard corn on the leather-bottomed feed bags brought the mules in double-quick time. That morning, however, I shook the bags, and later, for better effect, rattled some corn in a tin can, without attracting the attention of any-thing except some cottontail rabbits scampering beneath the sagebrush.

The coffee having been made in the meantime, I decid-ed to first eat breakfast. Afterward I climbed the highest mound in the neighborhood to see whether or not the animals could be located from that vantage point. No mules anywhere! Although I was able to see for miles in every direction, the teams were not visible. This put me in a perplexing situation: to leave the wagons with their valuable loads by themselves, unguarded, would be ex-tremely risky; on the other hand, it was imperative to trail the animals without further loss of time in order to prevent them from straying farther away than they had already gone. I did not believe that they had started hobbling toward Pueblo Bonito; that was still too far away. The thought came to me that they might have fallen in with a herd of Navajo ponies. Mules have a tendency to follow some old mare, and I considered it quite likely that in the night a stray band of broomtails might have approached the teams, and that the latter had joined the ponies when they moved off during their grazing.

To determine whether it was possible to pick up their trail, I started toward the spot where I had noticed the mules in the middle of the night. It was not difficult to discern the hoofmarks of the teams. They had been freshly shod while in Albuquerque and they left clear, distinct marks upon the ground. According to their plain story, the mules had followed a fairly straight course down a declivity between two ranges of low mounds, but presently their tracks intermingled with numerous hoofprints left by unshod, "barefooted"—therefore Indian ponies. From the spacing of the imprints made by the hoofs, and judging from the unusually disturbed condition of the trail, it was easy to deduce that the bunch of horses with which I was now sure the mules had mixed had been *driven* off! Obviously, some Indian had brought horses and mules together, driven them away, and in all probability was now holding them in some hiding place. Without a mount, and wearing high-heeled cowboy boots, I was unable to follow the trail for any great distance, especially as I did not know for how long a period of time the stock had been gone. The mules might be ten miles away from camp.

Sanders had warned me. He had told me that this was one of the favorite tricks of some Indians for picking up "rewards." He had insisted that I must be on the lookout every night between Cabezon and Pueblo Bonito for just such a play, but here I was, a victim of the wiles of the red man upon my very first independent trip. However, there was nothing to do but to return to camp and await developments. I knew that before long somebody would show up and offer, for a consideration, to be sure, to hunt the stock for me.

Already I could hear the guffaws of the boys should they learn how easily the teams had been spirited from under my nose. The humiliation, much more than any pecuniary loss entailed, made me determined to turn the tables, if possible, on friend Navajo. And so, while I evolved my strategy, I kept surreptitious watch for the caller that very likely would put in an appearance at any moment. In that assumption, I was not mistaken.

After leisurely cleaning the breakfast dishes, I began greasing the axles, a job that is done without jacking the wheels off the ground. The freighter wishing to apply a fresh lot of axle grease takes off the nut that holds the wheel to the axle. He then pulls on the upper rim of the wheel and by gently rocking back and forth gradually exposes the larger portion of the axle. Of course, one must be careful not to pull too energetically or to rock too vigorously as that might mean slipping the wheel entirely off the axle. While there is a certain knack of doing the job correctly, it can be mastered in a short time, and only a few operations are required to give one proficiency in the undertaking. On a long trip such as we were making, it is necessary to grease the axles several times while en route.

I was in the midst of this occupation when a Navajo rode up, slid off his pony and greeted me. In a noncommittal manner, I acknowledged his salutation, continuing with my work. Evidently, this was not what he had expected. I made no effort to ask his assistance in locating the team; in fact, did not speak about any lost or strayed mules at all. When he wanted to know how soon I intended to break camp, I replied that I had not yet decided.

"Where are your horses?" he desired to learn.

"Oh, they are feeding," I told him, still busying myself with camp chores. For a while, conversation languished. Whistling blithely and unconcernedly, I attended to various details, such as going over the fastening of the tarpaulins, stowing away the feed, putting more wood on the fire, checking the contents of the water barrel lashed to the side of the wagon, and sharpening my ax against a suitable piece of rock.

Two hours or more passed, and by that time I had my visitor thoroughly puzzled. Obviously, he was nonplussed and could not imagine why I had not, immediately upon his arrival, asked him to help me find the lost mules. Such should have been the natural reaction upon discovering the absence of my team. The fact that I appeared absolutely unruffled and completely unconcerned did not tally with his expectations. That was not playing the game according to Hoyle.

Noon was approaching, and still he "visited," and I had not yet done a single one of the orthodox things a freighter might be counted upon to do under similar circumstances. In a tantalizing manner I began to inspect the grub box, as if debating in my mind just what to prepare for the midday meal. How Poor Lo opened his eyes as I brought one good thing after another. Various kinds of canned fruit, including canned grapes, so much liked by the Navajos; canned tomatoes, pork and beans, coffee, flour, biscuits left over from the breakfast batch, and, to top it all, a sizeable piece of bacon! From the slab I cut some half dozen or more thick slices and laid them to one side, then got the frying pan and the coffeepot ready.

While my visitor kept outwardly calm and unconcerned, I could see the hungry glitter in his eyes, and it needed no great amount of perspicacity to imagine a watery mouth. Having thus set the stage most effectively and brought about the desired mental attitude, I opened the conversation.

"Do you often come to Pueblo Bonito?" I began.

"Yes, indeed," he replied. "I am a frequent visitor there."

"Then you know my boss, Mr. Wetherill?"

"Oh, he and I are old friends. I trade with him, my father trades with him, and all of us like him; he is our friend."

"Hm, I remember having seen you, and now I recognize you," I agreed. "Wasn't it you who traded some horses to the boss not so long ago?"

That was a perfectly safe supposition, since almost all Indians within a radius of at least a hundred miles traded horses and other stock with Wetherill, but he did not realize the purpose behind the inquiry.

"Yes, I was in Chaco Canyon only three weeks ago," he confirmed, "but I did not have any horses to sell at that time. I brought in a couple of blankets."

"Well," I conceded, "perhaps it was a brother of yours whom I must have mistaken for you."

"That is quite likely," he assented. "My brother goes there as often as I do." I tried my next tack.

"What's your brother's name?"

He fell squarely into the trap, his answer coming unhesitatingly: "He is Black Horse, the silversmith; everybody knows him."

"Oh, yes, I know him well," I hastened to assure him, continuing: "Isn't he the son of Tall Man who lives near Seven Lakes?"

It is not good etiquette to ask an Indian outright, at least not a Navajo, to tell his name; generally one learns it in some roundabout fashion. Of course I was not interested in knowing the name of my visitor just for the sake of making the acquaintance of the family. No, in establishing the identity of the men I would be able to obtain recourse, should such be necessary. That there was

some ulterior motive or design in my questions did not
seem to dawn upon friend Navajo. He answered readily
and without pausing; it was evident that his replies must
be true.

He corrected my assumption that made Tall Man his
brother's father, giving me instead the proper family line-
up. According to that, his father was Many Horses, a
medicine man of some repute. That, and some other details he vouchsafed, put me in possession of considerable
information regarding the unsuspecting brave. I knew his
family connections, their respective locations, and had
learned that all were regular customers, "yes, great
friends" of Wetherill.

With the gist of our long conversation stored in my
head, I thought it was time to play the trump hand, and so
I grew loquacious on my part. I told him it was my intention to rest the teams for an extra day, and because of that
reason had not gone after the mules in the morning.
There was fine feeding and plenty of good water at that
camp, so I would give the stock an extra day's chance to
get in readiness for the last lap of the trip. Still, it might
be a good idea to drive them back toward the camp, to
keep them from grazing too far and to give them their
accustomed rations of grain. Therefore, would he be
good enough to let me use his horse for a few minutes in
which to round them up? The mules were hobbled, and
with the abundance of grass and water at this camp, must
be quite close, perhaps just beyond the next hill, and I
would be away for just a few moments. As quickly as I
got back with the mules, we would prepare lunch and
have something good to eat.

My request was so natural that to refuse it would have
created suspicion—I had my good friend where I wanted
him. Now *he* was in a quandary: if he let me use his horse,

I could hardly help but uncover his well-laid plan to collect ransom; he knew that I would read the story of the tracks and discover his scheme. Possibly he had removed the hobbles from the mules when he drove them off in the early morning hours, and it would look strange, to say the least, to find the animals hidden away in some Indian brush corral in the company of a bunch of his own horses. His ponies could easily be identified as such by their marks, and he had been bragging about the great number of horses his family owned, and described their brands. His countenance showed the rapid working of his mind, but he came through the ordeal nobly.

"Please don't bother about the team," he suggested. "Let me go and bring them here. You can start the meal while I am away; I shall not be gone very long for, as you say, the mules will not be far from camp."

And without waiting for a remonstrance, he stepped over to his pony, mounted, and was gone, riding in the very direction that I had followed earlier that day when I discovered the tracks. He *knew* which way to go without having to hunt for tracks which, of course, confirmed my suspicions. The whole setup was so obvious, and the discomfiture of the poor fellow so apparent, that I could not refrain from smiling. My worries were over, of that I felt confident, so I set about making preparations for a much more bountiful lunch than it was my habit of cooking for myself when without guests.

The coffee had just begun to boil, and the aroma of sizzling strips of bacon was filling the air, when Mr. Navajo, the son of Many Horses, came galloping up the shallow ravine, driving before him the six mules. Sure enough, they were unhobbled, the hobbles resting across his thighs as he sat in the saddle.

"I freed their legs so they could run easier," he volunteered, jumping off his horse and putting the hobbles alongside the wagon. With his assistance, we put short tie ropes on the mules and fastened all of them to the rear end of the trailer. Although their feed was already apportioned and the nose bags awaiting for them, I did not give the grain to the animals, but left them where we had tied them.

"There is no hurry about feeding the mules; we shall be here all day," I told him, adding the invitation, "let us eat now before our food and coffee get cold."

The meal was ready, and both of us enjoyed the good provender that had come out of the well-stocked grub box. After eating, I pulled out a sack of Bull Durham tobacco and a packet of Mexican cigarette papers, so-called "saddle blankets" on account of their large size, and we smoked the more modern equivalent of the medicine pipe. After leisurely finishing the smoke, and without betraying any signs of hurry, I hung the nose bags over the mules' heads. A short while later, my Indian friend departed.

He had spent several hours in camp and, undoubtedly, a considerable length of time during the night watching for the most opportune moment in which to make off with the stock. Now he left without the silver dollar or more that he must have intended to demand for his troubles in finding the lost animals. True, he had been treated to a meal, but I could discern that he was troubled and uneasy. His actions indicated that he was puzzled over the failure of the well-laid plan. Clearly, something bothered him. Possibly he sensed that there was something rotten in Denmark. Had this young man, by chance, in some manner or other, gotten the better of him? That *something* had gone amiss, he knew, but he was unable definitely to put his finger on the factor that caused the slip-up. Also, he may have been pondering the chances for repeating the experiment in the night to come, since I had already told him of my intention to camp in that spot for another twenty-four hours, to rest the teams.

With the question "You are going to stay here overnight?"—to which I gave an affirmative answer—he mounted his horse, waved good-by, and within a few moments had disappeared from sight.

However, hardly had he crossed the ridge that made him lost to view, when I began harnessing the mules, taking off the nose bags, and hitching the team to the wagon. Despite my repeated assurances to friend Navajo, it was not my plan to remain in that camp any longer than necessary; I had no desire for a second experience like the one just brought to a conclusion. The dishes had been cleaned and put away before we smoked, a shovelful of earth covered the embers of the fire, and the rest of the coffee completely eliminated the danger of any sparks remaining alive and glowing.

Git up there, mules! On to Pueblo Bonito!

By evening, we had covered many miles. I kept urging the mules to step briskly to be sure of putting as much territory as possible between the morning camp and the place where we, after driving nearly till dusk, stopped for the night. Only two more days driving and we should be in Chaco Canyon; I was determined to be extra watchful to prevent a repetition of the previous night's experience, and also to keep the stock from straying toward home. That was a probability that had to be guarded against every time the teams, whether horses or mules, were camped within easy distance of the home stables, corrals, and pasture.

The late drive made us reach our camping place after

sunset. By the time the teams had been relieved of their harness and the nose bags placed over their hungry mouths, it was completely dark. In my hurry to get camp established, feed distributed, a fire started, and the grub box unloaded, I neglected to keep the mules tied to the wagons while they were eating their grain. That oversight cost me dearly and taught me another lesson that became fixed in my memory forever. It did not require more than that one experience for it to become a permanent part of the subconscious.

The first flames of the fire were blazing up under my coaxing when suddenly I came to the realization that I had not removed the nose bags from the mules. Those ornery critters, instead of waiting to be relieved of them, had wandered away although they could neither drink nor graze while they remained muzzled. Having looked so intently into the glow of the flames, I was virtually blinded. All about me was Stygian darkness, palpable: in my sightless condition next to impenetrable. I gazed into the blackness and toward the heavens, trying to get my eyes accustomed to the obscurity and to bring the pupils into focus, but it was some time before I was able to distinguish anything beyond the immediate radius lighted by the now briskly burning fire. From out of the darkness I could hear the mules, snorting into the nose bags, evidently fighting to rid themselves of those appurtenances. Foolish beasts!—they might even drown, should they stick their noses under water and get the tightly woven canvas bags filled with water.

It probably did not require more than some ten minutes to track the animals by their sounds, and to remove, one by one, the nose bags that hampered them in their desire to drink and begin grazing, although to me it seemed like so many hours. I was bathed in perspiration by the time I had secured the last of the bags and had fastened the hobbles on the sixth mule. In the darkness I had stumbled and slipped kicked my toes against stones and prickly cactus, and collided with short, stubby, brush· clumps that were invisible but substantial enough to make me lose my balance. Several times I had walked up to a deeper shadow in the darkness, imagining another mule in the dim outline, only to find my reaching hands encountering the branches of a pinon tree. However, I had now collected the nose bags, so back to camp and supper.

Following and trailing the mules by sound rather than by sight had led me in a zigzag route from the camp to the spot where I located the last mule. Thus, when I turned to retrace my steps, I was in an entirely different line from camp than the one described by me as I staggered along from one animal to the other, first to the left, then again bearing off toward the right. All the while the impenetrable darkness made it impossible for me to see where I was going. And so it came to pass that I stepped into a deep, narrow, rut, or washed-out place.

One moment I was looking toward the campfire as a guiding beacon, the next found me sprawled out, my face resting upon some sharp-cornered rocks, the nose bags scattered about me, my nose bleeding, cheeks and forehead badly scratched, and the right arm and right leg hanging in the treacherous pitfall. I was stunned; the sudden drop had just about knocked the wind out of me. My right leg was wedged in the narrow cut and refused to budge, my right arm felt paralyzed from the impact. Moving my hand and fingers convinced me that I had not suffered a broken wrist, hand, or arm, but the sharp pains were just as intense as if they resulted from a fracture.

I must have lain in that position a considerable length of time before I finally succeeded in freeing the leg that was imprisoned by the hard 'dobe walls of the rut, held clamped as if in a vise. The fire had burnt down to a small, reddish glare, now and again showing a brighter gleam as the slight evening breeze fanned it into upflickering life. I felt sick; the discomfort and pain nearly nauseated me. For the moment, walking was impossible. I found this out when I attempted to rise. My hands groped for the nose bags strewn about. Somehow I managed to collect all of them despite the darkness that shut in from all sides, then, with those pieces of equipment retrieved, I crawled on hands and knees toward the fire. Camp seemed miles away, but, eventually, I reached it. My overalls were torn, my shirt sleeves ripped, my boots badly stratched. Just how sadly and thoroughly my face had been abused I did not know, as I had no mirror with which to frighten myself.

Preparing and eating supper proved an awkward performance. However, the efforts to reanimate the fire, the boiling of coffee, and the opening of cans and the dozen other details coincident with making a meal, helped to bring about a certain amount of relief; to some extent, I forgot the shock and pain caused by the nasty spill. After drinking several cups of scalding hot coffee and gulping down some food, matters began to look much improved. A more careful inspection disclosed that my leg from the groin to below the knee had suffered abrasions and cuts from the contact with the sharp-edged, concrete-like adobe. I knew that the angry red of the contusions would change to sinister hues of purple, blue, and black, but I was happy and grateful that nothing more serious had befallen.

With supper out of the way, I turned nurse. In a

galvanized-iron water bucket, I heated water to nearly the boiling point. I tore two strips from one of my bed blankets and used those to make hot packs, alternating them as soon as they cooled. For perhaps an hour or longer, I applied the hot packs to the places that were the sorest, and this treatment had the desired effect: I found that it relieved me of a great deal of discomfort. Then, much later than was my wont, I turned into bed, rolling myself between the blankets and trying to find a comfortable position. The aches and pains were not diminished in my hard resting place, but eventually I dropped off to sleep, to find forgetfulness and recuperation.

I awakened to a steel-grey dawn with an arctic tang, stiff in every joint. Even breakfast failed to bring its accustomed cheer. Due to stabbing pains in the groin, I could only walk with a limp, hobbling along with an effort; my right knee, too, had swollen to nearly twice its normal size. But for once, almost providentially, the mules were within sight and quite close—they had grazed as if in a circle and were almost within stone's throw of camp. Rattling the grain in the nose bags enticed them to hobble directly to the side of the wagons, where I tied them and hung the bags over their long ears. That, in any event, saved hunting for the stock, which would have meant a painful exertion and might even have been impossible in my temporarily disabled condition.

The routine of harnessing and hitching to the wagons, the stowing away of bedroll and camp equipment, ordinarely such an easy matter and so quickly accomplished, became hard work on this morning, causing beads of perspiration to break from the forehead. Forced to awkward slowness, our start for the penultimate day's drive was delayed by perhaps an hour, but once under way, the mules started off with a will. The coolness of the fall morning and the proximity to the home stables combined to stimulate their efforts; mile after mile rolled beneath the wagon wheels, the animals requiring no urging. The usual noon rest period was cut short, and the afternoon's drive extended to regain at least part of the time lost through the late start. When at last we made camp for the night we were within easy driving distance from Pueblo Bonito, even if we failed to break camp the next morning earlier than we had done this day.

Within such tempting nearness to the ranch, it would have been unwise to turn the mules to grazing. Even with their legs hobbled, they probably would have started for the home corrals instead of feeding. Rather than remain near the wagons, they would have hob-skipped the intervening miles, traveling all night if necessary, to reach the stables that meant the end of the trip for them. Knowing this, I kept them tied to the trailer, three at each side. After they had finished their grain rations, I put some baled hay before them. That had been brought along from Albuquerque for just that purpose, and in this last night the mules had to be satisfied with it instead of browsing on prairie grass. Before they were finally tied to the wagon, to stay there until morning, I had taken them to a water hole, conveniently near, to quench their thirst.

Those chores attended to, I unrolled my bed, to sleep one more night away from Pueblo Bonito, feeling reasonably certain that nothing more would or could mar the trip between then and the safe arrival at the Wetherill ranch.

Even earlier than the regular schedule, we bestirred ourselves upon the following morning. The painful swelling of the groin glands was reduced, and my soreness had virtually left me, although I was still a little hesitant about using my right leg freely; it was dragging with a slight limp. The bruises had turned a bluish-black; I must have been a pretty sight, what with torn clothing, unshaven face disfigured with scratches and cuts, the left cheek swollen, as if afflicted with the mumps, and discolored—in fact, the sort of a disreputable scarecrow that one associates with slums, dives, and saloon brawls. Luckily, I was ignorant of the discreditable appearance of my person. Otherwise I probably would not have been trying to whistle a happy tune through puffed-up lips as I was putting the teams before the wagons for the last lap of our journey.

Shortly after noon we came to the steep trail leading from the mesa into Chaco Canyon. It was a bad piece of road and required careful handling of teams and loads. To prevent the wagons from forcing the teams downhill at a pace too fast, one that might result in disaster to animals and wreck the equipment, I blocked the rear wheels of the first wagon with short lengths of trace chains, hooking those to the wagon bed in such a manner as to stop the wheels from turning. The lead mules were already standing on the downward slope of the steeply slanting trail, awaiting the command to proceed into the canyon. I gave one more look, saw that the chains were properly adjusted, firmly grasped the reins in the left hand, the right hand clutched about the long rope connected with the brake pole of the trail wagon, then braced myself against the footboard and spoke to the mules.

The steady, deliberate pull of the team brought the lead wagon over the edge of the down-dropping trail. The four lead mules of the string were held back by me to slacken their pull on the traces. The wheel team was reined back sharply to brace against collars and breeching, thus straining backward against the weight that pushed from behind. They knew what was expected of them and held with all their might; the first four mules, guided by the pressure of the reins, moved ahead slowly, just fast enough to keep from tangling up with the ones in the rear.

As soon as the trailer followed the first wagon over the precipitous decline, I exerted as strong a pull as I was able against the brake rope, in that manner effectively locking the rear wheels of the second wagon. Nevertheless, the combined weight of the two heavy wagons, piled high with freight, accelerated our speed despite the chained wheels of the first wagon and the solidly locked brake on the trailer. The rear wheels of the two wagons did not turn; they slid along on their iron tires without braking power sufficient to restrain the momentum of the bulky mass, and before we reached the canyon floor the wagons were rocking and sliding along at a dangerous pace.

Several pieces of stone, each almost as large as my head, had rolled from the rocky side wall and fallen into the rough, crooked ruts of the trail. When the wheels bumped over those obstructions, the jar nearly dislodged me from my insecure perch, threatening to pitch me forward onto the mules. However, I held on and within a few moments the wagons rolled safely onto the floor of Chaco Canyon. Only three more miles to go!

The wagons pulled to a stop. A slight backing up of the team eased the pressure on the chains and enabled me to unfasten them. The wheels loosened, and the brake released on the trailer, we were ready for the home stretch. Between the sheltering walls of the canyon the sun shone warmly, and while yet high in the heavens, watched us swing through the tall gateposts of the ranch yard. We were home again after an absence of over three weeks.

Wetherill had known of our coming for two days; Navajos told him of the progress made by the wagons. Who his informers were, I did not know; I had not noticed any Indians except the one who had such poor luck in bringing off the stunt of running away with the teams and later "finding" them for me. Hearing the wagons roll by the door, he emerged from the office, shouting a cheery "Howdedo!" I had just awkwardly clambered down from the high driver's seat when he came abreast of the wagon and got a good look at me. With one comprehensive glance he took in the sorry spectacle of my figure, and the pleased expression was wiped from his face.

"Didn't I warn you not to touch booze?" he queried, with unconcealed anger and disgust in voice and expression.

"Boss," I replied, "please believe me, this is not the result of drinking. I had an accident."

I wanted to tell him about my mishap, but he waved explanations aside. I could not very well follow him about as I had to attend to spotting the wagons in front of the large warehouse for unloading, and the mules wanted to be unhitched and taken care of. Later, when I desired to broach the subject, he asked me not to bother him with excuses, then made his refusal to listen to my story of woe more hurtful by adding that he certainly was disappointed in me.

"I don't know what to think of you," he said, "but I will give you credit for bringing the teams and the loads back in fine shape." And with that left-handed compliment I had to be satisfied.

Mrs. Wetherill, who had strolled from the house during the process of unloading the goods and storing them in the warehouse, exclaimed, upon seeing my bedraggled appearance: "Why, Joe, you have been fighting again!"

She, also, remained skeptical when I told her in a few words of what had actually taken place. Both she and the boss thought that I had concocted a fine story to excuse my fall from grace. I do not think that they ever came to accept as the truth the real version of the affair.

The boys, too, indulged in quips and caustic remarks, explaining to each other at great length and in shocking detail just how a cowboy, who had no business to steal a freighter's job in the first place, could acquire battle scars in saloons and houses of ill repute. They drew lurid word pictures in language utterly unfit to repeat and still less permissible to print, until they had me so exasperated from the cruel taunts and brazen innuendos that I offered to fight one and all if they persisted in teasing and tormenting me. For many weeks thereafter I could hear such gratuitous warnings as "Be careful not to step into holes" whenever I happened to be saddling my horse preparatory to taking a ride to the mesa or upon some other errands.

Chapter 9

NAVAJO INDIANS

Before continuing with any more personal experiences, I shall tell something about the Navajos, in whose territory Wetherill had established his ranch. Let it be observed that their name is pronounced Navahoes, although the word is spelled N-a-v-a-j-o.

The tribal lands of that interesting people surround Chaco Canyon on every side and for many miles in all directions. There were many Navajos assisting in the work connected with the excavations. Others had been hired by Wetherill to provide a steady supply of fresh beef and mutton for the commissary, very much on the order of the buffalo hunters that furnished meat to the early railroad construction gangs. Still others were busy bringing in firewood at regular intervals. A number of Indians were engaged in freighting, and several were occupied in looking after cattle and sheep, owned by them in partnership with the boss.

I was in daily contact with them, and during some thirteen years spent in virtually every section of the extensive Navajo reservation, both in New Mexico and Arizona, came to know the Navajos intimately. I worked with them, played their games and sports, camped among them, attended their medicine chants and other religious ceremonials, ate their food. In later years, as owner of several trading posts, we had many pleasant dealings; I was not merely storekeeper and trader, but banker, adviser, doctor, undertaker, mediator, and judge to them, and at all times, and predominatingly, I trust, their good friend. Their history, legends, ceremonials, habits, peculiarities and idiosyncrasies were a constant source of interest. Despite their many shortcomings, I felt genuine affection for them, and when I left the reservation, not intending to return my eyes grew dim and moist, and a big lump obstructed my throat.

So I shall relate something of the supposed origin of this fine people and tell of their mode of living, certain customs, and other things that will not come amiss in a story whose locale is in the heart of the Navajo country.

We first hear of Navajos, or the Apaches of the North, in old Spanish reports and histories dated about 1630. They are, in origin, an Apache division of an Athabascan people who came, according to their own legends, from the North. It is probable that they originated on the Asiatic mainland and effected the crossing of the Pacific either by way of the Aleutian Islands, or by Bering Strait. Possibly, at that time, there was a solid link between the two continents which are now separated by the waters of the great ocean.

Their own assertions that refer to this legendary hegira are borne out by findings of ethnologists. While they do not have the "slanted" eyes of the Chinese (we know, of course, that they are not slanted at all), and are copper-colored instead of yellow-skinned, yet among them we find many types of a decidedly Mongolian cast. If one were to dress those Navajos in Chinese clothes and mingle them with natives of the Flowery Kingdom, it would be difficult indeed to distinguish our aboriginal Americans from the Asiatics.

With an innate pride they call themselves *Dinneh*— "The People"— and look down upon the Hopis and other Indians with a poorly concealed contempt. Toward the white man they have adopted an attitude which is a mixture of pitying tolerance and sardonic mockery. They possess an inborn dignity which is unshakeable; the inferiority complex is lacking entirely.

Today the Navajos form the largest tribe and are the most virile of the North American Indians. Their numbers have consistently increased decade after decade, and, where in 1870 their total was estimated at approximately 9,000, they number now between 30,000 and 35,000. Some writers and census people go as high as 45,000 in estimating the present Navajo population.

Through hundreds of years, up to this very day, they have preserved faithfully their identity and ancient usages. Old religious customs are carried on unchanged, impervious to modern influences and deterioration. They have never adopted masonry houses, except to allow themselves temporarily to be cooped up in the white man's house as children in Indian schools operated by the government or forming a part of missionary establishments, or, perhaps, while patients in hospitals. They have fought off the sedentary life, remaining true nomads, and except to a quite limited extent, they are not agriculturists.

During the pre-Spanish period as well as later, they were the scourge of the Pueblo Indians and eventually of the Mexican-American settlers, too, swooping down upon them, burning, killing, raiding. One of the common customs of the Navajos in those raids, or while waging warfare with other tribes or Mexicans, was to make wives of captured women and slaves of the imprisoned young men, provided the latter proved tractable. The raiders would drive off the stock of the vanquished foes, thus gradually acquiring herds of horses and cattle, goats, and especially sheep, from which their living is still derived to a large extent. Even now, horses and sheep continue to be the units by which they measure wealth.

They were cunning and aggressive in war, and to pursue an existence resembling the raiding practices of Genghis Khan and Attila suited the Navajos very well, although this existence was not conducive to the enjoyment of life, liberty, and happiness on the part of their neighbors. And although Hughes, the historian of the Doniphan expedition (first military expedition into the Navajo country, 1846), spoke thus highly of them: "They are celebrated for intelligence and good order—the noblest of the American aborigines," the continuance of their depredations caused a number of punitive and conciliatory expeditions to be sent against them. Treaties were made with them by the various American commanders of forces sent to the Indian country; invariably, the Navajos failed to adhere to the covenants of the agreements, furnishing ample precedent for the later doctrine that such pacts are but "scraps of paper." At last, however, the task to make them behave was given to one who knew better than his predecessors how to meet the emergency. This was none other than Colonel Christopher (Kit) Carson, commanding officer of the First New Mexico Volunteers, operating from bases at Fort Wingate and Fort Defiance.

Between the years 1862 and 1865 Kit Carson, with his troopers, rode through the Navajo country, reaching its farthest and most inaccessible fastnesses. At first, he tried kindness. When that was refused by the Navajos, who probably saw weakness in it, he showed them the many tricks an old tracker and border fighter had acquired and had at his command. He gave them no respite—nothing could stop him. To the Indians it must have seemed as if he never slept. Day after day, week after week, yes, even days *and* nights, he pursued them relentlessly. The climax came with the rounding up of some twelve thousand Indians. They were taken from reservation territory to the concentration camps in the Bosque Redondo (Fort Sumner, New Mexico).

To this very moment the Navajos remember the terrible experience of extermination, ruthlessness, hunger, misery, starvation. Unused to any confinement, they died by the hundreds. It was the end of their warring and raiding. There have been occasional outbreaks since, it is true. A score or more of miners, prospectors, and traders have been murdered in the course of the years, but the cry "The Navajos are coming" no longer resounds in the Indian pueblos or blanches the cheeks of colonists and townspeople.

Now they are a peace-abiding, pastoral people, making their living principally from their sheep, with a small portion of their income derived from agriculture. Their nomadic habits cannot be changed while they live as herdsmen and under the conditions and circumstances that describe their existence. The animals, whether sheep, goats, horses, or cattle, must be moved from one range to another, depending upon the seasons, feed conditions, water supply, and other pertinent factors. Corn, potatoes, beans, and onions are raised in small patches, frequently without the benefit of any irrigation or with just the merest trickle of water to moisten the parched ground. To help out the rather meager larder, they exchange commodities with their neighbors, the

Hopis, from whom they obtain peaches, corn meal, squashes, pumpkins, and other fruits and vegetables. They also barter for pottery, baskets, hand-woven Hopi squaw belts, and other products, giving in exchange saddle blankets, silver jewelry, both plain and ornamented with turquoise matrix, and livestock.

The Navajos are self-supporting. They do not receive pensions, subsidies, treaty payments or other financial help from the government. To be sure, such assistance was promised them at various times, but "Washindon," the collective term used by the Indians when speaking of the Great White Father's administration in Washington, has managed to side-step most adroitly those solemn obligations. Whatever material wealth they may possess comes mostly from stock raising. Sheep are by far the greatest source of revenue, although a number of Indians have sizable herds of cattle and horses. However, without sheep, the Navajo would be Poor Lo, indeed. Mutton is one of his staple items of food; the sale of lambs, sheep, wool, and pelts brings him a fairly steady income through the different parts of the year.

The lambing season varies with the separate localities. Efforts have been made by the government, through the stockmen and veterinarians attached to the Indian Service, to educate the Navajos not to permit mating between ewes and rams at a time that would cause the lambs to be born too early, while temperatures are still too chilly and while snow blankets the land. Generally, the lambing season comes between March and May, followed by the woolshearing season.

Wool is sold to the traders in the unscoured state. "Smart" Indians attempt, now and then, to increase the value of their clip by various unfair means, such as "salting" the wool. By this is meant the distribution of a generous amount of fine, flourlike sand sprinkled between the wool. Or they will bury the wool under a covering of wet sand, letting the fleeces absorb as much of the moisture and sand as they can, to make them heavier. In the resacking of wool that is brought in by an Indian inclined to swindle, it happens sometimes that lumps of rocks or pieces of old iron fall out. The experienced trader, wise in the ways of the wily native, becomes expert and knows whether the scale weights indicate normal, untampered-with fleeces, or "doctored" wool. He has the bags emptied at once, in the presence of the vendor, then makes his bid for the offered wool in accordance with the condition and quality of the commodity.

The Navajos are matrilineal; their clans bear names of localities, but are exogamous; no man will marry a woman having the same clan name as his own.

No community life such as we know it exists for the Navajo. This lack may account for the ever-present inclination to visit trading posts, to attend dances and sings and other gatherings. Distance never deters the brave or his squaw; the fact that he does not know the party giving the dance, or that he failed to receive a special invitation cannot dampen his enthusiasm. Everybody is welcome at the gathering, whatever its nature.

All Navajos are hospitable, even to an utterly unwarranted degree. The frequent visitors are entertained and fed until all food on hand is likely to be consumed. Besides lavish hospitality, gift giving is another integral part of Navajo life. Their desire not to be outdone, and to "keep up with the Joneses," often causes the incurrence of heavy indebtedness and may wreck completely the financial structure of the family. Payments for "sings" and dances, fees and gifts to medicine men, food for guests, stock, and other valuables gambled away in the gaming

that is an inevitable part of the festivity, all these draw
heavily upon resources.

Not infrequently the trader is asked to accept old family jewels, tanned buckskins, yes, even saddles and blankets
in pawn for coffee, sugar, flour, and other staples with
which to feed a horde of unbidden, hungry guests that
are sure to arrive when the word is spread that So-and-so
is about to stage a "sing" for his ailing wife, or for whatever the occasion for the assembly may be.

It is difficult to estimate correctly the conduct of another race. This is especially true when dealing with
aborigines or primitive people. The temptation is strong
to overemphasize their bad points and to go over their
good qualities with a light touch. As with all other people,
there are good Navajos, and bad ones.

Murder is not uncommon, but to the credit of the
Navajo it can be said that it is by no means as prevalent,
figured on a percentage basis, as among whites. Gambling
is a universal failing among the Navajos, principally indulged in by the men. Drunkness is rarer, thanks to the
rigid supervision exercised by the Indian superintendents
through the native police. Bootlegging is a serious offense.
For an Indian trader, located upon reservation lands, to
deal in intoxicating beverages spells heavy fines and the
forfeiture of his trading licence. Sexual crimes are virtually unknown; rape is considered by the Navajos themselves a very serious crime. Attacks upon white women
are unheard of.

The Navajo has a rather hazy idea of the meaning of
meum and *tuum*. Stealing and pilfering are favorite
pastimes, particularly relished during festivals and dances.
Traders generally protect their stock and shelf displays
behind wire screens and build extra-high and wide
counters to forestall, as much as possible, the inescapable

shoplifting. Too, the store windows of trading posts usually are heavily barred. Nevertheless, with an almost unbelievable agility, the Navajo makes away with merchandise, other goods, implements, and utensils. To leave an ax buried in a log at the woodpile means that another one will be needed by the wood chopper when he returns to his work after even a momentary absence. This applies to almost anything and everything that can be moved without too much trouble or danger of detection.

To be caught in some dishonest act does not bring the blush of shame to the countenance of the culprit, or cause consternation. Navajos will merely laugh and treat the whole thing as a joke, but none of their own race will think any less of them for the attempted or perpetrated fraudulent act.

Wetherill told of an Indian who had actually got away with a small, but very heavy, anvil from the blacksmith shop, and in later years I happened to catch a Navajo trying to sneak out of the store with a Western stock saddle, weighing in the neighborhood of forty pounds, concealed under his Pendleton blanket robe.

The Navajos consider white women lacking in modesty. They hold the American woman's mode of dressing distinctly immodest, and frown upon promiscuous kissing, the rowdiness so often exhibited by tourists of the gentle sex, the loud, boisterous laughing, the shouting, the uncontrollable flair for posing for snapshots in all sorts of ridiculous situations, and other breaches of good behavior. To the Indian, those actions bespeak lack of dignity and a total absence of self-respect. In marked contrast, the Navajo women and girls show a restraint and mannerliness that might profitably be copied by their white sisters.

The Navajo lives entirely in the present and is serenely unconcerned over past and future. Unlike 99 per cent of the "superior" white races, he will not take himself too seriously, and is ready to admit that he does not know it all. He is possessed of a keen appreciation of humor and loves to indulge in practical jokes. Even the one upon whom the prank is played enjoys it, and joins in the amusement without showing resentment or hurt feelings. Instead of being peevish or sullen the victim will do his best to turn the tables and get the laugh on his erstwhile tormentor.

The white man's house has found small favor with the Navajo, although more and more of the Indians are becoming accustomed to them from having lived in permanent dwellings while at the government boarding schools, in reservation offices, hospitals, or while having worked in or near railroad towns. The true, unspoiled, and uncontaminated Navajo, however, scorns whatever advantage the more modern housing provides. Considering his mode of life he is very likely, perhaps instinctively, right. It is, unquestionably, much better for him to live in a hogan whose earth floor is swept frequently than to be in a floored house where dirt would soon accumulate and breed filth and disease. Perhaps the principal reason for his preference is the obvious one: a nomadic people have no use for tenements or apartments, or bungalows and cottage-courts.

Hogans are almost always made of pinon or cedar logs, laid in a circular manner, tapering gradually toward the roof until that assumes a semispherical shape. The cracks are chinked up with small boughs and cedar bark, and the whole structure covered over completely with adobe and earth. A smoke hole is left open in the middle of the roof of this rude home, and there is a door opening that faces, invariably, east. Ordinarily, this doorway is covered by a blanket or pelt suspended from nails or pegs inside the hogan. This sort of substantial hogan may be used year after year, even though the occupants move away from it during certain seasons of the year. Families may own several hogans of this type, going from one to the other with their flocks.

In summertime a light, temporary hogan is constructed of brush and boughs, affording the merest shelter. Pieces of tarpaulins as well as old pelts and skins are used to help out in the erection of walls and roof for these transient quarters. Usually they are occupied only while the sheep are being shorn, or during late lambing season, or when the family is tilling small patches of arable land that may be located at some distance from the main hogan.

Should a member of the family die in the hogan, it becomes unclean and can no longer be used for a residence. It is then abandoned or burned down. To prevent the taboo upon the hogan and circumvent the consequences attendant upon a death in the house, ill persons are sometimes taken outside when it appears that death is imminent. Even the wood of an abandoned hogan, deserted because of death, will not be used by any Navajo. Firewood is extremely scarce in many regions, but no Navajo will pull down the cedar logs of the framework of a *chindee* hogan, as the contaminated home is called.

Various types, differing in construction and shape, are used by the Navajos, but the commonest type of hogan is the one described above. A variation found in many places is the sweat hogan, a miniature house built for the purpose of taking sweat baths and for certain rites of purification. Heated rocks are brought into that particular type of hogan when a person wishes to take a sweat bath; the door opening is closed tightly with blankets or pelts, and the inside temperature promptly rises to a degree that induces free perspiration. The bather may come out and plunge into cold water, or roll in dry sand, then return to sweat some more. Sometimes this is repeated several times until the desired results have been obtained.

For their big dances and chants, notably the *yeibitchai* ceremonies, a special type of hogan is constructed. Instead of laying the logs horizontally, the walls of these medicine lodges are formed by logs standing upright, tilting slightly inward. From a height of about five feet above ground, the house is completed in the same manner as the hogan first mentioned, the roof having the common, mound-like appearance.

Some of the *yeibitchai* hogans are very large and will accommodate hundreds of Indians. During certain parts of the rites the medicine men make the famous sand paintings upon the smooth, beautifully leveled floor—those intricate ceremonial pictures that are made entirely of different colored sands.

Medicine men are both doctor and priest. Theirs is a difficult profession, and they spend years in learning the many chants for the various kinds of illness. They must also master the making of the elaborate sand paintings, different ones being required for the distinctive occasions.

The Navajos are an industrious race, particularly the women. The men are able to work with a will, but do not relish long, sustained effort. The Navajo does not care for "steady" jobs, is perhaps unable to see any special advantage in working just for work's sake. His philosophy does not give him the idea that time is money, or that the accumulation of material gain should be the Alpha and Omega of earthly existence.

A large percentage of the Navajo women and girls are expert weavers of blankets. "Blankets" really is a misnomer; it is more correct to speak of the product of the

Navajo hand looms as rugs. Formerly the blankets were an entirely native product, even to the dyes used in making the different colors, these being mostly of vegetable origin. Now the blankets have become modern, and less valuable; many are put together with a cotton warp or are made of factory-spun wool yarn. Hardly any are woven nowadays that are not colored with aniline dyes.

The secret of the old native vegetable dyes is virtually lost, so far as actual use is concerned. The formulae are known, it is true, but Mrs. Blanket-weaver does not employ them, but gets her dyes ready-made from the trading post, at ten cents a package.

Blankets made from native, vegetable-dyed wools have long since been snapped up by collectors and museums, or are held, in smaller numbers, by old-time residents and traders. George Wharton James, the well-known author of many books dealing with the Indians and the Southwest, has written a volume, *Indian Blankets and Their Makers*, that treats the subject exhaustively. An exceptionally fine collection of Navajo rugs. both the authentic old ones and the finest of the modern product, can be seen in the Fred Harvey showrooms in the various hotels operated by the Santa Fe Railroad, as in the Alvarado in Albuquerque, the La Fonda in Santa Fe, and in El Tovar at the rim of the Grand Canyon.

While as a people the Navajos are versatile and adaptable, and skilful in crafts, it is especially the silversmith who has developed his calling to a high degree of artistry. The ornaments he creates are hammered from silver obtained by melting Mexican pesos. The articles that come from his forge and anvil cover a wide range, from small, narrow-banded finger rings, without turquoise sets, to heavy, gorgeously embossed conchas for belts and beautifully designed silver headstalls for horses.

The demand that followed the indiscriminate tourist trade, aided and abetted by the urgings or promptings of careless traders, gave birth to articles that were unknown in the old days. Furthermore, they are altogether foreign to the native taste and origin, embracing such things as brooches, lodge emblems, teaspoons, salad sets, napkin rings, cigarette boxes, and many other abominations. Instead of remaining true to the pure Indian types, a great deal of the silver-ornament output of the modern Navajo silversmith has degenerated into meaningless stuff, intended solely for the souvenir-buying visitor.

At least one smart storekeeper in Albuquerque has put the making of "hand-made Indian jewelry" on a basis that takes full of advantage of modern mechanical aids. Young Indian boys and men work with electrically driven machinery. They wear uniforms bearing in large letters the name of the shop owner. Their product is fashioned from standarized patterns. Technically, it is not a falsehood to state that the product is, in reality, an Indian-made article, but one must admit that each piece turned out in that frenzied machine shop has about as much originality as a dime.

The old-time silversmith fashioned unique pieces only —no two articles coming from his hands were ever alike. They were produced with loving care and innate artistry. Symbols really had a meaning and deep significance, but the machine age, as applied to Navajo jewelry, is working a sad transformation. It is now possible to buy spoons by the dozen, brooches and rings by the gross, lodge emblems by the boxful, and all articles as much alike as if stamped out on a punch press. They are made by Indians, that is true, but there the story ends.

Here is a quotation from the article on Navajo silversmiths by Dr. Washington Matthews appearing in the

Second Annual Report of the Bureau of Ethnology
(Smithsonian Institution) published in 1880-1881:

> Among the Navajo Indians there are many smiths . . . who
> work chiefly in silver. When and how the art of working
> metals was introduced among them I have not been able to
> determine—many believe they are not indebted to the Euro-
> peans for it. . . .
> The appliances and processes of the smiths are much the
> same among the Navajos as among the Pueblo Indians. . . . A
> large majority of these savage smiths make only very simple
> articles . . . those who make the more elaborate articles are
> few. . . . Their tools and materials are very simple . . . iron,
> pliers, hammers and files they purchase from the whites. . . .
> Files are used not only for their legitimate purposes, but the
> shanks serve for punches and the points for gravers with
> which figures are engraved on silver.

That is as true today as it was then, so far as the real
silversmith of the unspoiled and un-Americanized reservation is concerned. With the workers on the mechanized
assembly line, it is a different story.

The real, truly Indian pieces show great ingenuity of
design and rare skill of workmanship. They combine
beauty of pattern with correctness in weight, symmetry,
and balance. Many belts, made of oval silver disks handsomely patterned in embossed figures and strung upon
narrow strips of buckskin or other leather, are exquisite
showpieces. Armlets, *gatos,* that protect the wrist against
the snap of the bowstring, are worn by the men exclusively, but both sexes adorn themselves with bracelets, rings,
belts, and beads.

The tools used by the artisan are the most primitive
imaginable, the bellows for his forge a homemade affair,
and his anvil, as often as not, just a stone. If the smith is
lucky he has found a piece of an old railroad rail, or
similar chunk of iron or steel, that can be used for an

anvil. If not, a suitable piece of hard, smooth rock serves the purpose. He will use a simple punch, some three-cornered and flat files, a hammer, ordinary knives, and some odd-shaped pieces of metal. The traders supply him with flux and some of the other things necessary for handling the silver, also the material itself from which he fashions the ornaments, the Mexican dollars or pesos.

The white man's religion never gained a real foothold in the Navajo country. The Spanish padres began the attempt to Christianize the Indians hundreds of years ago. Their success, based upon percentage of population, is about on a par with that of the missionaries who have toiled, generation after generation, to induce the Chinese to follow Christ.

The various churches and missions scattered through the Navajo reservation and maintained by the Catholic fathers, Baptists, Methodists, and other denominations, may do some good. I am not able to deny or affirm the possibility. But as for making true, honest Christians of the Indians, particularly the Navajos, their combined efforts have achieved infinitesimally little. It seems a case of love's labor lost.

Missionaries may claim converts and object to my statements, but I know from my many years of residence in the heart of the reservation and my intimate daily contact with the Indians, that the Navajo of today is probably as much a pagan as he has been from time immemorial. He does not attend church except for the Christ-birth celebration, and then not from the devout urge, but because Christmas to him is synonymous with free food and gifts. *His* religious manifestations find outlet and expression in the medicine lodge, in the *yeibitchai* dances, in the chants and sings.

If one doubts whither lies the Indian's conviction, let him watch the stolid, unimpressed and completely blank expressions of the natives in any Christian church. It is painfully obvious that they have only the slightest conception, if any at all, of the meaning or import of the ritual, prayer, communion, sermon, or other phase of the service. Then observe those same Indians attending, and perhaps actively participating in one of their own dances, chants, or similar religious performances! Nowhere can be found deeper interest, a manifestation of keener feeling, or more abundant proof of utter and absolute oneness with the ceremony and all it implies. Bodies tense, eyes flashing, every nerve keyed to its highest pitch, unreasoning and unquestioning belief are startingly portrayed—a grim contrast to the apathetic, lethargic demeanor in the missionary's chapel.

While I was on the reservation, my own observations, corroborated by the experiences of other traders, ranchers, government employees, and others, proved that polygamy among the Navajos was practiced quite generally. Not infrequently, a man would have a mother and her daughter for wives; more often two sisters would share the hogan and the affections of a proud brave. As a rule, couples mated while rather young, but as with the whites, sometimes a girl became the bird in the gilded cage of some old man.

The young women particularly are a fine-looking lot, comely, straight, beautifully featured, possessed of a splendid carriage, and boasting glossy, blue-black hair. Almost all of them are small, delicately boned. Their active outdoor life, plentiful physical exercise, regular horseback riding, and ignorance of corsets, stays, bust supporters, high-heeled pumps, and other atrocities produce for them ruddy health, firm, gracefully rounded breasts, straight, flat backs, and slim, beautiful bodies. The coarse food of their diet necessitates thorough mastication which, in turn, accounts for the flashing whiteness of their teeth.

Under the circumstances and conditions, it was, therefore, not strange to find traders and others occasionally falling victims to the charms of the copper-hued beauties, so shy, maidenly, pretty and soft-spoken.

As a consequence of virtually living their life in the saddle, they have finely formed small feet. That applies to the men as well—even a big, strapping husky standing six feet tall will probably take a shoe that could not accommodate the underpinning of a ten-year-old white boy.

Many curious superstitions and taboos are connected with the family and domestic life. The son-in-law must carefully avoid his mother-in-law; some believe that blindness follows the breaking of the taboo, others hold that it merely signifies disrespect. Relatives, friends, or acquaintances will warn the son-in-law or mother-in-law of each other's presence to prevent accidental meetings. Consequently if a man marries more than once, he is obliged to keep out of the path of a corresponding number of mothers-in-law, unless his wives are sisters.

If a squaw desires freedom from marital bonds, she indicates her wishes by simply putting the saddle and bridle belonging to her spouse outside of their hogan. The Navajo understands the meaning of this act; he betakes himself elsewhere and the divorce is an accomplished fact.

Indian women, generally, do not suffer so intensely in childbirth as do white women. This is probably due to strongly developed abdominal muscles gained through walking, horseback riding, climbing over rough country while herding sheep, and other physical pursuits. Too, the squaws are not so highly sensitive or of such delicately adjusted nervous temperaments as are the more highly civilized white women.

Children are always welcome. Should the mother die, some relative takes them. Illegitimacy has no stigma for either mother or child. A child born to an unwed mother belongs to her clan just the same, and she does not have to simulate or feel shame on account of the birth.

Navajo mothers are almost always kind to their children. Crying children are hushed promptly through gentle means; corporal punishment does not seem to exist. One does not hear screaming or wailing children, or leather-lunged viragos scolding and berating the little ones.

The Navajo women are shrewd bargainers, whether buying or selling, and quite a match for the trader, himself a keen merchant. They will ride many miles, without being perturbed over the distance, to take a blanket or some pelts to the particular trader whom they prefer over others. Later, when they leave the trading post, it is safe to wager that neither buyer nor seller got the worst of the deal; such is the effect of friendly bartering that each party believes he has come off best in the transaction.

The United States government has been grossly neglectful in carrying out the promises made to the Navajos upon diverse occasions. Those included proper grazing grounds, assistance in the matter of restocking and maintaining herds, financial subsidies and adequate school facilities, to list just a few. The military leaders who made the treaties and agreements that embodied those obligations acted in good faith, but the politicians charged with putting the promises into effect failed miserably.

When the Navajos returned from their enforced stay
in the Bosque Redondo, the reservation assigned to them
comprised 3,328,000 acres, virtually all in mountainous
regions with a mean altitude of over 5,000 feet. The
government furnished, to these Indians that came back,
30,000 sheep and 2,000 goats. The present boundaries
take in close to eight million acres, or somewhat over
twelve thousand square miles. This is about one and
one-half times the size of the original reservation domain,
but it is still inadequate, inasmuch as the Indians themselves have multiplied between five and six times in
numbers. Thus, by purely mathematical reckoning, they
should have for their requirements and needs a territory
at least double the present size.

The promised cash payments never materialized. Some
schools were built, closed after a while, then reopened.
In lieu of providing educational facilities at home, as had
been agreed upon, many Navajo youngsters are sent to
Indian schools in Oklahoma, southern Arizona, California, and other places. This transplantation is not a
wise move from a humanitarian or practical viewpoint.

Education is supposed to be compulsory among the
Navajos. The older people have always resented it for a
number of reasons. In the first place they claim that their
boys and girls are needed at home, to help herd sheep and
attend to numerous other chores. Then, and quite
rightly, they feel aggrieved because the enforced separation from home and family has never yet served any
practical purpose. On the contrary, it has been a detri-
mental factor and has caused hardships, griefs, disappoint-
ments and disillusion.

To take a child of six or seven years of age from the
reservation and keep him for a number of years in some
such Indian school, as, for example, Riverside, California,

is cruel and stupid. The boy, grown almost to manhood, returning to his people, may have been trained in some manual art and be a good carpenter, mason, or cabinet-maker. As a rule, he has become proficient in some (from his people's viewpoint) absolutely useless accomplishments. He is unable to use or capitalize his knowledge at home—the Navajos have no need for masons or bricklayers. His school clothes, white man's shoes, the stiff mannerisms and false ideas acquired at school, all grate upon his relatives. He is neither white man nor Indian; a white raven, and just as conspicuous.

This applies equally as well, or even more so, to the girl who comes back to her family after an absence that ranges from early childhood to puberty. Her changed standards of life conflict starkly with the mode of existence in the hogan. It must be a bitter struggle indeed for those hapless youngsters to slough off the thin veneer of a false civilization that has been forced upon them.

About 1900, rumors of gold having been found in the Indian country started a mild gold rush from different points but failed to mature any projects into new Klondikes. Some gold was produced by various parties, claimed to have been found on the reservation, but verification was lacking. The Indians were averse to having white prospectors overrun the reservation. It is probable that some of the gold seekers were killed by the Indians. Other prospectors gave up the chase when their hopes grew dimmer with each succeeding day spent in the desert.

The Office of Indian Affairs, organized well over a century ago, was mismanaged for so many years as to make it a national scandal. The commissioners—political appointees—seldom knew anything about the Indians or the reservations. Over a thirty-year period, from 1868 to 1897, the term of office for the commissioners barely averaged two years. In later years, and as a result of numerous complaints and "exposes," the Indian Bureau underwent a general house cleaning, but it has, nevertheless, managed to continue as one of the most stiff-necked, arbitrary, and autocratic divisions of our Department of the Interior.

Congress, at various times, set aside funds and appropriations for the benefit of the Indians. That gave the Indian Bureau a chance to charge the Navajos with expenditures from appropriations for purposes entirely without benefit to the Indians. At one time the sum of $100,000 was charged against the Indian's monies to help build a bridge at Lees Ferry, Arizona. That place is far removed from the Navajo reservation, and, at the time, not one Indian lived within twenty-five miles of the proposed bridge site, that is, on the reservation side. However, interested counties wanted to build roads, bridges, culverts, modern highways and other improvements to lure the tourist or to facilitate the white man's travel.

That many other unjustified expenditures diminished the funds appropriated and set aside for the benefit of the Indians is indicated in the *Annual Report* of the Board of Indian Commissioners for 1936, which stated, in part:

We have cited this Lee's Ferry bridge case to point out what we regard as unjustifiable use of Government authority in making reimbursable appropriations. They have been made without the consent of the Indians and in most cases, even without their knowledge. The fact that such appropriations might benefit the Indians does not justify the placing of what is practically a forced mortgage upon the property of an Indian tribe.

In the particular instance of the Lees Ferry bridge an aroused press, agitated by friends of the Indian's cause, the action of Congress subsequent to the exposure, forced a reversal and the cancellation of the orders which had made the appropriation for the building of the bridge a charge upon the funds of the Navajos.

In more recent years, oil and gas leases were granted to whites, entitling the leaseholders to drill in specified sections of the Navajo reservation. So far, those ventures are without any commercial significance. It is undoubtedly true that mineral and oil deposits exist within the tribal lands, but their development may never reach the importance of the Oklahoma fields. What is known positively is that wide sections of the far-flung reservation are underlaid with enormous coal fields. When the nation finds it necessary or desirable to exploit those riches, we may discover that the barren desert can produce untold wealth.

And so Dame Fortune, always capricious, toys with the fate of my friends, the Navajos, successively making them the dread lords of all they survey; defeated warriors, blasted from their ancestral hunting grounds; peaceful, nomadic husbandmen. Tomorrow—who knows—they may be millionaire oilmen and coal barons!

Chapter 10

THE OUTFIT

One of the outstanding characters of the Wetherill retinue was Old Man Hunt. He had become a fixture on the ranch, spending his days doing odd jobs. Before the passage of the years had made him unfit for the dangerous work of breaking horses or the equally strenuous freighting, he had been rated a top hand with stock and teams. Now, stiffened from the many hard jolts received during the years spent as broncobuster, and partly from the effects of innumerable days and nights on the range in all sorts of inclement weather, he puttered about, making himself useful in storeroom and saddle and harness shop, looking after the stock of feed and hay, directing the wood choppers at the big pile of cedar and pinon logs, lording it over the chickens and pigeons and throwing generous handfuls of grain to those voracious fowls.

However, while Hunt's physical condition did not permit hard manual labor or muscular exertion, his mind had not deteriorated with time; mentally he was bright and just as keen-witted as the younger people; when he commenced telling tales of the earlier times in the Southwest there was always an attentive audience to listen to his stories. Quite likely, some of those tales were drawn with a fine disregard for too close adherence to actual facts; undoubtedly his narrative was colored to suit his fancy, and it was evident that in the course of years he had developed a sharp appreciation of dramatic values. Still, that did not make the telling less interesting—no, rather the contrary.

Hunt told his version of the forming of the arroyo that bisects the entire length of Chaco Canyon, the gulch's deep-cut walls of from twenty to forty feet sloping down gradually to the very canyon floor, where the Chaco merges with the Escavada Wash. According to him, the bottom of the canyon did not show any tendency to form a ditch or gully, let alone a full-sized arroyo, when he first saw it. At that time, according to his story, the floor of the Chaco was one solid unbroken expanse from wall to wall. But later the buffalo herds roaming through the canyon followed a path straight down the middle and wore away the surface to such an extent as to cause the rains of the following years to convert the fairly deep trail into a flume. Thus the channel started by the sharp hoofs of the buffalos widened, and with each succeeding season became deeper until it reached the proportions with which we are now familiar.

He told of the stampeding of a large herd of buffalo in a driving snowstorm. The animals were galloping across the mesa, in that part which we had transformed into our pasture, and when the thundering ranks reached the cliffs of the canyon walls, the leaders, blinded by the stinging flakes, failed to see the terrible drop yawning beneath their feet. Hundreds of the buffalos plunged headlong down into the abyss, the fall killing the first ones, the succeeding ones in turn being annihilated by the mass of bone, horn, and hoof that descended from the top, piling layer upon layer. According to our narrator, the bones that were left, after the wolves and coyotes had feasted on the carcasses for months, made a heap from ten to twelve feet high.

The old fellow could recount some fascinating stories of his early trading with the Indians. He told of freighting when that work had to be done with ox teams, of set-tos with the red men, of shootings and killings. It was certain that he had known personally many of the men who, a few years previous, had made crimson history in the Southwest. He had rubbed elbows with peace officers and outlaws who dominated the scene in such places as the Texas and Kansas cow towns, and, later, in the Colorado camps and in Tombstone, the vermillion spot of Arizona. Inasmuch as those encounters had taken place within some fifteen to twenty years of the telling, it was reasonable to suppose that they had retained most of their original color in the mind of the old cowboy. Other old-timers, drifting into the canyon on different occasions, would corroborate the tales unfolded by Hunt, although there might be some divergence on dates or years, excusable in a period and country that gave little heed to fixing exact calendar time.

Lorenzo Hubbell, of Ganado, another old Indian trader, also told many amusing incidents of dealing with the Indians when all supplies had to be brought overland by ox teams, long before the completion of the Santa Fe Railroad. He related how he used to swap a single sewing needle for the equivalent of twenty-five cents' worth of pelts, hides, wool, or other goods bartered by the Indians. When a Navajo objected to the high cost of the needle, Hubbell would tell him to return it, suggesting at the same time that he go back to camp and himself make a needle. Every package of needles, costing Hubbell less than ten cents, brought a return of five dollars or more! And neither he nor his clerks ever gave out more than a single needle to an Indian—the natives did not even see that those little implements arrived in packages.

Many of the stories were verified by the boss. Wetherill had not only lived through the same turbulent years but had gathered authentic information about notorious events and outstanding happenings from friends, acquaintances, and, last but not least, from his brothers. There were five of the Wetherill boys, all of them explorers, stockmen, Indian traders, and, to hear their enemies, some—or all of them—cattle rustlers, thieves, and crooks. *"Mehr Feind, mehr Ehr!"* as the German proverb has it. I never saw anything that was not perfectly legitimate in the actions or conduct of any of the Wetherills with whom I came in contact. However, in those rough-and-ready days it was easy to acquire the reputation of being a cattle thief. Anybody who managed to have and to hold cattle was dubbed an old rustler, and often the term was bestowed with tolerant approval. In any event, Wetherill of Chaco Canyon, or Pueblo Bonito, had been in the thick of unruly Western activity for a number of years and could speak with authority upon the phases of frontier life which were of interest to those who listened to Hunt and other tellers of tales.

Wetherill has been credited with being the discoverer of the Mesa Verde ruins at Mancos, Colorado. He was engaged in taking Eastern tourists and sportsmen on camping and hunting trips when he learned of the existence of those magnificent cliff dwellings. And from the Mancos ruins he came to the communal buildings in Chaco Canyon. There he found such a wonderful field for exploration and excavation that he enlisted the financial support which should make it possible to let the world at large share in the benefits of his finds. This needed help came to him through a friend from the East, Mr. Fred Hyde, who organized and financed the Hyde Exploring Expedition. The avowed purpose of that undertaking was the uncovering of the buried archaeological treasures of Chaco Canyon, and it was brought to a most successful conclusion in the years that followed.

Fred Hyde was a member of a New York family that had amassed considerable wealth from manufacturing soap and kindred products. He had been everywhere, knew all sorts of out-of-the-way corners of the world, but as many others before and since, fell in love with the irresistible charm of the desert country. Well over six feet tall, rangy, clear-eyed, strong, fearless, a student and worker, he presented an ideal type. He described personal experiences in Egypt, demonstrated Japanese swordsmanship with the two-handed sword, related tales of old Mexico, and spoke convincingly of trips and happenings in various countries of Europe. The enormous cost of the proposed undertaking was no deterrent to him; undiscouraged over the burden of heavy financial outlays, he furnished the money necessary to begin and complete the first excavation of the great communal buildings that had slumbered undisturbed for virtually a thousand years.

Fred's restless energy found manifold outlets during the work of uncovering the riches that had remained in obscurity so many centuries. He also plunged into the variety of work connected with the establishment of depots, freight stations, trading posts; supervised the hauling of supplies, expedited the shipments of objects taken from the ruins, and actually assisted in handling teams, men and livestock; he was a guiding light in the transformation of the exploring expedition into a trading and ranching business when the principal purpose of the Hyde company had been accomplished.

"Black" Phillips' birthplace was in the Kentucky mountains. Just how he got to Pueblo Bonito and became one of the "boys" was not disclosed. He had been one of the gang for some years when I arrived as a new recruit to the Triangle Bar Triangle outfit. His nickname indicated the shock of black, unruly hair that topped his head. Of tall, handsome appearance, he held himself rather aloof and was easily the most uncommunicative of the fellows that shared work and fun on the ranch. While easy-going and polite, he could turn viciously wild and uncontrolled upon occasion, particularly when in some of his more morose moods he would take exceptions to joking remarks about his southern drawl or home mountains. Innocent little innuendos assumed in his mind the proportions of personal slurs and insults, and it behooved everybody to keep "Black's" idiosyncracies in mind and not to overstep the proprieties as they were interpreted by the lanky Kentuckian.

Palmer had come from Kansas, was taciturn by nature and not a good mixer. However, Fred was not only a top hand and all-around expert cowboy, but also a first-class blacksmith. Under his skilful hands iron became like wax, and from his forge emerged beautifully made branding irons, exquisitely tempered spurs, bridle bits inlaid with silver, candleholders, door knockers and other things. Small wonder that he could be found more often in the blacksmith shop than on the range or in the corrals. The enormous breadth of shoulders and thickly muscled arms bespoke the tremendous physical strength of the man. His prowess was best demonstrated when he had to shoe half-broken broncos. Then it seemed as if his grasp would nearly pull out the animal's leg when the horse reared back or tried to kick the daring human who held him.

His principal diversion, aside from working in metals, was pistol practice, and in the course of time and through the expenditure of thousands of rounds of ammunition he had become uncannily proficient in the use of Mr. Colt's equalizer. Fred could keep an empty tin can dancing in the air until all chambers in his six-shooter were fired. No discarded bottle, regardless of distance, size, shape, or color was safe—if Palmer took aim it meant shattering the target. He prided himself upon never shooting a jackrabbit except squarely through the eyes. "Them eyes do make the best targets," he would drawl, when another of the luckless bunnies sprawled between the sage and cactus, struck down in its track as if by lightning. But despite his expertness with the six-shooter, he shot himself as clumsily as the veriest greenhorn who never before in his life had handled a gun.

It happened one winter day, when several of the Triangle Bar Triangle boys were driving a bunch of horses toward winter pasturage beyond the San Juan River. The weather was bitterly cold, and the water of the San Juan flowed blackly between the banks. For some two feet toward the middle of the river, extending from the water's edge at both banks, ice had formed, and the horses shied away from the slippery surface. With nostrils almost touching the unfamiliar substance, they snorted and reared back, time and again breaking away from us, refusing to make the start into the river and crossing to the other bank. We whooped and yelled and slapped our ropes against the chaps, but the horses would not be persuaded—nor could they be frightened into making the plunge. Fred became impatient. He jerked his Colt from its holster and began firing at the heels of the horses nearest to him. All of a sudden he let out a yell of pain and, swaying dizzily in his saddle, reined his mount to the rear. Phillips and I rushed over to him, wondering what had happened, when he shouted: "I'm shot!"

While firing his shots, intended to scare the horses into a sudden lunge through the band of ice, his own mount had made an unexpected side movement, for the fraction of a second throwing Fred off balance. That happened just at the moment when he had "thrown" his gun downward for another shot at the ground. Instead of hitting back of the horses, the bullet had furrowed down his leg from just below the knee clear to the bottom of the foot, coming out through the sole, but stopping in the boot! Well, he was a pretty sick boy, but kept to his horse until we could get him to a doctor in the small Mormon settlement of Fruitland. Of course, we had cut away his boot, and stopped the flow of blood, but it took a good deal of stamina to ride with the badly injured leg through the icy waters of the San Juan and beyond until we could secure medical assistance for Fred.

The horses, for the moment having been left to themselves, got up courage and picked their way through the ice and the river, making the crossing without offering any further resistance. They had begun to browse on the few tufts of grass not covered by snow, and nibbled on the sere branches of the sagebrush and young cottonwood trees growing near the river's edge. One of the boys took charge of the remuda and drove the horses in a leisurely fashion toward the alfalfa pastures that had been our destination.

The doctor of the Mormon village attended Palmer's

1. Author on horseback. *Copyright G. Haven Bishop.*

2. Author's trading post, Keams Canyon, Arizona, from painting. *Copyright G. Haven Bishop.*

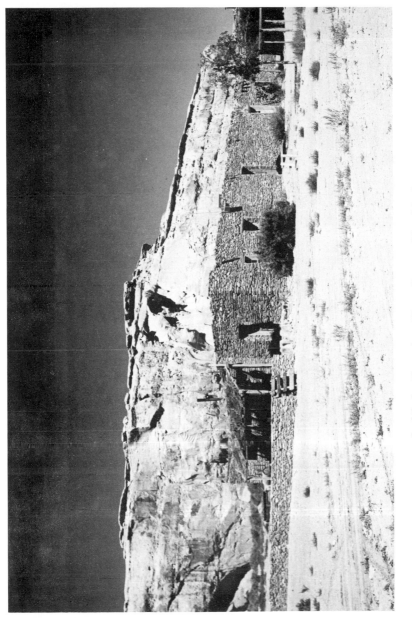

3. Wetherill ranch at Chaco Canyon, New Mexico.

4. Author's home at Keams Canyon.

5. Spider Woman Rock, Canyon de Chelly, Arizona.

6. Wagon freighting to Chaco. *Photo courtesy National Park Service, Chaco Center.*

7. Walpi, a Hopi pueblo in Arizona, 1870s. *Photo by J. K. Hillers.*

8. Arizona ranch scene, turn of the century.

wound. It was almost a miracle that no more damage than the examination disclosed was done by the heavy .45 caliber slug of lead that had torn through the chaps and coursed through the fleshy parts of the leg and into the foot. Fred was bandaged and left in the home of the Mormon settler who looked after the pick of the remuda (saddle horses) for Wetherill during the winter months. It was several weeks before the doctor permitted the patient to mount his horse and return to Chaco Canyon. From the unfortunate accident Palmer remained ever after slightly lame in the right foot.

Chapter 11

MORMONS

At the time when I was riding for Wetherill, most of the country in northern San Juan County, watered by the San Juan River and its tributaries, was occupied by Mormons. They lived in flourishing farming communities, veritable oases in that otherwise arid desert section. Hay, grain, alfalfa, potatoes, cabbages, other garden truck, and a wide variety of fruits and berries, were grown in abundance by those patient, hard-working husbandmen. They kept cows and actually had fresh milk, rich cream, and home-churned butter upon their tables.

They were beekeepers, and the women put up large quantities of preserves, spiced and watermelon-rind pickles, and other good things to eat. From the pigs raised by them they cured hams and slabs of bacon and enjoyed home-rendered lard. There were sausage makers among them, and others who could make cheese. Out of "green" rawhides they fashioned the seats of large, sturdy, comfortable chairs. The women still did a certain amount of spinning and weaving, utilizing the wool from their own sheep.

Those Mormons were expert farmers and stockmen,

frugal, thrifty, strictly honest and upright, although narrow-minded and undoubtedly bigoted in questions of religion. Their viewpoint in church matters was as restricted as that of the early settlers of New England. Many of the blue laws of the Puritans and the ordinances of the Mormons ran parallel. They did not permit smoking or drinking; gambling and even the mildest forms of card playing were taboo. Modesty and unblemished purity distinguished their women, young and old—they had no sex crimes, "jazz babies," cocktail-swigging debutantes, and other distorted outcroppings of the later and "more modern and advanced" social life. They were, one and all, zealots in the matter of gaining converts for their religious belief; proselytizing had become one of their favorite pastimes.

Polygamy, although supposedly outlawed, was still practiced more or less openly by many of the adherents of Mormonism living in the remoter districts of virtually inaccessible country. They found that the easiest way to circumvent the law, accepted by the majority of Mormons, was to establish several homes, and many took advantage of this opportunity and maintained families in different places.

Hatcher, one of the freighters occasionally working for Wetherill, kept and reared families in three places, and would visit his wives at convenient intervals. Whenever he came through Chaco Canyon on those trips, we would see a number of new faces. Young women, middle-aged women, but, above all, a swarming horde of children of every age and both sexes, almost overflowed the confines of the huge, covered wagons that were their temporary homes. Hatcher used to indulge in such flimsy explanations. He had just been to see some relation—he was bringing back with him some kinfolk—his niece, or cousin, or aunt, was moving—his wife's married sister was coming to visit his home. The odd thing was that never another man accompanied those treks—invariably it was Hatcher who had charge of the wagon or wagons. If there should be more than one vehicle, the second or third would be driven by some of the capable young women, guiding the teams with strong, sun-tanned hands.

At every other time, when freighting for Wetherill or going through Pueblo Bonito with a load of produce from the San Juan farms to Albuquerque, Hatcher was in the habit of making camp near the corrals and the water troughs of the ranch. However, upon those occasions when traveling with one of his families, he kept away from our little settlement in the Chaco. Then he would drive past and beyond the actual confines of the ranch and pitch camp some two or three miles farther up, or down, the canyon. There, out of sight and hearing of the Wetherill outfit, he would stop, unhitch the teams, start the fire and prepare for the night. The children would tumble out of the high wagons, attend to various chores, gather firewood, help the women, take the horses and mules to water, or just play about, evidently happy to be on solid ground instead of in the swaying wagons.

Two or three times I happened to ride by Hatcher's camps, but I received such a cool, almost unfriendly greeting that I gave up trying to see something of the more intimate, domestic arrangements of his perambulating harem. It was obvious that he did not relish or welcome neighborly calls when engaged upon the serious business of moving certain parts of his widespread family. While generally of a pleasant, jovial nature, at those times he became distant and standoffish, barely making civil answers to perfectly innocent remarks or questions.

Quite often I found myself a guest of different Mormon

families in the San Juan country, whither my duties as
rider for Wetherill would take me. I do not recall even
one instance when I was not made much of; I was always
treated as an honored and most welcome visitor. The
best room in the house was mine; special dishes were
prepared for me; my horse was looked after by the man
of the house himself or by some other member of the
family.

Invariably there came frankly expressed invitations to
become a member of the Mormon colony; to take up a
homestead; to give up the rider's unrestrained and unpro-
fitable existence and change to the more stable life of
farmer and stockman; to select a girl from the many in
the village and marry; above all, to take the proper view
of the Mormon belief and adopt the true religion! Unquestionably, a conversion would have been a profitable
move for me, it would have meant an immediate acceptance into the full confidence of those hardy pioneers. It
would have assured many material advantages, generous,
unstinted assistance in the way of getting a start as hus-
bandman, and last, but by no means least, a virtually undisputed choice among the daughters of the land not
already betrothed.

With considerable acumen, the men of the family or
settlement left the attack upon the long-legged, red-headed
rider to the diplomacy and subtle persuasions of the
women. From the moment I dismounted and gave greeting to my host until the very second when I touched spurs
to my horse, leaving the hospitable shelter bestowed in
so friendly a manner, I was surrounded by young and
attractive girls and women. They gave tremendous and
hard-to-resist weight to the arguments and used all wiles
known to the female to bring about a decision that would
have resulted in me quitting the range and joining the
Mormons.

However, the gentile resisted the sweet maneuvers as nicely as his inexperience permitted, and he must have succeeded rather well because the friendships persisted and were not marred by the refusal to accept the bountiful offerings. Some of my happiest recollections of the days in the old Southwest are memories of the gracious hospitality extended by my Mormon friends and enjoyed to the fullest by me when still a boy, hungry for the pleasant warmth of family life, home atmosphere, and affection.

Chapter 12

CHRISTMAS

Telling about visits to the Mormon villages brings the recollection of an experience that befell me one winter day when I was returning from an errand to the San Juan, headed for Pueblo Bonito.

It was two days before Christmas, the weather bitterly cold. The day before I had spent with an old Indian trader, a squaw man, who had put me up for the night, fed both me and my horse, and warned me about the approaching storm when I left for the river. Wetherill's message delivered, I turned my horse, pointing him homeward, refusing the cordial invitations of the Mormon to remain for the Christmas celebration. I was eager to be back in Pueblo Bonito, to spend the holiday on the ranch that meant home to me. Mrs. Wetherill, I knew, had been very busy in the kitchen for some ten days, making cakes, plum pudding, and all sorts of other good things. There was to be a Christmas tree, and there would be some small remembrances for each and every one of the large ranch family. No wonder I did not wish to miss the festivities.

Some three miles south of the river the trail leading to Pueblo Bonito forked; my road branched off to the left, taking me back by way of the trading post, only twelve miles from the San Juan. This was not the first time I had ridden over the road; I was well acquainted with the trail and did not need to worry over losing my way. From the point where the saddle trail ended at the trader's place the wagon road began, leading all the way to Chaco Canyon. The distance I had to cover was some sixty miles, a long road, indeed, but not too far for the powerful brute I was riding. Another fact to consider: the season was in our favor, as heat and sandstorms were not likely to bother us at Christmas time.

With my mind filled with happy thoughts, I set out upon the ride toward Pueblo Bonito. The sky was dull, leaden, heavy with snow-bearing clouds that presaged the onrushing storm, but before the eye of my soul danced the image of the bright lights of the Christmas tree that was to be lit in Chaco Canyon. The horse, knowing as well as I that we were homeward bound, required no urging; he was stepping out at a mile-eating gait. Although the weather looked far from promising, we had no thought of aught but a speedy return to the Wetherill ranch.

However, hardly had we crossed the ford of the river when fitful winds brought the first snow flurry. Soon we were engulfed in a swirling sea of flakes that came with stinging sharpness, breaking against our faces and striking directly at our eyes. Instead of turning about and accepting the situation philosophically, as I should and would have done under ordinary circumstances, I kept prodding the animal to face the swiftly developing storm, and continued on the trail. I did not know what a lesson the elements had in store for me.

Long before we came to the place where the trail divided, the storm had us blinded. I knew, and admitted to myself, that I could no longer see the road, but de-

pended entirely upon the keener senses of my horse.
However, the poor beast was not much better able than I
to face the stinging lash of the driven snow, dashed furiously against us. He kept shaking his head, bending his
neck to escape the full blast of the storm, and by those
maneuvers side-stepped into an old trail that some Indians
had made when going after wood. Neither the horse nor
I realized that we had quit the trail that was to take us
past the Indian trading post; we were following a sufficiently defined path that we thought was the Pueblo
Bonito track. But in his attempts to evade the beating of
the snow scourge, the horse was steadily sheering off to the
west instead of going southeast. It was impossible to see
a distance of even a few feet; in fact, while seated in the
saddle, the ground was invisible.

I carried no watch, hence did not know just how long
we had traveled, but after what seemed an agelong time,
I came to the realization that we had missed the right
trail, and I was ready to acknowledge that we were lost.
And lost we would, perforce, remain, until the storm
should clear and enable me to see the landmarks with
which I was familiar. Only after the storm abated would
I be able to orient myself and obtain proper bearings.
For the moment there was nothing else to do but to stay
on the trail we were following. I counted upon the possibility that it might lead to a Navajo hogan, which would
have meant food and shelter. Thus we continued, hour
after hour, all day long, but failed to come to a hogan; nowhere a trace of an Indian camp or settlement. Gradually,
the greyness that had enveloped us from almost the time
of our start began to thicken, until at last it was so murky
that we did not dare continue for fear of falling into unsuspected arroyos or other pitfalls.

The snowing eased up toward nightfall, and about an

hour after we stopped, ceased entirely. I had dismounted in a clump of pinon trees, thinking they would provide a bit of shelter and, possibly, some firewood. I fastened my horse to one of the low-crowned trees, placing him on the protected side, spreading the saddle blanket on his back to prevent chilling. There was no feed for him, of course, or, for that matter, anything for me to eat. But even more than food we missed water. Both of us tried eating snow, but that made the thirst more tantalizing and intensified the desire for a drink.

After a number of attempts, I succeeded in lighting a small fire. From the trees surrounding our dismal camp, I broke off as many dead branches as I could find, shredding the first bits of wood to make tinder, and slowly, piece by piece, feeding the larger chunks to the flame until we had a respectable campfire. The horse kept nuzzling me, plainly begging for his oats and corn, but I had to disappoint the poor fellow. In the warmth of the fire, which required constant attention and replenishing, we felt a bit more cheerful, but it was a long vigil through the night before dawn began to disperse the shadows of darkness.

Day broke clear and bright, the snow-blanketed ground dazzingly white in virginal purity. Then, after climbing to the highest hill near by and surveying the landscape, and after noting carefully the position of the various peaks, buttes, mesas, and other landmarks, I was confronted with the disenchanting reality that, despite our long ride of the previous day, we could not reach home in time for the Christmas celebration—we had drifted at least forty miles out of our way! Away off to our left were the familiar outlines of the canyons and ranges of the Wetherill domain—it would require most of two days riding to cover the distance separating us from them. Well, we were here—nothing could change the fact—and

so, instead of fretting any longer over the missed plum
pudding, the luscious turkey dinner, and other delectables, I gave heed to the more pressing need for food and
drink, at the moment the matter of greater importance.

From the knoll that I had climbed to gain a better
observation point I looked long and earnestly in every
direction, watching for the surest sign of humans: smoke
curling upward. There! Less than two miles off on our
right a blue, thin, smoke cloud spiraled on high. It must
come from a fire in some hogan. Marking the direction
in my mind, I saddled the horse and cut across country
toward the place where the smoke had shown itself. The
poor animal was gaunt from lack of water and feed, but
he struck out energetically, knowing instinctively, perhaps, that I was guiding him toward sustenance.

Before long, we approached a Navajo campsite. A
pack of rough, half-wild dogs set up an ear-splitting bark-
ing and howling, announcing our arrival to the Indians,
but, queerly, none opened the flap over the hogan entrance to see who the guest or guests might be. That was
rather unusual, but explained itself when I had dismounted, fought off the snarling dogs with quirt and
rope's end, and lifted the blanket that was door to the
hogan. Only two young girls were at home, and they were
palpably frightened over the coming of the tall young
white man. They cowered as far away from the door
opening as the wall of the hogan permitted, dark eyes
peeking out from under the big blanket they had thrown
over themselves.

Greeting them in Navajo, I inquired after their
family or relations. The only word they uttered was
"Attin," meaning that none else was there. I told them
that I was one of Wetherill's men, but the information
failed to have any soothing effect. I spoke of having been

lost during the preceding night because I had missed the right trail on my way back to the ranch. I mentioned the fact that neither my horse nor I had eaten or drunk since the morning of the previous day, but my words did not appear to make the slightest impression. Not one word in answer—only the peculiar stare of the four eyes, watching me as if mesmerized.

At last, becoming impatient, and thinking them quite unusually stupid, I ordered them to prepare coffee and to make some food ready for me, also to find some ears of corn for the horse. Still no movement under the big blanket, only the hypnotized glare from those smoky-black orbs, the dilated pupils indicating very clearly how frightened their possessors were. I could not account for this strange behavior, so utterly at variance from the usual hospitality extended to everybody in all Navajo hogans. My patience had become exhausted by that time, so I walked over to the two girls, grabbed one by an arm and pulled her from under the blanket upon her feet. Then I saw why they had acted so oddly: one of the girls was nude entirely, and the other virtually without clothes!

Now was explained the obvious fright and horrible discomfort of those two youngsters, not more than perhaps fourteen and sixteen years old, respectively. To ease the situation and reassure the girls, who were scared out of their wits, I laughed and laughed until they, too, began to see some humor in their predicament. Casting about for some articles of clothing, I grabbed a handful of what I thought might be skirts and waists and tossing those over to them, directed the girls to dress hurriedly because I would be coming back into the hogan in just another moment or two! Leaving them, with that threat hastening the job of dressing, I lifted the blanket that protected the entrance and strode out into the open. Another burst of howling greeted me, the dogs taking their job seriously, no doubt about that.

After a short interval I re-entered the hogan and found both girls, now fully clothed, busy about the fire. Water was being boiled for coffee, some meat had been brought to light, also some cold biscuits, evidently the remains of supper from the evening before. One of the two scared beauties was engaged in tearing the husks from a heap of corn, getting it ready for my horse. Presently, hot, steaming coffee was warming my innards, while the horse was contentedly crunching the hard corn spread out before him upon an old piece of wagon cover. By that time, my two young hostesses had lost their shyness and were able to converse and could even indulge in some sly smiles.

They said that their father and mother had gone after "Krissmuss," by which they meant the customary Christmas distribution of free food and presents at some mission or trading post. They had been left at home to look after the sheep and goats, still penned up in a small stone-walled corral under a rocky ledge, barely visible from the hogan. They gave me explicit directions about taking a short cut that would put me back on the trail I had lost the day before, and when I left, after giving each one a silver quarter, they were laughing gaily and waving good-by to me as long as I could see them.

Late in the afternoon of that same day, Christmas Eve, I came to a trading post, and the trader had no difficulty whatever to make me accept his invitation to stay over-night with him. The horse was bedded down in a regular box stall, an almost-unheard-of luxury, generously provided with hay and grain, and I found a comfortable bunk for myself adjoining the storeroom. The combination dinner and supper tasted mighty good, and the bed, although lacking innerspring mattresses, seemed as soft and downy as if so equipped; horse and rider made up for the night spent under the pinons.

True, I had visions of the festivities on the Wetherill ranch—Christmas Eve was to be the big time for feasting and opening of gifts. I was still kid enough to feel keenly the inability to be present at the merrymaking, but being thoroughly tired out, and having a stomach full of warm food, I did not let those dreary thoughts keep me awake for long. Within a few minutes after going to bed, I must have been sound asleep.

Christmas morning found us about twenty miles from home, mount and man well rested and eager to be on their way. I thanked my trader friend for his hospitality, for which one could not proffer payment without insulting the host. We knew now that in the course of a few hours we would be back in Pueblo Bonito, even if the weather should change suddenly and bring another storm. Within a radius of those last few miles, we could not get lost. However, the day started auspiciously and remained bright and clear. Riding mile after mile, we came, eventually, to the mouth of the canyon. We crossed the widespread Escavada Wash, then trotted up Chaco Canyon. By that time we were no longer by ourselves, for a number of Indians had joined us, all bound for Pueblo Bonito and the big free meal that Wetherill was in the habit of providing for them each Christmas. And presently we rode between the two tall gateposts into the big, open lot, the stable buildings on one side, the excavated ruins at the opposite, the boss's house in front, and in the far background the overhanging cliff of the mesa wall. I unsaddled, turned my horse into one of the corrals, then walked over to the office to make my report.

Coming in among the group of Indians, my return had not been noticed. The office had no windows to the rear of the building, consequently one could not observe from there what was or might be happening in the lot. In this way, it came about that none of the ranch family had become aware of my arrival. All the boys were assembled in the office, as well as Mr. and Mrs. Wetherill and their children. When I opened the door and entered the house, Mrs. Wetherill jumped from her chair, rushed toward me and before I knew what was happening, had hugged and kissed me! Laughing and almost crying, she exclaimed: "You bad, bad boy, where have you been?" and went on to say how worried everybody had been about me when I failed to come home at the time they expected me. They had experienced great anxiety when the storm engulfed the canyon, figuring that in all probability I was out in it. With the easy facility of worrying mothers, who invariably fear the worst, she had pictured me lost in the terrible snowdrifts, maybe hurt, surely starving to death, perhaps losing consciousness in the cold and gradually freezing into another existence. "Aren't you ashamed, scaring me and all of us like this?" she wanted to know.

While this loving tirade burst over my head, I stood in front of the gang blushing like a simpering schoolgirl. What had just happened to me, being kissed before the assembly, was something that would be hard to live down. I felt so terribly embarrassed that Mrs Wetherill, suddenly sensing my utter discomfiture, thrust me before her and took me through the living quarters to the kitchen, at the other extreme from the office. There she made me tell just what had kept me from returning earlier, and while I was trying to relate my story she stuffed me with cookies and hot coffee. Then she told the news that has lived in my memory ever since: Hoping that I would surely return that day, she had postponed the Christmas celebration—the feast had been delayed by her until that very evening—the gifts had not yet been distributed! They had waited for my return. Christmas was not to be celebrated until Joe was there to enjoy it with them.

Hearing the news, so wonderful and unexpected, I broke down and cried like a baby; great, heavy tears rolled down over my snow-chapped cheeks. While I was a tall husky, and always ready to assert myself a real man, still, underneath lived just a big, overgrown kid, with a child's sensibilities, hiding from a rough-and-ready company a side that most of them could not have imagined. Mrs. Wetherill, the splendid, wonderful woman, knew better, and her remarkable insight and fine understanding told her things that I would not have admitted to myself. Anyhow, she comforted the youngest member of the ranch family, told me to get myself cleaned up and ready for the big party, and she let me leave the house through the back door of the kitchen. That maneuver allowed me to escape from the quizzically inclined gang assembled in the office.

By dusk our Indian friends, who had been feasting on the fat yearling steer butchered for the occasion, and who had consumed huge quantities of freshly baked bread and gallons upon gallons of coffee, dispersed. Navajos, generally speaking, dislike being abroad after dark—there are entirely too many spirits, ghosts, and hobgoblins about for one's comfort! If it is at all possible, they try to reach camp in time to keep out of the way of encounters with the evil ones, admitting shrewdly that discretion is the better part of valor. With the visitors out of the way, preparations were started for own celebration.

In the bunkhouse I had to submit to a great deal of good-natured chaffing. Wasn't it disgraceful to have everybody wait just for the return of a no-good cowpuncher? What could one expect when sending out a green hand who could not even follow back on his own trail? Why should real men be obliged to put themselves out for a mere kid? Wouldn't it be better to have children stay at home, with their mothers, than to turn them loose upon a world already suffering too much? And did you notice how the boss's wife kissed the poor stray when he got back to the home corral?

Under some of the remarks, I wanted to explode, and felt like slaughtering the whole merciless crew. Presently, however, everyone was too much occupied with the problem of making himself presentable for the dinner table in the boss's house to continue the ragging, and I was left in peace. There was general shaving, bathing, changing to clean clothes, slicking down unruly hair. Faces shone as if polished; the hair of the boys clung to their scalps like fur to a drowned rat. Of course we could not "dress"—our wardrobe was limited to but two classes of clothing: clean and soiled. But for this special occasion everybody turned out in clean clothes, and with faces, hands, and bodies thoroughy scrubbed. Nothing different was expected; we were quite in fashion and met the demands of ranch etiquette.

We marched into the long dining room where a heavy table was laden with good things to eat. Mrs. Wetherill's two Indian maids, who assisted her in house and kitchen, waited on us and she, herself, saw to it that none lacked a generous helping of turkey or a big steak, tomatoes, corn, sweet potatoes, mashed potatoes, cranberry sauce and, for dessert, big slices of mince and pumpkin pie. We were offered our choice of coffee or chocolate. The latter beverage had been cooked for two days prior to the serving; when asked about, Mrs. Wetherill explained that only in such manner could the full flavor of the chocolate be brought out. She had simmered it on the stove for hours, allowed it to cool, then cooked it once more. She had whipped it with an egg beater, making it as smooth as velvet, and her efforts and patience had produced a most delicious beverage.

Except for attending to the necessary chores, such as feeding the stock in the stables and corrals, looking after the windmills to make sure that the pumps were not frozen up, and throwing rations of grain to the chickens and pigeons, no other work was performed on Christmas. Nobody gave fretting thoughts to the matter of fence riding or occupied his mind with any affair except the all-important one of the coming dinner and evening celebration.

After dinner began the real Christmas festivity; the gorgeously decorated tree shone in the light of the candles that were lit, and the boss, himself, began distributing the presents. First came the gifts for the children, who were least able to curb their impatience to see what Santa Claus had brought. Those joyful oh's and ah's! Those wild exclamations of sheer happiness as the boxes and bundles were demolished and the glittering or hoped-for contents revealed. After the children had finished unpacking and exclaiming over their things, the two Navajo girls, Mrs. Wetherill's maids, received their Christmas gifts, mostly articles of clothing, and some inexpensive pieces of jewelry. Then the boss began handing out packages, gaily decorated with fancy ribbons, to the boys.

There were spurs, hand-braided rawhide quirts, imported Mexican reatas with buckskin-bound hondas, silk bandanna neckerchiefs, gauntlets, work gloves, warm woolen socks, and a number of other things calculated to gladden the heart of a cowpuncher. Too, he distributed bags of Bull Durham smoking tobacco, rice cigarette papers, boxes of matches, yes, even plugs of chewing tobacco, although the boss did not use tobacco in any form. At the end, Mr. Wetherill, though himself a strict teetotaler, produced bottles and glasses, and everybody was treated to a long drink of good wine!

The boss and his wife exchanged personal gifts after all others had been made happy with presents and remembrances. Then, when everything seemed to have come to a close, the boys brought their combination presents to the boss and his wife: for Mrs. Wetherill we had a set of new dishes that she had admired some months previously when in Albuquerque during the fair. For the boss there was a long, odd-looking package that proved to contain a fine single-barreled shotgun, especially bored for long-range shooting, the very gun with which to greet the hawks that almost daily pestered the pigeons and chickens and guinea hens inhabitating the yard.

During the winter months, the duties on the ranch were light. At that season work was done in more or less perfunctory manner; we spent many hours attending to inside repairs in the blacksmith shop, or in rebuilding certain sections of the stable, feed room, or suchlike. Generally, in cold weather, saddles were taken apart and treated with neat's-foot oil to prevent cracking of the leather during the hot summer months to come, and chaps and boots were thoroughly rubbed with oil to make them withstand both wet and dry weather. A new supply of rawhide hobbles was made from the freshly skinned hides of the beeves butchered on the ranch for their meat. The hides were also utilized for making pack boxes, to fit the sawbuck packsaddles we used to put on mules for certain camping trips, or when on the trail unaccompanied by a chuck wagon. Those pack boxes, shaped over empty

wooden cases that had held two five-gallon cans of kerosene, were almost indestructible when thoroughly dried.
They were light in weight, but would wear like iron.

Of course the stock in the stables and corrals, and in
the big pasture atop the mesa, had to be looked after, but
we did not engage in many of the things we were in the
habit of doing during the summer and fall months. One
reason for that was the physical state of the stock: the
stallions and geldings were not strong enough to be
broken, the poor feeding conditions of the winter range
precluding excess energy, and the mares were mostly in
foal. Also, it would not have served any practical purpose
to train horses at that season, because we could not have
sold them. To break them in November or December
and then to turn them back onto the range for several
months would have meant the useless expenditure of time
and effort. It was a foregone conclusion that when the
beasts were rounded up in spring they would surely have
forgotten their first lessons and would have to be taught all
over again.

The real work of the year did not begin until spring
made the world green and the first warm sunshine carpeted the prairie with millions of wild flowers. Then, and
through the summer months till about Thanksgiving,
activities were many and varied and kept everyone busy
from early until late. Fences had to be repaired, after
suffering the buffeting of the winter storms and the
crushing impact of snowdrifts; the windmills required
overhauling and repacking; cattle and horses had to be
shifted to different sections of the range; colts and calves
had to be branded; broncs learned their A B C's in the big
corrals and became "gentled" through methods not so
gentle; roundups took place; stock was driven to the railroad for sale or shipment, and, in the late fall, winter sup-

plies were laid in, necessitating long hauls by freight wagon from the San Juan country in the north and from the different railroad towns, such as Albuquerque, Grants, Thoreau, and Gallup, in the south.

Chapter 13

BILL FINN

One of the characters not yet mentioned turned up in Pueblo Bonito on a day in early summer. I was in one of the large corrals at the edge of the arroyo, when I saw the cloud of dust in the upper canyon that announced the advent of a rider long before he could be distinguished. Indians were coming and going at all times, so I gave no heed to the arrival of a horseman until a quiet, drawling voice hailed me from outside the corral.

"Is this the Triangle Bar Triangle ranch?" it desired to know.

"That's right," I answered, taking in the appearance of the questioner. I saw a medium-sized man about twenty-six or twenty-eight years of age, sitting an exceptionally fine, cream-colored horse. The man wore the conventional cowpuncher's outfit: wide-brimmed Stetson hat, chaps, boots, spurs. All showed long and hard usage. From the fact that he had one end of his rope tied and knotted to the saddle horn, I deduced him to be a Texan, as that habit was peculiar to the cowboys of the Lone Star State. My assumption proved correct; as I learned later the rider had come from the Panhandle.

His six-shooter was slung low, extending farther down the thigh than was the usual custom of cowpunchers, and a piece of a leather thong held the bottom of the holster securely to one of the silver conchas adorning the chaps. This fastening permitted quick drawing of the gun and prevented the barrel from sticking to the holster. Seeing this, my interest in the visitor heightened—it might be worth while to learn something more about the lean, sun-baked Texan.

"Riding far today?" I inquired.

"No, I'm stopping here," came the astonishing information.

So we were to have the company of this hard-bitten young fellow! Hm, probably that would be attended with interesting developments, considering the general appearance of the caller.

"I'm Bill Finn," he volunteered after some moments, during which time he had scrutinized me, the corrals, stock, windmills, ranch buildings, and, in one comprehensive sweep, the entire landscape. He accompanied the statement with a cold, fishy, distrustful stare in which was mingled an expression that indicated clearly that I could go to hades if I did not like the sound of the name. Did my senses betray me, or could I really hear the unspoken threat: "I dare you to tell me you have heard the name before!"

I acknowledged the introduction and gave my name, then desired to know whether he wished to see Mr. Wetherill, at the same time pointing out to him the location of the office. He merely nodded, flicked his horse's neck with the rein, and rode over to the boss's quarters. From the corral I watched him dismount, leaving the horse stand with the reins dropped to the ground, then enter the office.

Ordinarily, a puncher coming to the canyon meant a message from some other rancher or an application for a job. I was certain that I had never before seen Bill Finn; conjuring up in my mind the images of a number of ranches, I could not place him among the various outfits with which I had become familiar. However, he might have come from a point a greater distance away than the ranches which the Wetherill hands used to visit upon occasion. His horse, a splendid animal, showed the strains of a long, hard ride, not merely the effects of a two-or three-day jaunt.

The broncos kept me busy for another hour or more. I had dismissed the Texan from my mind; but when I went to the feed house to get some hay for those horses that I meant to keep in the corral overnight, there was Finn's horse still standing where his rider had dismounted. Most unusual, I thought, that the man should be talking with the boss for nearly two hours. Bill, however, made an even more protracted visit; it was nearly suppertime before he emerged from the office, escorted by Wetherill, who, seeing me returning from the corrals, called out:

"Joe, this is Bill Finn. Show him where to put his horse and take him with you to the cookhouse. He is going to stop with us."

Thus Bill Finn came to Pueblo Bonito and joined the Wetherill outfit.

In the months that followed I came to like the man, although it was a difficult job to gain his confidence. He was thin-lipped and exceedingly closemouthed. Never once during the years that I knew him did he speak of his origin or talk about his life previous to his coming to Chaco Canyon. That part of his existence remained a closed book till the very end.

He proved to be an unusually skilful horseman and fearless broncobuster. The rope he used was longer by several feet than the reatas generally employed by the cowpunchers. He kept it fastened to the saddle horn to make sure, as he expressed it, that nothing would get away from him once it was roped. This bespoke expertness, for only a man absolutely confident of his own ability and his horse's training could take the chances of getting tangled up in a rope that was held at one end by the heavy stock saddle, without chance of loosening it, and pulled at the other end by possibly more than half a ton of maddened steer.

He demonstrated just how good he was with his long rope when one day he rode into the yard, a snarling coyote struggling feebly in the choking loop.

"That fellow was just a mite too cocky, so I thought I'd teach him better by bringing him along," Bill explained. He had spurred his horse into a sudden dash at the unsuspecting coyote, and the educated rope caught the animal cleanly around the neck.

He cleaned and oiled his six-shooter every night with religious regularity, and it was at one of those sessions that I noticed for the first time that Bill carried a second gun. This was not a Colt, but a double barreled derringer, a most extraordinary weapon for any cow hand to tote, and when I exclaimed in surprise, Bill drawled: "It's a handy little thing to have in case of sickness!" The possession of the derringer was in itself an astonishing circumstance, but even more out of the ordinary was the place where Bill carried it. This was in a specially constructed holster riveted against the underside of the flap of his left chap leg, entirely concealing the presence of the miniature cannon from view. To all outward appearances, whether Bill was astride a horse or afoot, he had but the one conventional type of gun, a heavy Colt .45; no bulge indicated the presence of another arm.

The wicked little instrument of sudden death received the same meticulous attention and loving care as its big brother, and the cartridges in both guns were changed each evening. Just what to make of this puzzled me greatly, but I never fathomed the mystery that may have been lurking behind this matter of the two guns, one carried openly, in approved fashion, the other one hidden, deadly as a rattlesnake coiled underneath a bush or between rocks, unseen and unsuspected, therefore doubly dangerous.

Bill showed that he know how to use his Colt by engaging in frequent competitions with Fred Palmer, up to the time of Finn's arrival the undisputed champion shot of the outfit. The scores were, as a rule, so closely matched that we began calling those two gun performers the Colt Twins.

At the time of Wetherill's murder, Bill was the only one of the boys who happened to be on the ranch that day, and he prevented a general massacre of the entire family.

"It was due entirely to Bill's courage and cold-bloodedness that we were saved from the same fate as befell my husband," was Mrs. Wetherill's statement afterward repeated to me several times in later years when she and her children were living in Arizona. "But for Bill's bravery, all of us would have been killed that day," she would add in emphatic tones.

Frustrated in their desire to continue killing, the blood-maddened Indians attempted to burn down the ranch buildings; again it was Bill who stood them off, all alone, but with a gun in each hand. And finally, when

the murderous crowd had left, it was he who brought
Wetherill's body from across the arroyo, where the lion-
colored sand was turning crimson, soaking up the red
blood of the slain.

The boys, in the absence of Bill, would speculate in a
mildly interested manner as to just which sheriff had been
eluded by the Texan when he found shelter and sanctuary
in Chaco Canyon. They were of the unanimous opinion
that he whom they discussed had been ahead of a posse,
but through superior riding or by artful dodging had
managed to shake off and lose his pursuers. Maybe they
were right, *quien sabe?* To me, it did not make any
difference; Bill and I were friends, and remained upon
good terms for many years.

His end came more peacefully than anybody expected.
Accompanying a shipment of cattle to Kansas City, he
caught a severe cold that developed into pneumonia. A
week later Bill Finn was dead, his cynical eyes closed
forever, his provocative drawl stilled, never to be heard
again.

Chapter 14

DIVERSIONS

Pueblo Bonito had no direct communication with the outside world, such as by telephone or telegraph. Mail was brought from the railroad point by Navajo Indian carriers, without adherence to a fixed schedule. During months when road and weather conditions made it possible, we received letters, magazines, and newspapers at frequent intervals, but in the time between November and March it happened often that we were without mail for weeks on end.

The Wetherills and Fred Hyde subscribed to more than a half dozen papers of national importance. Those included the *New York Times*, the *New York Herald*, the Denver *Post*, the Los Angeles *Times*, and the San Francisco *Examiner*. Besides these there came less important papers published in the New Mexico and Arizona cities and towns of Albuquerque, Gallup, Holbrook, and Phoenix. We also received newspapers from El Paso, Texas. In addition to this assortment of dailies that kept us abreast with the happenings in the world, a veritable deluge of magazines and books came to the ranch.

The weekly and monthly periodicals included the

serious magazines of the type of *Scribner's* and the *Atlantic;* the humorous side was represented by *Judge* and *Life.* The list included a number of publications that dealt with technical subjects, others pertaining to stock raising and breeding, some with mechanics. Of course there were the *National Geographic, Collier's,* and *The Saturday Evening Post.* Elbert Hubbard's *The Fra* and the *Philistine* came and were enjoyed thoroughly—his *Little Journeys* formed the topics of many discussions.

Occasionally, some foreign-language magazine would drift in, coming from France, Spain, or Germany. Of the latter type, I recall particularly two German magazines. possibly because at that time I was better able to read that language than French or Spanish. They were the *Simplizissimus* with its sharp satire and the *Kladderadatsch,* strongly socialistic in tone.

If the fare provided by the papers and magazines proved too tasteless, we could always dig up some copies of the *Iconoclast* and discuss the editorials of William Cowper Brann. That fiery Texan had been assassinated a short time previous, but his writings and utterances were very much alive. How we relished those vitriolic charges and reveled in the inflaming sermons against graft, corruption, social, economic and religious abuses, political humbug and other evils. Reading the *Iconoclast* gave us a postgraduate course in polite Billingsgate, select invective, and legally safe blackmail terms and expressions.

True, at the turn of the century we did not share in the "blessings" of universal radio communication. However, there were compensations to offset that lack. Just think—we were spared static disturbances, jazz programs at one o'clock in the morning, the peculiar forms of "entertainment" furnished by blackface comedians (God save the mark!) and obese lady singers who smugly and complacently admit, although it is quite needless, that they never received vocal teaching or proper training.

We did not have to listen to *fireside chats* that might better be termed *political bedtime stories*; aspirants for public offices did not address us fatuously as "My friends"; pre-election ballyhoo did not pollute the ether; our intelligence was not assailed by oft-reiterated but never fulfilled promises to "balance the budget."

Instead of wasting valuable time listening to false prophets and humdrum programs, we made more intelligent use of the hours, particularly during the long winter evenings, by reading books and magazines, or we would indulge in the gentle arts of conversation and discussion, which were still practiced in the land at that period.

Economic, social, and political problems, national as well as foreign, came in for their full share of attention. At a time when Hitler, Mussolini, and Stalin had barely graduated from diapers, we discussed another despotic dictator, Porfirio Diaz, the ironfisted ruler of Mexico. In later years, John Kenneth Turner published his story *Barbarous Mexico*, but long before the publication of that vivid exposé, we knew of the terrors that held the Mexican people gripped under the ruthless regime of Don Porfirio.

Lincoln Steffens was gaining prominence as the great American muckraker, the title he earned through his disclosures of corruption in politics and society. Ida M. Tarbell was making life interesting, if not hectic, for John D. Rockefeller and the Standard Oil Company. The country had just emerged victorious from the conflict with Spain. Dewey and Hobson shared honors with "Teddy" Roosevelt who had made the strategically unwise, but imagination-firing and gallant attempt to duplicate the feat of the Six Hundred at Balaklava by charging with his Roughriders the strongly manned and fortified hills of San Juan.

President McKinley was dead; "Big Stick" Roosevelt took over the post of chief executive of the nation. The Wright brothers had flown successfully the queer contraption that was the forerunner of the modern airplanes. Henry Ford was at the beginning of his career of making millions of inexpensive automobiles; Marconi's wireless was getting its first practical application; Professor Roentgen gave to the world his discovery of the X-ray, and our own Dr. Gorgas had solved the yellow-fever problem.

Enrico Caruso was thrilling the world with his wonder voice; John Philip Sousa held the spotlight as the American march king; Sarah Bernhardt's genius was acclaimed by enthusiastic audiences; Ignace Jan Paderewski maintained world recognition as a brilliant concert pianist.

An interesting period that, the beginning of the twentieth century, despite the fact that some of our *enlightened* moderns take pleasure in referring to the time as "the horse-and-buggy days."

It must be admitted, of course, that we lived in crass ignorance of many matters. None had as yet told us about our personal, including the most intimate shortcomings. Daily we were guilty of sins of omission and commission: figuratively, the darkness of illiteracy enshrouded our existence. We did not know of Halitosis, B.O., Cosmetic Skin, Telltale Gray, Dishwater Hands, the lack of proper Feminine Hygiene, and a host of other matters that have since become painfully popular terms.

The golden age of the genus *Advertising Man* was dawning; presently, we were to learn the meaning of such words as Reader Interest, Consumer Acceptance, Mass Reaction, Applied Psychology, and other highfalutin expressions bandied by the didactic. The manufacture of gadgets was destined to make millions of dollars for the "smart" men who took advantage of the developing mania of the American people to get some doodad or other for a multiplicity of purposes and uses. Advertising slogans could look forward to a quarter century of mushroom growth and application.

Yes, the high-wheeled buggy and old Dobbin may give rise to guffaws and engender a feeling of superiority in certain Washington circles, but we did have fun!

Possibly our happy spirits were brought about directly through a deplorable ignorance of the true status of our existence. Nobody enlightened us, telling us what a miserable life we were leading. Those men who like to play at the game of being gods had not yet sung their siren song of a brace of chickens in every pot or gilded the future with vivid and impractical mirages of a More Abundant Life!

It was left for the brighter and keener minds of some decades later to discover Revolving Pension Plans for the aged; to becloud sane thinking with imaginings that one can get something for nothing. What a farce! And what a pity that American political intelligence should sink to a level so low as to make the acceptance of the pseudo Messiahs by the masses a *fait accompli*.

Undoubtedly, it must have been a benighted age in many respects, but it was free from the locust plague of Washington crackpots and brain-trusters. The businessman was unhindered in the legitimate management of his own affairs, no farmer was compelled by a coterie of Official Advisers to the Demigod in the White House to restrict his potato acreage. Nor had the world been enlightened sufficiently to understand the theory that sees the furtherance of public good in a policy of destruction of natural resources.

The American intelligence of that period of backward-
ness would not have understood, and would not have been
ready to admit, that destroying the cotton growing in the
fields, and slaughtering cattle and pigs by the hundreds of
thousands merely to kill off the stock, would facilitate the
solution of the problem of clothing and feeding the
nation. Especially not, when simultaneously one-third of
that same nation is declared to be ill-fed, improperly
clothed, and poorly housed.

Naturally, our diversions were not altogether literary.
We indulged in all sorts of games; entertained, not only
ourselves, but, occasionally, some rare visitors, with home-
talent musicales; we would ride forty or fifty miles to
attend a dance, or to watch the Navajo ceremonial chants
and dances, such as the weird *yeibitchai* and the colorful
Fire Dance. A favorite pastime was just to sit about,
swapping stories, truthful or imaginary.

In the summer and fall we competed with the swiftest
of the Indians, not in foot races, but to determine the
fleetness of our favorite horses. As a rule the Indians
would win all races over short, sprinting distances, leaving
the honors to us in the long-distance events. To call our
bronco riding by such fancy names as ranch-gymkhana, or
rodeos, did not occur to us; you see, we were simply a real
horse outfit, not a dude ranch.

Chapter 15

MAKING COLLECTIONS IN
NAVAJOLAND

Many of the Navajos trading in Pueblo Bonito were indebted to Wetherill. Some of them failed to settle their
accounts at the time promised, and since a number of
those delinquents lived in places at a considerable distance
from Chaco Canyon, it happened at rare intervals that
one or two of the boys would be sent on a debt-collecting
trip. That meant starting with several unburdened
pack mules and returning with them carrying loads of
rugs, tanned buckskins, silver ornaments, medicine baskets, and other articles with an intrinsic, or definite, trading value. The boys looked upon those collection trips
with longing eyes. The tour was considered a sort of
vacation; it would break the routine of ranch chores, and
take the collector into many of the most remote sections
of Navajoland. Places that other white men hardly knew
about were visited by Wetherill's messengers upon those
trips; many Indian children became frightened when the
cowboys made their appearance, never before having seen
persons of another race and color.

Bill Finn and I were sent upon one of those excursions.

We started from Pueblo Bonito with four pack mules, carrying no other load than our camping equipment, which included bedding, grub, some grain, nose bags and hobbles, coffeepot, frying pan, Dutch oven, knives, forks, spoons, cups and a few other cooking utensils. The amount of grub was held down to a minimum, to be used only when absolutely necessary. It was our intention to live off the country, or more specifically, off the Indians, during the greater part of the journey.

Wetherill had turned over to us a list of Indians whose accounts with him were badly in arrears. He had also given us a condensed history of each customer, told us about his family or clan connections, the estimated amount of livestock he owned, indicated the location of his camp, and made us jot down in a small memorandum book other pertinent facts. Of course, we carried no authorization papers or power of attorney, but nobody ever questioned our right to act for the boss.

It was midsummer. The rains that usually fall during that season had been late in coming; we could look forward to getting caught in one or more of those heavy downpours which resemble, and often are, cloudbursts. That prospect left us undaunted. We had slickers and chaps to protect us; if our plans did not miscarry, we would have the shelter of friendly hogans for most of the nights that we should have to spend away from the ranch.

Our route, as suggested by Wetherill, was by way of Tohachi, Fort Defiance, Chinle, Round Rock, the Luka-chukai Mountains, thence in a circle toward Shiprock, and from there in an almost due easterly direction to Canyon Blanco. Turning south, we were to follow the canyon to its upper reaches, which course would bring us back toward the Chaco mesa, and thus to the ranch. We estimated the entire distance to mean a ride of between three hundred to three hundred and fifty miles, making allowances for washouts and other obstacles that would entail detours. Too, we kept in mind the possibility that some of the Indians we wished to visit might have moved to other, and more distant, locations.

According to our calculations, it would require approximately three weeks to complete the circle of the trip, but when ultimately we got back to the ranch we had been away from Chaco Canyon for two days over five weeks.

Bill and I being accustomed to camping, we did not need much time in which to make ready for the tour. Assisted by the cook, we got together the grub that we looked upon more or less in the nature of "iron rations." From the trading store the boss had brought a generous supply of Bull Durham tobacco, cigarette papers, and a large quantity of small brown paper bags filled with hard candy. The smokes were to put the grown-up Indians in a good humor, while the sweets unquestionably would be much appreciated by the children of all ages that we were sure to encounter in the various hogans.

Old Man Hunt stood ready at the feed house, where we picked up a couple of bags of mixed oats and corn, something to help make the mules forget their lazy existence in the home corrals and stables.

There were no special farewells or leave-takings; our journey was all in the day's work. Everybody knew that we would be as if cut off from the world while on our trip, that we should virtually be beyond the means of communication, that neither we, nor the ones remaining behind, would see or hear from each other until our return. Nevertheless, our goodbys consisted in merely waving a hand at the boys who watched our departure and shouting a "So long!" to them as we rode through the tall gateposts at the entrance to the large inclosed lot that was bounded by the stables, corrals, shops, the boss's house, and the excavated ruins.

During the first day we fastened the mules together, two and two, by tying a short piece of rope between their headstalls. That made driving them ahead of us much easier than having to watch four beasts, each one with a different idea about how to proceed, or rather, how to manage to make a break and get back to the ranch. By the middle of the second day they apparently had become reconciled to their fate, and we could allow them to travel independently of each other. Only over stretches where we struck across country, instead of following a road or trail, was it necessary to tie them together, or to lead them with a rope.

When we had to do the latter the first mule only was fastened to the lead rope. Each one of the other three was tied by a short halter rope to the tail of the animal in front, thus forming a veritable chain of mules walking the narrow pathway of the trail. Upon those occasions either Bill or I would take the lead, heading the procession. The other made up the rear to prevent any pulling back on the part of the animals behind the leader. In single, Indian file, we would march along until we again reached a road that permitted easier, less restricted travel.

It is seldom that hill collectors are greeted in a particularly joyous manner. Ordinarily, they are not made welcome as friends of the family or treated like guests of honor, but in every hogan visited by us we were made to feel that we should consider ourselves just that. The best place in the camp was cleared for us; we were served with the choicest pieces of meat; the comfort and welfare of the guests became the chief concern of the family. Our horses and mules, too, were looked after carefully; we did not have to worry over anyone making off with the livestock, or any other part of our equipment and outfit.

We had come to discuss old indebtedness to our employer and expected some sort of payment or part settlement, but that did not dampen the obvious and sincere enthusiasm of our hosts. They were quite agreeable to talking about the account; there was no inclination to deny the debt or to offer alibis for nonpayment. Certainly, they owed the money, and they were ready to pay what they could. And with a naïveté that was absolutely unstudied and unassumed, they would produce perhaps two or three small silver trinkets, such as rings or bracelets, worth maybe fifty or seventy-five cents each, and in all seriousness offer them as payment-on-account of a bill that might amount to four hundred or five hundred dollars! Their good friend, our boss, should get the balance as soon as they received some money from the sale of sheep, wool, or cattle.

It would have been poor policy to have refused such token payments, or to deride their insignificance. With becoming gravity we accepted whatever was offered, no matter how small the value of the proffered articles. We made a note of the items collected, wrote in our little book a short description so as to be able to identify them later, and gave our estimated, approximate valuation to the Indians, subject, of course, to confirmation and revision by Wetherill. Then followed the often long-drawn-out discussions that were to bring about results more satisfactory than the first offer.

In at least several instances those talks lasted for days. During that time we would take an inventory of the sheep and cattle owned by our host, make suggestions that we take over a certain portion of the stock, evaluate horses, inspect and appraise Indian-tanned buckskins, family jewels, and other valuables, and in general try in our most diplomatic, yet insistent manner, to effect a more substantial payment on account than the initial offering made by the debtor. In nine cases out of ten we succeeded. Frequently we persuaded the Indian to balance the old account, but caused a new bill against him to be entered when our salesmanship prompted him to ride to Pueblo Bonito to buy a new wagon, or saddle, or other desirables of which we spoke in glowing terms.

The horses that were turned over to us in payment were branded right then and there with the Triangle Bar Triangle. We would do the same if we were given cattle. In this job of branding the Indians would assist. For that purpose we carried with us some running irons, as the slender pieces of iron that were used under those circumstances are called.

Running irons were hardly more than two feet in length, and the thickness of the iron did not exceed that of an ordinary lead pencil. One end of the iron was turned back, forming an incomplete loop. The looped part of the iron was heated to the proper temperature for branding, then used to burn the design of the brand into the hide of the animal.

The boys working for Wetherill carried running irons under the skirting of their saddles, slipped between the loops of wide, heavy leather straps to which are fastened the *cinchas*. Even a small fire, easily made with a few handfuls of sagebrush branches, will heat a branding iron of that type sufficiently hot to mark a calf or yearling colt.

At certain periods and in various sections of the Southwest, possession or use of the running iron was frowned upon by the orthodox cattlemen. The reason? Too many rustlers came by sizable herds of stock by starting out upon their career with just two pieces of equipment: a long rope, and a quick running iron!

Such stock as we acquired upon our trip was driven to Pueblo Bonito by Indians we hired for the job unless, as happened repeatedly, the owner himself volunteered to make delivery at the ranch. In any event, all horses and cattle received on account of Wetherill's bills were branded by us, to prevent backsliding. The boss had instructed us not to accept sheep or goats, therefore we did not have to fret over mutton on the hoof. Indian jewelry, buckskins, wampum, baskets and other articles, as well as actual cash, we carried along with us, loading the mules with a steadily heavier-growing cargo of valuables.

We had been away from Pueblo Bonito about a week when, one afternoon, a tremendous downpour of cloudburst proportion overtook us. The heavens had been theatening with rain for two days, therefore we were not entirely unprepared for it, although we had hardly figured on being caught in a near tidal wave. The storm was accompanied by furious bolts of lightning, jerkily illuminating the scene, and the crash of thunder reverberated from the walls of the canyon through which we were riding at the time, the smashing noises suggesting the playing of an unearthly tympan in the orchestra of the elements.

The mules, luckily, were "necked," and Bill and I promptly threw ropes over the heads of the animals, holding them with our lariats. Otherwise they would have stampeded. Our horses did not relish the pelting of the raindrops, mingled with stinging hailstones, and for several minutes we were kept quite busy trying to avoid getting tangled up with the frightened animals, anxious to flee from the blasts of the unleashed elements. There was no shelter in the canyon; the walls rose sheer and offered no protecting niches or overhanging rocks.

The rain had been pouring from the heavens in torrents some eight or ten minutes, and despite our slickers and chaps we were drenched to the skin. We heard a peculiar rumbling noise, coming from the head of the canyon. We glanced backward, but could not discern the cause of the disturbance. All at once, Bill Finn, who was riding at the rear of our little caravan, shouted: "My God, look what's coming!" I reined in my horse and looked over my shoulder. There, about three hundred yards away, came a solid wall of muddy water down the arroyo, the dirty brown waves tumbling over themselves. The gulch was some ten or twelve feet deep. About a mile above we had crossed from the opposite bank to the side of the canyon we were following at the moment. The enormous quantity of water released by the thunderclouds had poured in swift streams down the bare hillsides and over the hard-baked adobe flats into the natural drainage canal of the canyon which sloped downward rather sharply. The arroyo, running the length of the canyon, was filled almost immediately, the water coming so fast and in such large volume that there was not time or space to fill the ditch by degrees.

Bill had hardly shouted his warning when the flood rushed by us, tumbling in a mad race down the canyon, filling the narrow arroyo from bank to bank. Huge boulders were tossed ahead by the swirling mass of water that forced all obstacles out of its way in a relentless and irresistible manner.

"Gee, fellow, you and I have more luck than brains," was Bill's comment. "Just imagine what would have happened to us and the mules if that sweet little drop of rain had fallen on us while we were busy getting into and climbing out of that arroyo!"

True, that wall of water would have swept us before itself like so much chaff. We could not have gotten out of its way fast enough to save ourselves or the animals, and in the tremendous rush none could have lived.

For a few minutes we sat our horses and watched the play of the water, thankful to be on terra firma. The rain was falling less violently; the storm moving off. After a while we continued on our way, in about an hour's time reaching an isolated Indian trading post. There we took care of our horses and mules, stowed the packs, saddles, and other equipment in the warehouse, then accepted the trader's invitation to come into the house and get dry.

To accomplish that, we stripped to the skin, donned some shirts and overalls from the trader's shelves, and hung up our water-soaked garments by a fire that had been kindled in the big fireplace which ornamented the living quarters of our hospitable friend. Our chaps, saturated with rain despite the treatment with neat's-foot oil, weighed as much as green beef hides; our boots felt as if they were soled with lead. The saddles were not very wet, our bodies having absorbed most of the rain and splashing water. An inspection disclosed that the packs had not suffered at all, the double thickness of strong tarpaulin proving itself impervious to moisture—it was actually waterproof. Therefore, the contents of the aparejos, principally grub and feed, had weathered the storm without being damaged in the slightest degree.

We rested that night in a warm, dry house, and slept, after filling our hungry selves, in a real bed, forgetting in that luxury the ducking and pelting of the previous afternoon. By the following morning our leather equipment was still damp but had dried out enough so we could use it. Horses and mules showed no ill effects from the cloudburst experience. After breakfasting with the trader, we saddled up; soon we were on our way, continuing the march.

Chapter 16

ON THE TRAIL TO WALPI

The journey had already taken us past Fort Defiance, into the neighborhood of Ganado, when our Indian host, with whom we had spent three days, informed us that we would be unable to see any more Navajos for at least another week. Hosteen Tso (Fat Man), explained that the Indians were going to the Hopi reservation to attend the annual Hopi Snake Dance. It was his opinion that for the ensuing week there would be small likelihood of finding in their camps any of the people we desired to visit. In about eight days they would have returned home, he thought. He, himself, was saddling his horse in the morning to leave for Walpi, the Hopi village on First Mesa. Wouldn't we like to accompany him?

Bill and I decided to avail ourselves of the chance to go along. We would have a guide, would see something new and interesting, and the mules could rest during the few days while we were away.

Our duffle was stored in Hosteen Tso's hogan. His squaw received instructions to guard it, and to look after the horses and mules during our absence. For our friend insisted that our own mounts needed the rest just as much as the pack animals. He had many horses, as had his father, and we could choose two good, sturdy ponies from his herd. That suited us very well—in fact, we welcomed the offer as an ideal arrangement. From every viewpoint it would be much more desirable that we ride Indian ponies instead of our own horses. We knew that Indian ponies do not seem to mind the almost continuous loping, hour after hour, over every kind of terrain. Navajos maintain that sort of grueling pace for long-protracted periods. Their ponies are inured to such traveling, but it will nearly kill any other type of horse. We also knew that our equipment was in safe hands, and that we should find it and the animals in good shape when we returned. Therefore, considering all those points, we acquiesed readily to the proposition with carefree hearts.

Very early in the morning we got away. During the night several other Indians had arrived at Hosteen Tso's hogan, all bound for the Snake Dance ceremonial. It was a troop of some ten or twelve riders that left the camp shortly after a hastily eaten breakfast. From almost the very start the horses were urged into a sort of a dogtrot, peculiar to Indian ponies, and kept at that gait hour after hour. This same speed was maintained even over terrain that would be considered all but impassable by horsemen of more civilized localities.

Our leader, a Navajo medicine man, slowed up but imperceptibly for the steep banks of deep arroyos or stretches of prairie undermined by thousands of prairie-dog burrows. Close-growing sagebrush, prickly cactus, low-branched pinons and cedars, heavy underbrush, glass-smooth, slippery rocks, and deep, loose sands, were all the same to him. They presented no obstacle, neither were they sufficiently important to bring the horses to a walk. He appeared oblivious of all hazards and continued to set the pace as, with a rhythmic swing of his arm, he plied the short braided-rawhide quirt, letting it fall against the rump of his pony. He was not beating the horse, no, the pony hardly felt the whip, but a Navajo simply cannot ride a horse without the accompanying motion of the flailing arm.

It is nearly incredible how that gait, maintained for long periods, eats up the miles. The astonishing thing is that Indian ponies, taken off the range, fed on only such grass and brush as they can forage for themselves, without the benefit of strengthening oats or corn rations, can stand up under that sort of treatment. Moreover, one marvels that they are able to continue in the same manner day after day. They perform as if made of spring steel and whalebone, giving evidences of surprising stamina and resiliency.

To ride a fine, well-bred American horse from dawn till dark over such a course would result in having a galled, footsore, and leg-weary beast, unfit for another ride for at least a week. That kind of abuse might even permanently injure the animal. Bill and I knew this, and therefore we had accepted with alacrity our host's offer to ride two of his ponies instead of our own mounts.

We camped that evening with some friendly Indians whose hogans were clustered in a semi-settlement in Steamboat Canyon, about halfway between Ganado and Keams Canyon. By now we were well beyond the unmarked boundaries of Wetherill's sphere of influence, but our temporary landlords were acquainted with the boss and had, at various times, visited Pueblo Bonito. They made us welcome to shelter and food as the visitors belonging to their own people, yes, they went out of their way to show us extra attentions and courtesies. Evidently they were pleased to entertain the two white men who had come to share camps and meals with the red men. It was obvious to them that we wanted to be friends of the Navajos, and they seemed glad to acknowledge us as such.

The horses were hobbled and turned out to graze; in the morning one of the young men or boys would round them up while we were eating breakfast.

The squaws prepared dinner for the troop of visitors, served it, and withdrew. The men ate, then grouped themselves against the wall of the hogan and began smoking. Judging from appearances, the daylong ride had not tired them; they started a discussion and continued talking until late into the night. Bill and I found a comfortable place upon some sheep pelts, our feet stretched toward the center of the hogan where a fire burned. For a while we took part in the conversation, but before long dropped off to sleep without being aware of having done so. The quietly monotonous drone of the speakers' voices would have lulled us into sleep, even if we had been able to resist the slumber-inducing warmth of the hogan.

Several times during the night I wakened, but only for fitful moments, scarcely conscious of the fact that I did so. Upon each occasion I beheld the same spectacle: the blanketed figures of the Navajos sitting in the half-obscurity, their immobile expressions showing in the flickering light of the fire, listening with grave attention to the softly modulated voice of the narrator. The cadence of speech remained the same always, with hardly a change in the inflection of the tone. At rare intervals one or the other of the auditors would grunt in an approving or confirmatory manner. No other noises punctuated the discourse.

The close attention of the listeners and the meticulous restraint from interruption might have betokened some weighty matter under discussion. That, however, was not the case. The subjects that were being talked about ranged from purely family affairs of minor importance to the prices paid for wool by the different traders, and the opening of a new trading post. Everything that was said pertained to common, ordinary neighborhood gossip, but from the consideration and respect accorded each speaker, one would have imagined that matters of particular moment were being debated.

Whether or not our Indian friends slept at all during that night, I do not know. Stirrings, comings and goings, and the voices of the women outside the hogan, engaged with the preparations for breakfast, awakened Bill and me just as dawn was breaking. We made our way to the open, there to shake off the last remaining traces of sleep in the exhilarating, bracing morning air. From a short distance away we could hear the arrival of the remuda being driven toward camp. The two boys delegated to bring in the horses had not removed the hobbles from the forelegs of the ponies but were driving them forward while still hobbled. Close to the hogans they left the animals to themselves, but none attempted to stray or return to the grazing. Nevertheless, those cayuses would not permit themselves to be saddled and bridled without first feeling the rope about their necks; each pony had to be caught with the lariat before it would stand still and allow the rider to approach closely.

After saddling the horses, we returned to the hogan and ate our morning meal, prepared and served by the squaws and young girls. It consisted of freshly baked corn bread, mutton ribs broiled over the open fire, and black coffee. There was no milk, but we could sweeten the bitter draught with lumpy, discolored sugar.

Within a few minutes after everybody had finished breakfast, we were mounted and once again on the trail to Walpi. We passed out of Steamboat Canyon, so named because of a peculiar mass of rock resembling a sharp-prowed ship without masts or funnels, rising steeply from the canyon floor and in its solitude dominating the landscape. The horses followed a trail through rolling, hilly country, eventually coming to the top of an immense mesa. Several times during the day we crossed deep-cut canyons and smaller arroyos, always regaining the widespread tableland.

In the afternoon we reached Keams Canyon, seat of an old-established trading post well known throughout the Navajo country. Little did I dream that I was destined to spend nearly eight years in Keams Canyon, as owner of that post and other trading establishments—my hopes and ambitions failed to include that possibility.

Toward evening, shortly after sunset, we made camp on the bank of a wide wash about a mile and a half from Walpi. All about us campfires blazed brightly, indicating plainly that many visitors had come to witness the weird spectacle of the Snake Dance. There were campers from the towns on the Santa Fe Railway, Holbrook, Winslow, and Flagstaff; delegations from Prescott, away off to the west; others had made the trip from Albuquerque and Gallup in New Mexico. Many of the sight-seers were Indians from the various pueblos; others could be distinguished as members of the Apache tribes in the southern parts of Arizona. We also saw Utes, Piutes, and Sioux during the time we spent at Walpi.

The majority of the Indians had come on horseback, although a few arrived in wagons, accompanied by their families. The white spectators from the far-off towns and cities had hired teams and mountain buckboards in those places where they had to leave the railroad and begin the drive overland toward the heart of the reservation. In later years, the automobile appeared on the scene, but at the time when I first saw the Snake Dance, all visitors arrived on horseback or in horse-drawn vehicles.

The day had been stiflingly hot, but as the sun began to drop below the western horizon, the atmosphere cooled quickly. Soon the golden ball rested upon the rim of the world, and the earth took slice after slice out of it until the light-and-heat-giver had disappeared completely. Ever-lengthening, flaming rays shot into the sky, first of a fiery golden hue, then by degrees running the entire gamut of the solar spectrum. The color nuances included every shade of orange, pink, mauve, crimson, purple, burnished gold, and amethyst, painting in an indescribably beautiful manner the bluff sides of the mesas and tinting the towering ranges in the dim distances.

Up above, the sky changed from pearly gray, suffused with blushing pink, to the vivid blue of turquoise, then to purple and afterward to blackish blue. As the sun disappeared, the moon rose. First she just peeped over the horizon's edge, as if doubtful of the cue to strut the stage. Then she grew bolder, pushing her round face upward, the immense, orange-colored disk glowing like an over-ripe pumpkin. Once in command of the field, she paled to a silvery slate and finally revealed herself in virginal whiteness, flooding the desert with her cold, penetrating light.

The uncounted millions of stars sprinkled across the universe shone with a brilliance and sparkle unknown to the dwellers in lower countries. Falling luminaries would, for a brief moment, leave their flashing trail against the liquid-indigo of the skies. Not a single cloud smudged the vast expanse of ether, bathed in the shimmering radiance of the moon. Surely, a most unpromising outlook for rain. The indications were that the Snake clan priests had a real job ahead of them for the morrow, to persuade the Ones Above to open the sluice gates of the heavens!

From Walpi no sounds could be heard. The village gave no outward signs of life, not even the flicker of dim lights was to be seen. Under the dazzling whiteness of the moon's light, the bulk of Walpi showed blackly against the night sky, vaguely outlined, like the silhouette of a crouching beast. But everybody knew that in the underground kivas there was much activity, and that the Hopis in the pueblo were engaged busily with the preparation and final touches for the ensuing day's ceremony. The restlessness and fevered anticipation that undoubtedly filled the minds of the active participants in the coming affair, and also occupied the thoughts of the many visitors, created an almost palpable tenseness in the atmosphere.

About the campfires was much life, and none seemed ready to go to sleep. Groups and individuals passed from one camp to another, visiting, renewing old acquaintances, gossiping. The horses and mules, hobbled and turned out to graze, had a hard time finding forage. The squealing, and the other noises of the snorting and kicking beasts indicated fights for a bunch of grass or the possession of a desirable strip of brush. Now and again the high-pitched braying of a burro would quiver through the darkness.

Despite the arduous ride of the day, that should have left us worn out and dead tired, it was well past midnight before Bill and I rolled ourselves into our blankets to snatch at least a few hours sleep. Almost before we had got well into the business of recuperation, the Hopi roosters, those trumpeters of the sun, were sounding the coming of a new day, and although it was still some time before dawn, the campfires were already being fanned into new life; every group was occupied with the preparations for breakfast.

The stiffness that inevitably accompanies sleeping on the hard ground was soon shaken off; we hunted our horses, removed their hobbles, took them to water, and then returned to camp. There the animals received a modest feed of mixed grain, spread out before them on an old piece of tarpaulin because, Indian-bred, they were not accustomed to eating their rations out of nosebags.

In the meantime our own morning meal was being cooked in the camp of a Navajo who had arrived by team and wagon and had brought along his wife and children. They had established themselves comfortably, and the cooking facilities permitted the extension of hospitality to their guests, although they were virtually self-invited. However, we paid at least partially for the meal by forcing some silver coins upon the woman. To make the gift more acceptable, and to prevent a crass breach of good manners, we suggested that she take the money and use it for the purchase of more coffee and sugar from a Hopi Indian who operated a small trading post in the flat at the base of First Mesa. We added the promise that we would return and drink some of the beverage.

Chapter 17

THE HOPI SNAKE DANCE

Saddles, chaps, guns, blankets, and other equipment that would have impeded our movements were left in the camp of the friendly Navajos. We had decided to walk up the steep, stairlike trail to the pueblo atop First Mesa rather than ride our horses to the summit of the flat rock. That proved a wise precaution, for when we reached the place of the Snake Dance it was evident that we should not have found sufficient room for picketing horses. The small area about the Snake Rock lacked space adequate to the needs of the audience that was beginning to assemble; most decidedly, it furnished no opportunity to stable the saddle horses.

No finer dramatic setting could be conceived than the scene of the Walpi Snake Dance. The open space where the antelope and Snake priests perform their ceremonial is undeniably limited. The front of this natural stage is bounded by the drop of the perpendicular wall of the high cliff on which Walpi perches, while the background is formed of the terraced houses of the Hopis. That miniature plaza, if one may thus designate the small, narrow strip of open ground between the abyss and the dwellings, is the platform; the glorious sky constitutes the roof of the playhouse.

A strikingly decorative effect is brought about by a lone rock, of circular shape rising some twelve feet from the mesa floor, standing in the upper end of the Walpi plaza, the Snake Rock. During the performance of the dance it becomes a reserved grandstand seat for as many spectators as can scramble to its flat top and balance themselves in a precarious manner in their aerie.

Many accounts of the Hopi Snake Dance have been written: Dr. Jesse Walter Fewkes, of the Smithsonian Institution, declared that the greater portion of them were worthless. Rather than go into long-winded details, I shall confine myself to just a few facts that have been clearly established, some which will not confuse or befuddle the issue.

The ceremony is a prayer for rain. That is the paramount objective, and there is no Hopi Indian, man, woman, or child, pagan or Christian, that questions the unfailing efficacy of the petition. The Indians do *not* pray for the life-giving downpours in the chapels and churches and other places of worship established by the white men's missions. They are convinced that theirs is a *surer* way of persuading the gods to listen favorably to their supplications.

The snakes used in the ceremony are wild snakes, and many full-grown rattlesnakes are included in the lot. Their fangs and poison sacs are *not* removed, nor have the snakes been rendered harmless in any other manner, as by treatment with numbing potions or otherwise. They are caught several days before the dance, kept in the kiva of the Snake clan, and when the dance has come to its concluding climax, are set free on the desert.

During the confinement of the reptiles in the kiva, the

Snake priests go through certain parts of the ritual that include rites of purification and the washing of the slithery captives. Various writers have attempted to weave an air of Delphic mystery about those rites. With smug complacency each one announces that he is one of the extremely few who have been accorded the privilege of witnessing the sacred washing ceremony. Piffle! Dozens and scores of white men, at various times, have been present in the kiva when the Snake priests worked with their reptilian prisoners.

President Theodore Roosevelt, and the party accompanying him, witnessed the snake washing, as did, on other different occasions, a number of Indian traders, scientists, artists, and others. George Wharton James, the author of many authentic books on the Indians of the Southwest and the desert regions, was allowed to enter the snake kiva during those ceremonials. J. Lorenzo Hubbell, an old-time Indian trader in that part of the country, was present repeatedly, generally with other whites, invited friends, when the priests were engaged in their kiva rituals.

As late as 1925, Leo Crane, an Indian agent, wrote of his experience in the snake kiva during the washing of the serpents. He added, naïvely, that "perhaps not more than a score of white men have witnessed this ceremony." That was probably flattering to his vanity and indicative of his feeling of superiority, but decidedly inaccurate in fact.

For many years it has been possible for almost any white man to gain admittance to the kiva during the performance of the rites preceding the Snake Dance, provided he came properly introduced to the Snake priests or other influential members of the Snake clan, or happened to be on a sufficiently friendly footing with other Hopis of

standing. In later years—meaning after my first attendance at the dance, when I was established as Indian
trader in Keams Canyon and made the Hopi country my
home for the better part of a decade—upon two occasions
I saw the washing of the snakes, but refused subsequent
invitations to the kivas in the years following.

One may be sure that none of the missionaries attend or
countenance the Snake Dance. To them it is devil's
work. They speak with bated breath about the horrifying
spectacle, bewailing the fact that the government permits those heathenish rites. They ought to be prohibited!
They are positively scandalous! How can one expect to
convert the pagans when they are allowed to continue
staging the performance of that indecent dance?

Those are the expressions one hears from the devout
field workers, if one can get an opinion at all. The never-
diminishing native attendance at the dance, the fervid
expressions on the faces of good, Christianized Indians,
which are wooden and stolid when in the missionary's
Sunday school, the intense ardor of active participants
and Indian watchers alike, all combine to spell complete
refutation of the value of Christian teaching. For hundreds of years, efforts to convert the Indians have never
ceased, and regularly, each year during Snake Dance
time, the theory that the missions are making headway
goes to pot. In the course of centuries, the workers in the
Lord's vineyard have not gained a measurable foothold.

The dance itself, that is, the public part of it, consumes
not more than half an hour. First to put in an appearance
are the Antelope priests, entering the plaza in single file.
The upper parts of the priests' bodies are nude, painted
with zigzag lightning designs traced in white. They shake
gourd rattles while marching solemnly about the open
space. After completing the circle of the stage several

times, they line up in a straight formation, their backs toward the houses, faces to the plaza and the edge of the cliff. Their arrival and marching is marked by a quiet, dignified mien, in sharp contrast to the noisy, rushing entrance of the Snake priests, who burst upon the scene in their fantastic and hideous array.

On their faces are smears of red paint; a circle of thickly daubed white outlines the mouth. Their long hair is in disorder, hanging in untrimmed strands down their naked torsos and backs. They wear Hopi-woven, embroidered ceremonial skirts of knee length, belts about their waists. Their feet are encased in buckskin moccasins with rawhide soles. The priests are decorated with all sorts of finery: armlets, necklaces, wampum beads, bracelets, feathers, fox pelts dangling from their belts, clappers, made of horn, fastened to their legs below the knees. In some of the strings of beads, or in the ornaments tied to the belts can be seen bright, shiny buttons, small pieces of mirrors, and other odds and ends picked up here and there.

Directly behind the line of the Antelope priests is a rude bough shelter, tied together with ropes, and immediately in front and center of the line, in a hollowed depression in the rock, covered with a stout piece of board, the snakes are kept. As the Antelope priests circle the plaza, each man stamps vigorously with his right foot on the board of the *kisi* sheltering the reptiles. This procedure is followed by the Snake priests; as they march, every member of the dancing fraternity gives a resounding thump on the board with his foot as he passes.

The Snake priests then line up in a row facing the Antelope priests. An old Indian passes between the two lines of dancers, sprinkling water from a bowl, while the priests of both clans sway their bodies to the rhythm of a low, monotonous chant. A short pause, then the Snake priests break formation. They realign themselves in pairs and begin dancing in a sort of half-crouching position toward the *kisi*. The left member of the team has his right arm about the shoulders of the man by his side, who, as he reaches the *kisi*, stoops low, inserts his hand and arm into the snake hole and produces whichever one of the writhing and objecting reptiles he happens to grasp.

His partner, carrying a short stick decorated with feathers, the snake whip, brings that into play, stroking the creature with it until the other dancer, who has been holding the serpent by its middle for a few moments, places the squirming animal in his mouth. There he goes, in the peculiar hop-skip dance, the two ends of the snake dangling and twisting from the sides of his mouth!

In the rear of the dancing pair follows the alert "gatherer." It is his duty to retrieve the snake as it is dropped by the dancing pair when they have completed the circle of the plaza. This he does with incredibly swift motions. The dancing pair, meanwhile, repeat their performance, extract another one of the captive squirmers from under the board of the *kisi*, and continue their dance. The other pairs of priests, of course, have not been idle, but have joined in the dance, going through the same routine as the first couple, each team passing successively by the *kisi* and delving into the hidden mass of snakes. The spectators thrill to the appearance of especially vicious-looking rattlers, or the coming to light of an unusually large bull snake, with body so long that the ends trail the ground while the humped-over dancer carries it in his mouth.

When the last snake has been taken from the *kisi* and danced with, dropped and gathered up, two priests describe, with consecrated corn meal, a large circle on the rocky ground. The dancers crowd around this circle and drop all the snakes into it as more meal is sprinkled by the priests. Suddenly, probably upon some signal, certain of the men who may have been designated previously for the task, swoop down and gather between their hands as many snakes as they are able to hold. With this squirming burden they rush from the scene, push through the packed cordon of the spectators, race to the four points of the compass and liberate the reptiles in the desert below. The consecrated snakes are now messengers to the Ones Above, carrying with them the prayers for rain and corn growth, needed so imperatively by the dwellers upon the barren cliffs of the Hopi sky city.

There is a singularly hideous thrill, at the same time repellant and attractive, in watching the handling of the mass of reptiles, so revolting to humankind as a rule. Particularly blood-chilling is the final act of the dance when the snakes are dumped in one mass into the circle of sacred corn meal, and thence grabbed with both hands by the Indians who return them to freedom. Even the stoutest nerves shake a bit when a member of the priestly clan, thus engaged, races by and all but thrusts his wriggling burden into one's face!

The snakes set at liberty, the runners return to the mesa top. The dance itself is over, but one more phase of the spectacle remains, a sort of purification indulged in by the performing participants in the ceremony. The Snake priests gather at the edge of the mesa and gulp down long draughts of an emetic, prepared beforehand and waiting for them. As in accord, they bend over and vomit up the hellish-looking concoction they have just swallowed. Although a most indecorous position and performance, they are able to maintain a certain solemnity and dignity. They drink several times, promptly losing each draught. The vomiting itself does not seem to be accompanied by that retching and agonizing effort which distinguishes *mal de mer*.

Opinions differ as to the meaning and purpose of this last phase, some holding that the emetic is in fact a powerful antidote to counteract the effect of the snake bites suffered during the dance. Others insist that it is merely a final act of purification, part of the ritual of the ceremony. Personally, I do not know, and shall not offer any interpretation of my own. If the drink is a mixture that offsets the infection from snake bites, it is remarkably effective. None of the dancers seem to suffer from the sustained and intimate contact with the reptiles; the handling of the revolting animals, many of whom are unquestionably poisonous rattlers, appears to bring about no ill effects.

Maybe it is a bit unwarranted skepticism to hold that the rains would have come regardless of the invocations of the Snake priests. But try to find a Hopi to admit any such suggestion! Wasn't the weather dry and scorching for weeks and weeks on end? Wasn't the land crying for moisture to quench its parched surface? Didn't the heavens darken time and again with masses of clouds, only to frustrate the hopes of the people for the much-needed rain? And can anyone deny the strange fact that almost invariably and immediately upon the heels of the dance, the gods cause the sluice gates of the heavens to be opened, so the life-giving waters can pour forth?

The Hopis claim that there has not been a refusal from their gods in a thousand years—invariably, their petitions for rain are granted. The white people know that it has been true for a long time because, through decade after decade, they have attended the dance in ever-increasing numbers.

Scientific explanation fails in the face of pagan faith.

Possibly the Hopi medicine men have learned to foretell the approaching rains through primitive scientific methods, developed out of hundreds of years of observation of natural phenomena. However, the almost incredible exactness of the arrival of the rains at the climax of the ceremony seems to rule out even this.

With my own eyes I have seen the rain clouds pile up in thick, black masses, and I have watched the cloudbursts transform the level plains into lakes almost simultaneously with the ending of the dance. Possibly a perfectly natural event, but, to the superstitious Indian mind, conclusive proof of the granting of his prayers. And when this phenomenon occurs year after year with a regularity that astounds even the most sophisticated, it is easier to understand how much of a handicap has been placed against the missionaries and their teachings. The Indians are quick to arrive at the simple conclusion that their own priests are much more adept in getting favorable responses from the deities than are the preachers of the white men.

The visit to the Hopi pueblo of Walpi and the witnessing of the Snake Dance were the high lights of our trip. Accompanied by Hosteen Tso and the medicine man who led the party to the sky city of the Indians, we returned to the former's hogan. There we spent another day, winding up our business with the host, then continued with the less dramatic duties of visiting other camps and attending to the collections, the purpose of our trip.

In the neighborhood of Chinle we made another protracted stay, visiting Navajo encampments in Canyon de Chelly (pronounced de Shay) and Canyon del Muerto, as well as hogans located at the mouth of the canyon and in the wide plains fronting the big gap. Canyon de Chelly apprehension into the umbrageous thickets, half expecting, not goblins, perhaps, but some of the large bears that inhabit the Black Mountains to break forth.

The nights, in those rare heights, were bitterly cold, the mornings as frosty as November. The few hogans we visited harbored a sullen crowd, entirely different from the occupants of the camps in the country below. The children in several of the Indian homes in the Lukachukai region began crying upon seeing white men, obviously frightened out of their wits. They had never before seen any other people than Navajos, and even after we had persuaded them to accept our candy offerings, they could not quite overcome their fear and discomfort over being so close to the unknown and unimagined persons.

Bill and I experienced an unconscious feeling of relief when the gloomy range had been left behind and we were, once more, riding through the sunnier plains, en route to Shiprock. Before we reached that famous land mark of the Navajo reservation, in the extreme northwestern corner of New Mexico, Hosteen Tso Begay had left us, properly thanked and rewarded. Between the plains that surround the upthrust pile of Shiprock and the mouth of Canyon Blanco, we made but three or four stops of short duration, then headed our caravan for home.

Canyon Blanco is well-named: the walls of that gash are nearly white. We followed its course for two days, calling on several of our friends who had established permanent camps in the beautiful canyon. They were tilling sizable patches of ground, resembling, in that otherwise arid and uncultivated desert country, small farms. We knew by name almost all the Navajos we met; they lived in such close proximity to Pueblo Bonito as to make Wetherill's trading post their logical source of supplies, and, therefore, they were frequent visitors at our ranch.

holds a remarkable assortment of stately spires, massive rocks resembling huge altars, immense bastions, towering obelisks, heaven-piercing columns and enormous slabs of stone standing on edge, all chiseled, through untold ages, by the infinite patience of Dame Nature from sandstone of delicate red and pink hues. Many of the fantastic examples of erosion have fluted tops, or give the impression of being gigantic pipe organs.

It is impossible to describe the grandeur of the mighty scene, or to give an adequate picture of the effects produced by the arrangements of awe-inspiring canyon walls and eroded rocks in grotesque attitudes. One is bewildered by the green of vegetation, the bright stream, mirroring the fleecy clouds overhead, meandering its own course through the canyon, the color of small patches of cultivated land blocked off in rectangular or odd-shaped pieces, and the nearly pure-white sands covering other sections like cake frostings. And, like a celestial canopy, over all the manifold colors and somber shadows spreads the Western sky of intense blue.

One of the most interesting sights in that canyon of natural wonders and scenic surprises is the White House, a cliff dwelling built upon a ledge in the unscalable, sheer wall of smooth sandstone that forms one of the sides of the upper canyon. The peculiarly colored adobe clay that was used by the original builders when they constructed the prehistoric dwelling has faded to a light dove-grey. In contrast to the red stone of the canyon wall, and the darker shadows of the cavernous recess of the ledge, the ruins are made to stand out sharply, appearing nearly white in color, hence the designation.

This particular part of the country of the Navajos yielded the best collections from the Indians whom we approached about settling their accounts with Wetherill.

They gave us a number of exceptionally fine blankets, also a considerable amount of jewelry and some baskets. However, most of the silver ornaments, *gatos*, bracelets, belts, and rings, were not turned over as outright payments, but given to us to be held as pledges. Those articles were to guarantee the payment of the debt at some future time; Wetherill was to keep them until their owners could redeem the pawns. That, of course, was an acceptable proposition and we knew that the boss would agree gladly to those stipulations. In any event, it was preferable to have the outstanding accounts secured by the collateral of pawned goods than to carry them without more assurance than the oral promise of the debtor to settle the bill at some undetermined date in the time to come.

Thus far on our peregrinations we had traveled without a guide, except that we followed the lead of our friends when we visited the scene of the Snake Dance. From place to place we had made our way by riding over trails that already were familiar to us, or by following the directions of the Navajos who told us how to find our next objective. In several instances we had missed the mark, but each time regained the proper direction without really becoming lost. Now, however, we were about to explore a part of Arizona unfamiliar to both of us, *terra incognita* to Bill and me. The Indian trader at Chinle, when asked about it, warned us that we would find the country beyond very difficult territory to travel over.

Possibly we could have continued on our tour unassisted, but both of us realized that nothing would be gained through the attempt. Therefore we asked Hosteen Tso to let his eldest son go with us, to guide us over the trails until we should be safely on the road to Shiprock. Thence we knew the way that was to take us, by going through Canyon Blanco, to Pueblo Bonito.

Hosteen Tso Begay (Fat Man's Son) became our He was a fine young fellow, straight as an arrow, serious, an Indian Adonis. His grave mien indicated he considered his job a great responsibility, and whil no manner servile, conveyed the impression that he honored in being selected for the job.

During the next week we had several opportunties proving to ourselves that the engagement of the India youth was a wise move. It would have been exceedingl difficult for us to find the trails leading into the Luka chukai Mountains by way of Round Rock, and equally hard to follow those dim paths. Each succeeding day saw us in more rugged and wilder country; many times Bill and I wondered how we would manage to get our horses and mules over passes that appeared positively insurmountable. But without hesitation our guide continued ahead, never swerving from the path that was, in many parts, virtually indistinguishable. And thus we forged onward and upward, climbing dimly outlined trails that took us to the roof of our particular world, the dark, forbidding Lukachukais (Black Mountains).

The hardships of the arduous climb to the heights were repaid and every effort made worth while through the scenic beauties that unfolded themselves before us. The high altitude of the jagged, torn range, covered with tall pines, firs, beeches, and many other trees, afforded unforgettable glimpses into abysmal canyons; our unbelieving eyes beheld views that appeared to embrace all creation. However, there was about us an indefinable *Something* that struck an awe-inspiring note. Even the mountain meadows, lush with green grass that owed its abundant verdancy to the many trickling springs issuing from the rocks, could not change the somberness of the scene as a whole. Involuntarily, one would cast hasty glances of

The purpose of our coming had been heralded; they had learned, through the mysterious channels that relay information in the Indian country, of the object of our visit. Dealing with old friends and acquaintances facilitated our mission, and before we knew it we had packed the mules for the last day's trip—the next, and final, stop was to be Pueblo Bonito.

Five weeks and two days had elapsed since we left the home ranch when, in the middle of the afternoon, we drove the pack mules to the door of the office, dismounted, and announced our return to Wetherill. He was busily engaged in checking some accounts, and had not noticed our arrival. Hearing our cheerful "Howdy, boss!" he gave us a hearty greeting, then helped to unpack the loads. After we had stacked the collected blankets and other articles in his sanctum, he suggested that we leave the recital of our trip, and the listings of the results, until evening. Thus, after supper, we returned to the office and made a full report.

The memoranda, jotted down in our notebook, amplified by our oral explanations, gave him all necessary information pertaining to the collections. Neither Bill nor I realized just how much our efforts had produced, and we could hardly believe our eyes and ears when the grand total, including the value of livestock that we had sent to the ranch, amounted to nearly four thousand dollars.

Wetherill's remark, at the end of the lengthy session, "You boys will each have five dollars a month more to spend from now on!" was proof that he considered our trip a profitable one. As for Bill and me, the happy news more than made up for any privations endured on the long trek.

Later that evening, in the bunkhouse, we had to listen to much chaffing. The boys asked a number of questions, such as: "Did you two have a good time while in Mexico City?" and "How was the swimming in the Pacific Ocean?" while a third came out with the cheerful information: "I heard that the boss was about ready to send the sheriff after you; I believe he figured you had skipped the country!" All affected grievous injury when they learned that we had been rewarded with an increase of pay for, as they put it, "gallivanting all over the country while we had to do the work that rightfully should have been done by you!" Underneath, of course, they were glad with us, and helped celebrate our success.

Chapter 18

GOOD-BY TO PUEBLO BONITO

John Ferguson, a school friend of mine, and, like myself, inclined to adventuring, sent a long letter to me from San Francisco. He had just reached the city by the Golden Gate after making the passage around Cape Horn as a member of the crew of a full-rigged sailing vessel; the voyage from Newcastle, England, to California had required 182 days. He wrote that we ought to meet somewhere in New Mexico or Arizona, and proposed a tour into Old Mexico. The selection of a meeting place and the date of the rendezvous were left to me. It was his suggestion that I acquire several horses and pack animals, and the necessary camp outfit, to enable us to go on a trip of perhaps five or six months' duration. He claimed to have enough ready money to defray the expenses involved in the undertaking and, according to his letters, was prepared to spend all of it in order "to see some dry land after half a year upon the briny deep."

For some time I had been restless, but failed to diagnose properly the reason for my disturbed tranquility. John's first letter threw light upon the state of my mind; the wanderlust in me was making itself felt, and I could no longer neglect to obey the urge. It was inevitable that, sooner or later, I should have saddled my horse and ridden away in search of new countries to explore; John's invitation merely gave impetus to the long-dormant desires. And while engaged in the preliminary preparations for the proposed camping tour on horseback and with pack mules, my soul grew peaceful. Nevertheless, to leave the outfit and to bid good-by to the canyon, to Pueblo Bonito and the other places that held so many happy associations, was a distinct wrench. And I knew, deep down in my heart, that I should miss the mesa and breathtaking rides after the wild, beautiful horses that had been my charges for so long.

The last few days on the Wetherill ranch were melancholy ones for me, even though I looked forward with pleasure to the long trip in company with one of my earliest friends. I visited all spots that were within reach, impressing upon my mind the picture of each, realizing sadly that in all probability I should never again see those scenes.

I rode to the place where the trails of the forty-niners had carved ineradicable lines across the face of the country. The sight of those deep ruts, running parallel over a broad strip of prairie and unerringly pointing westward, affected me like a visit to some shrine. But then, wasn't I on hallowed ground? Shouldn't I bow in reverence before the memory of those brave pioneers whose slow-moving, cumbersome wagons marked the first paths across this desert?

Today, after nearly half a century, my admiration remains unstinted when I think of the sturdy stock of Americans of an earlier age that lived in a period which did *not* belittle ox teams, covered prairie schooners, and horses and buggies. The events of current times prove

that the venturesome, independent trail makers had little
in common with certain modern groups, Americans also,
but of emasculated spirit and flagging courage. Those
intrepid pioneers, men, women, and children, braved the
unchartered wilderness with its dangers, hardships, and
privations. Their philosophy would not have understood
or countenanced following self-styled leaders into an alley
that has no turning, and blind guides ostensibly looking
for the corner beyond which Good Times were supposed
to be lurking.

Then, long decades ago, the people knew nothing of
regimentation; furthermore, they would not have submitted to it. They were *free* Americans, moved by lofty
ideals, ready and eager to carve out their own destinies.
Alphabetical relief agencies and boondoggle departments,
covering up national waste and inefficiency and portending political serfdom, found no place in the order of things
considered fit and proper by the Americans of that period.
Tens of thousands of husky, able-bodied men did not
waste their time, and the money sweated out of taxpayers,
by raking leaves, picking up pieces of paper, or leaning
idly against hoe handles. Those Americans of another
day occupied themselves differently; they were busy
building a nation!

A stone cabin stood beside the deep-rutted trail of the
California-bound emigrants, abandoned and half tumbled
down. It had been one of the stations used by the Pony
Express riders when those fearless fellows carried messages across an Indian-infested country. In its time there
had been a stout door to the small, one-room house. That
disappeared long ago; somebody had taken it and used
the wood to feed a fire. The window opening, for added
protection high up in the wall, almost under the roof

line, was bare of frame and shutters. Like a cyclopean eye it stared unblinkingly over the vast expanse of range that had been the scene of wild dashes, blood-curdling war whoops, and heartbreaking toil.

One more look at those mementos of a glorious past; in silent salute I raised my hand, greeting the shades of those indomitable Americans who had left an inspiring message printed deeply in the very earth they crossed over on their way to conquest.

Every morning during my last week on the Wetherill ranch I rode over the large pasture atop the mesa, visiting the different bands of horses and saying my adieus to them. How it thrilled me to see them, to watch them break into a sharp canter, heads high, ears alert, manes and tails streaming in the wind.

There they go!—the glossy bays, the tall roans, the flea-bitten grays, sleek sorrels, one or two silken-coated blacks, the gay and giddy pintos, and, most impressive of all, those gorgeous palominos, cream-colored, with platinum manes and tails, looking for all the world like statues come to life. Good-by, my darlings! Farewell to you, my beloved friends! I pray that you will never lack lush pastures and cool water—may it be your fate to find kind masters. Good-by, you wonderful animals!

The camp outfit, gotten together by me, was complete. In addition to my private saddle horse, I had acquired another good riding animal and three pack mules, also the necessary equipment in the way of saddles, aparejos, tarpaulins, cooking utensils, and suchlike articles. John and I had agreed to meet in Thoreau, a station and unimportant settlement on the line of the Santa Fe Railway, some thirty miles east of Gallup, New Mexico. He was to come by train from San Francisco; I intended to wait for him on the ranch of a friend, near Thoreau.

holds a remarkable assortment of stately spires, massive rocks resembling huge altars, immense bastions, towering obelisks, heaven-piercing columns and enormous slabs of stone standing on edge, all chiseled, through untold ages, by the infinite patience of Dame Nature from sandstone of delicate red and pink hues. Many of the fantastic examples of erosion have fluted tops, or give the impression of being gigantic pipe organs.

It is impossible to describe the grandeur of the mighty scene, or to give an adequate picture of the effects produced by the arrangements of awe-inspiring canyon walls and eroded rocks in grotesque attitudes. One is bewildered by the green of vegetation, the bright stream, mirroring the fleecy clouds overhead, meandering its own course through the canyon, the color of small patches of cultivated land blocked off in rectangular or odd-shaped pieces, and the nearly pure-white sands covering other sections like cake frostings. And, like a celestial canopy, over all the manifold colors and somber shadows spreads the Western sky of intense blue.

One of the most interesting sights in that canyon of natural wonders and scenic surprises is the White House, a cliff dwelling built upon a ledge in the unscalable, sheer wall of smooth sandstone that forms one of the sides of the upper canyon. The peculiarly colored adobe clay that was used by the original builders when they constructed the prehistoric dwelling has faded to a light dove-grey. In contrast to the red stone of the canyon wall, and the darker shadows of the cavernous recess of the ledge, the ruins are made to stand out sharply, appearing nearly white in color, hence the designation.

This particular part of the country of the Navajos yielded the best collections from the Indians whom we approached about settling their accounts with Wetherill.

They gave us a number of exceptionally fine blankets, also a considerable amount of jewelry and some baskets. However, most of the silver ornaments, *gatos*, bracelets, belts, and rings, were not turned over as outright payments, but given to us to be held as pledges. Those articles were to guarantee the payment of the debt at some future time; Wetherill was to keep them until their owners could redeem the pawns. That, of course, was an acceptable proposition and we knew that the boss would agree gladly to those stipulations. In any event, it was preferable to have the outstanding accounts secured by the collateral of pawned goods than to carry them without more assurance than the oral promise of the debtor to settle the bill at some undetermined date in the time to come.

Thus far on our peregrinations we had traveled without a guide, except that we followed the lead of our friends when we visited the scene of the Snake Dance. From place to place we had made our way by riding over trails that already were familiar to us, or by following the directions of the Navajos who told us how to find our next objective. In several instances we had missed the mark, but each time regained the proper direction without really becoming lost. Now, however, we were about to explore a part of Arizona unfamiliar to both of us, *terra incognita* to Bill and me. The Indian trader at Chinle, when asked about it, warned us that we would find the country beyond very difficult territory to travel over.

Possibly we could have continued on our tour unassisted, but both of us realized that nothing would be gained through the attempt. Therefore we asked Hosteen Tso to let his eldest son go with us, to guide us over the trails until we should be safely on the road to Shiprock. Thence we knew the way that was to take us, by going through Canyon Blanco, to Pueblo Bonito.

Hosteen Tso Begay (Fat Man's Son) became our guide. He was a fine young fellow, straight as an arrow, slim, serious, an Indian Adonis. His grave mien indicated that he considered his job a great responsibility, and while in no manner servile, conveyed the impression that he felt honored in being selected for the job.

During the next week we had several opportunties of proving to ourselves that the engagement of the Indian youth was a wise move. It would have been exceedingly difficult for us to find the trails leading into the Lukachukai Mountains by way of Round Rock, and equally hard to follow those dim paths. Each succeeding day saw us in more rugged and wilder country; many times Bill and I wondered how we would manage to get our horses and mules over passes that appeared positively insurmountable. But without hesitation our guide continued ahead, never swerving from the path that was, in many parts, virtually indistinguishable. And thus we forged onward and upward, climbing dimly outlined trails that took us to the roof of our particular world, the dark, forbidding Lukachukais (Black Mountains).

The hardships of the arduous climb to the heights were repaid and every effort made worth while through the scenic beauties that unfolded themselves before us. The high altitude of the jagged, torn range, covered with tall pines, firs, beeches, and many other trees, afforded unforgettable glimpses into abysmal canyons; our unbelieving eyes beheld views that appeared to embrace all creation. However, there was about us an indefinable *Something* that struck an awe-inspiring note. Even the mountain meadows, lush with green grass that owed its abundant verdancy to the many trickling springs issuing from the rocks, could not change the somberness of the scene as a whole. Involuntarily, one would cast hasty glances of apprehension into the umbrageous thickets, half expecting, not goblins, perhaps, but some of the large bears that inhabit the Black Mountains to break forth.

The nights, in those rare heights, were bitterly cold, the mornings as frosty as November. The few hogans we visited harbored a sullen crowd, entirely different from the occupants of the camps in the country below. The children in several of the Indian homes in the Lukachukai region began crying upon seeing white men, obviously frightened out of their wits. They had never before seen any other people than Navajos, and even after we had persuaded them to accept our candy offerings, they could not quite overcome their fear and discomfort over being so close to the unknown and unimagined persons.

Bill and I experienced an unconscious feeling of relief when the gloomy range had been left behind and we were, once more, riding through the sunnier plains, en route to Shiprock. Before we reached that famous land mark of the Navajo reservation, in the extreme northwestern corner of New Mexico, Hosteen Tso Begay had left us, properly thanked and rewarded. Between the plains that surround the upthrust pile of Shiprock and the mouth of Canyon Blanco, we made but three or four stops of short duration, then headed our caravan for home.

Canyon Blanco is well-named: the walls of that gash are nearly white. We followed its course for two days, calling on several of our friends who had established permanent camps in the beautiful canyon. They were tilling sizable patches of ground, resembling, in that otherwise arid and uncultivated desert country, small farms. We knew by name almost all the Navajos we met; they lived in such close proximity to Pueblo Bonito as to make Wetherill's trading post their logical source of supplies, and, therefore, they were frequent visitors at our ranch.

The purpose of our coming had been heralded; they had learned, through the mysterious channels that relay information in the Indian country, of the object of our visit. Dealing with old friends and acquaintances facilitated our mission, and before we knew it we had packed the mules for the last day's trip—the next, and final, stop was to be Pueblo Bonito.

Five weeks and two days had elapsed since we left the home ranch when, in the middle of the afternoon, we drove the pack mules to the door of the office, dismounted, and announced our return to Wetherill. He was busily engaged in checking some accounts, and had not noticed our arrival. Hearing our cheerful "Howdy, boss!" he gave us a hearty greeting, then helped to unpack the loads. After we had stacked the collected blankets and other articles in his sanctum, he suggested that we leave the recital of our trip, and the listings of the results, until evening. Thus, after supper, we returned to the office and made a full report.

The memoranda, jotted down in our notebook, amplified by our oral explanations, gave him all necessary information pertaining to the collections. Neither Bill nor I realized just how much our efforts had produced, and we could hardly believe our eyes and ears when the grand total, including the value of livestock that we had sent to the ranch, amounted to nearly four thousand dollars.

Wetherill's remark, at the end of the lengthy session, "You boys will each have five dollars a month more to spend from now on!" was proof that he considered our trip a profitable one. As for Bill and me, the happy news more than made up for any privations endured on the long trek.

Later that evening, in the bunkhouse, we had to listen to much chaffing. The boys asked a number of questions, such as: "Did you two have a good time while in Mexico City?" and "How was the swimming in the Pacific Ocean?" while a third came out with the cheerful information: "I heard that the boss was about ready to send the sheriff after you; I believe he figured you had skipped the country!" All affected grievous injury when they learned that we had been rewarded with an increase of pay for, as they put it, "gallivanting all over the country while we had to do the work that rightfully should have been done by you!" Underneath, of course, they were glad with us, and helped celebrate our success.

Chapter 18

GOOD-BY TO PUEBLO BONITO

John Ferguson, a school friend of mine, and, like myself, inclined to adventuring, sent a long letter to me from San Francisco. He had just reached the city by the Golden Gate after making the passage around Cape Horn as a member of the crew of a full-rigged sailing vessel; the voyage from Newcastle, England, to California had required 182 days. He wrote that we ought to meet somewhere in New Mexico or Arizona, and proposed a tour into Old Mexico. The selection of a meeting place and the date of the rendezvous were left to me. It was his suggestion that I acquire several horses and pack animals, and the necessary camp outfit, to enable us to go on a trip of perhaps five or six months' duration. He claimed to have enough ready money to defray the expenses involved in the undertaking and, according to his letters, was prepared to spend all of it in order "to see some dry land after half a year upon the briny deep."

For some time I had been restless, but failed to diagnose properly the reason for my disturbed tranquility. John's first letter threw light upon the state of my mind; the wanderlust in me was making itself felt, and I could no

longer neglect to obey the urge. It was inevitable that, sooner or later, I should have saddled my horse and ridden away in search of new countries to explore; John's invitation merely gave impetus to the long-dormant desires. And while engaged in the preliminary preparations for the proposed camping tour on horseback and with pack mules, my soul grew peaceful. Nevertheless, to leave the outfit and to bid good-by to the canyon, to Pueblo Bonito and the other places that held so many happy associations, was a distinct wrench. And I knew, deep down in my heart, that I should miss the mesa and breath-taking rides after the wild, beautiful horses that had been my charges for so long.

The last few days on the Wetherill ranch were melancholy ones for me, even though I looked forward with pleasure to the long trip in company with one of my earliest friends. I visited all spots that were within reach, impressing upon my mind the picture of each, realizing sadly that in all probability I should never again see those scenes.

I rode to the place where the trails of the forty-niners had carved ineradicable lines across the face of the country. The sight of those deep ruts, running parallel over a broad strip of prairie and unerringly pointing westward, affected me like a visit to some shrine. But then, wasn't I on hallowed ground? Shouldn't I bow in reverence before the memory of those brave pioneers whose slow-moving, cumbersome wagons marked the first paths across this desert?

Today, after nearly half a century, my admiration remains unstinted when I think of the sturdy stock of Americans of an earlier age that lived in a period which did *not* belittle ox teams, covered prairie schooners, and horses and buggies. The events of current times prove

that the venturesome, independent trail makers had little in common with certain modern groups, Americans also, but of emasculated spirit and flagging courage. Those intrepid pioneers, men, women, and children, braved the unchartered wilderness with its dangers, hardships, and privations. Their philosophy would not have understood or countenanced following self-styled leaders into an alley that has no turning, and blind guides ostensibly looking for the corner beyond which Good Times were supposed to be lurking.

Then, long decades ago, the people knew nothing of regimentation; furthermore, they would not have submitted to it. They were *free* Americans, moved by lofty ideals, ready and eager to carve out their own destinies. Alphabetical relief agencies and boondoggle departments, covering up national waste and inefficiency and portending political serfdom, found no place in the order of things considered fit and proper by the Americans of that period. Tens of thousands of husky, able-bodied men did not waste their time, and the money sweated out of taxpayers, by raking leaves, picking up pieces of paper, or leaning idly against hoe handles. Those Americans of another day occupied themselves differently; they were busy building a nation!

A stone cabin stood beside the deep-rutted trail of the California-bound emigrants, abandoned and half tumbled down. It had been one of the stations used by the Pony Express riders when those fearless fellows carried messages across an Indian-infested country. In its time there had been a stout door to the small, one-room house. That disappeared long ago; somebody had taken it and used the wood to feed a fire. The window opening, for added protection high up in the wall, almost under the roof

line, was bare of frame and shutters. Like a cyclopean eye it stared unblinkingly over the vast expanse of range that had been the scene of wild dashes, blood-curdling war whoops, and heartbreaking toil.

One more look at those mementos of a glorious past; in silent salute I raised my hand, greeting the shades of those indomitable Americans who had left an inspiring message printed deeply in the very earth they crossed over on their way to conquest.

Every morning during my last week on the Wetherill ranch I rode over the large pasture atop the mesa, visiting the different bands of horses and saying my adieus to them. How it thrilled me to see them, to watch them break into a sharp canter, heads high, ears alert, manes and tails streaming in the wind.

There they go!—the glossy bays, the tall roans, the flea-bitten grays, sleek sorrels, one or two silken-coated blacks, the gay and giddy pintos, and, most impressive of all, those gorgeous palominos, cream-colored, with platinum manes and tails, looking for all the world like statues come to life. Good-by, my darlings! Farewell to you, my beloved friends! I pray that you will never lack lush pastures and cool water—may it be your fate to find kind masters. Good-by, you wonderful animals!

The camp outfit, gotten together by me, was complete. In addition to my private saddle horse, I had acquired another good riding animal and three pack mules, also the necessary equipment in the way of saddles, aparejos, tarpaulins, cooking utensils, and suchlike articles. John and I had agreed to meet in Thoreau, a station and unimportant settlement on the line of the Santa Fe Railway, some thirty miles east of Gallup, New Mexico. He was to come by train from San Francisco; I intended to wait for him on the ranch of a friend, near Thoreau.

It lacked a week before we were to see each other, but I was impatient to be on the road, so, early one morning, we set out. Driving the extra stock before me, I started up the canyon, past the impressive ruins of Pueblo Bonito, past Chettro Kettle in its crescent-shaped recess, and beyond to the head of the Chaco, where towers La Fajada (The Belted), a massive, circular rock guarding the entrance to the cut. Emerging from the canyon, we traveled over the far-spreading, slightly undulating plains toward our first objective, the trading post of Old Man Howard, at Seven Lakes, some twenty miles away.

Keeping to a leisurely gait, we reached Howard's place in the early hours of the afternoon. The trader, friendly, hospitable, and insistent, persuaded me to stay with him overnight. Horses and mules were put in one of his corrals and fed with hay and oats; for me, Howard arranged a comfortable bed in a spare room. Upon hearing that I was leaving that part of the country he prepared a regular feast, not to celebrate getting rid of me, but to honor the parting. I had already been made much of at the leave-taking in Chaco Canyon, and now, for the second time in two days, I was treated to a ceremonial dinner. It was a *beau geste* on Howard's part, a visible token of affection and good will.

Besides looking after my physical welfare, my host regaled me with stories, knowing from experience how avidly I absorbed those recountings of earlier days. We sat up until an advanced hour, both of us reluctant to go to bed. Howard had no obligation to rise early, his customers were not in the habit of arriving at the store much before noon during that season; so far as I was concerned, it would not matter for once whether I made ready for the ride at six o'clock in the morning or at ten. I was without the responsibility of chores or routine work, free to do as I might please. Feed and water were in the corral, so, consequently, I had no need to fret over the demands of the stock.

Notwithstanding the late hour of my going to sleep, and disregarding the knowledge that no duties called, I was up and about the corral at the usual early hour the next morning. Habits become firmly fixed, and I could not have remained abed and felt comfortable after the hour struck at which I was accustomed to dress and begin my day's work. Howard, who lived alone, was puttering about the kitchen, preparing breakfast, while I "grained" the stock. Even the mules received some mixed oats and corn, a luxury they did not enjoy very often.

Having eaten the morning meal, I got my outfit ready for the trail, and with a hearty good-by left Old Man Howard standing in the door of his store. He watched until a slight rise in the road took us from view. On the crest of the last hummock I reined my horse. There I turned and waved my hat in final farewell, then followed the extra horse and mules that had ambled along in the well-worn path leading in an almost due southerly direction toward Midnight Canyon, and through that pass to Smith's Lake, as that body of water is called nowadays. It used to be just "the lake" till in later years an Indian trader, named Smith, built a trading post in the vicinity, thereby christening the shallow, stagnant pool.

The second night out from Pueblo Bonito was spent with Many Horses, the same Navajo whose son had failed in his attempt to collect ransom for the stock driven off from my camp when I returned from Albuquerque on my solitary freighting trip. Many Horses was glad to see me. He did not know of his son's little game, and I did not enlighten him, but we were well acquainted, having seen and met each other many times in Chaco Canyon.

His name was bestowed fittingly: he owned a large herd of fine-looking horses, and it was from Many Horses' band of ponies that Wetherill had obtained the splendid palominos which were the pride of the Triangle Bar Triangle remuda. Most of his horses were racers; the fleetness of Many Horses' stallions was known throughout the Navajo Indian country.

Upon the third day, I reached the ranch where I meant to stay until John should arrive from the coast. The rancher, Childress, had a contract with several large lumber-camp commissaries, calling for a steady supply of fresh meat for the men employed in the woods. The butchering was done on the ranch, and the freshly killed beef delivered to the logging camps in the mountains to the south.

Childress owned two broncos that had been giving his "boys" some trouble, so I set about to "break" them for him, in that manner paying at least partially for my keep and the feed of my horses and mules. One of the animals. a powerful four-year-old bay, proved a handful, indeed, and I had to ride him some five or six times before the other men felt inclined to take him out of the corral. The rancher's foreman, Harris, a Texan, was the shortest cowpuncher I ever saw in my life: he stood barely five feet tall in his high-heeled boots. He "adopted" the bay after the horse was gentled, and it was amusing to see this little shrimp of a man bestride the big, deep-chested stallion.

Despite his undersized stature, Harris was a competent cow hand, and performed the duties of foreman in an expert manner. I had met him for the first time while on a roundup two seasons before, and had been amazed over the Texan's dexterity with a rope. When he heard that I had quit the Wetherill outfit, he promptly offered me a job under him, but this I declined. After I explained my reason for the refusal, he was good enough to say: "Anytime you want a job on the Childress ranch, Red, it's yours!"

Chapter 19

THOREAU

Thoreau, still only a mere speck on any map, was at that time even less imposing. The Santa Fe Railway maintained a station there, in charge of an agent who combined under that title the duties of ticket seller, general agent, expressman, baggage handler, warehouse superintendent, train dispatcher, freight soliciter, and possibly half a dozen others. A burly section foreman was in command of a corporal's guard of railroad laborers, quartered in the section house diagonally across the tracks from the rusty, two-story station building. Those workers, swarthy sons of Mexico, and their families, lived in a row of small, one-room structures built of discarded railroad ties, the chinks filled with adobe mud. The roofs of the little cabins, also, were adobe; thick layers of the native soil kept out the penetrating heat of the sun's rays, and most of the water when it happened to rain.

The McGaffey Company operated a general merchandise and trading store. They dealt with cow and sheep outfits, supplied ranchers, miners, and prospectors, had considerable interests in the lumber camp and sawmill operations in the mountains to the south and in Albuquerque, were wholesalers to traders on the reservation, and engaged in barter and retail trade with the Indians.

From Mexican and Indian woodcutters they bought large quantities of firewood, chopped into short lengths; long rows of the fragrant, resin-exuding pinon and the stringy-barked cedar, stacked in sections measuring two cords each, flanked the embankment of the railroad siding. Many carloads of the sweet-smelling fuel were shipped from Thoreau to Albuquerque and other points.

McGaffey's was the only store of importance in that part of the country, drawing its customers from an extensive area. The nearest of the other large trading posts, comparable because they carried heavy stocks and offered wide assortments, were located many long miles away from Thoreau. Those competitors had their establishments in Grants, at the base of mighty Mount Taylor, or in Gallup, heart of the coal-mining region. Thus, whether traveling eastward, or riding into the west, one had to cover at least thirty miles before finding a variety of goods similar to the display at McGaffey's.

There were perhaps ten or twelve nondescript shacks and buildings, in addition to the railroad station and the general store, that made up the whole of an unsightly blot on an otherwise lovely landscape. Such effeminate luxuries as hotels, taverns, restaurants, or inns did not exist. However, the weary and hungry traveler could buy canned sardines, lukewarm tomatoes *á purée,* dried-out cheese of uncertain vintage, and a bagful of stale crackers in the store, spread the unappetizing viands upon a piece of newspaper, and with some such feast restore the burnt-up energies. The rider's animals invariably fared better: oats, corn, and hay were to be had, although sold at outrageously high prices.

Under the guise of a half-baked eating house, old lady

Sanchez operated a thriving rumshop. Perhaps her customers were on a liquid diet, *quien sabe,* but the fact remains that the menu, recited by the Macbethian, witch-like duenna, listed only such items as vile gin, rot-gut whisky, doctored tequila, and a sulphurous concoction designated, catholically, as vino.

Two sons, considered by all to be the slickest cattle thieves in six counties, and suspected of having their fingers in every unsavory pie, assisted the elderly woman in handling the "business." Range justice overtook all; some time later one of the sons and his mother were "requested" to leave town and warned not to return. The younger of the two boys was killed in a saloon fight; he stopped a heavy slug coming from a gun quicker than his own.

Thoreau, bearing the name of a great American nature lover and essayist, lay sprawled in all its unredeemed ugliness beneath a flawless sky, surrounded, but unaffected, by sublime grandeur of scenery when I rode into the settlement to make inquiries for letters or telegrams from John.

Although I had been waiting for more than ten days on the Childress ranch, and had ridden to the railroad point twice during the interval, so far I was without additional news from my friend. And upon this third time, I was disappointed again, neither post office nor telegraph station held messages from him.

To rest my horse, I put him in McGaffey's corral and treated the faithful beast to a big feed of grain. For myself I bought a lunch in the store, selecting some canned fruit and plain crackers as least thirst-provoking. The horse and I had quenched our dry, dusty throats at a place about three miles east of that settlement, the water in Thoreau being virtually undrinkable.

While seated upon the high store counter munching my modest lunch, I overheard the conversation between two of the store clerks and a small assembly of ranchers, cowboys, and lumberjacks grouped in the center of the building. They were discussing the exciting news of the day: Tom Goodrich had marched Joe Lewis down to the tracks and at gun's point forced him to board the semi-weekly local freight train. As Joe climbed the steps of the caboose, Tom had shouted his farewell warning: "I'll kill you if you ever come back here!"

Big, overgrown, slow-thinking Tom had at last discovered what had been an open secret and the topic of range gossip for more than half a year, the fact that slim little Joe had made systematic attacks upon the virtue of Mrs. Goodrich. Months ago the tale had been carried to the Wetherill ranch by some freighter, but found little credence. Later information, however, strengthened the first reports. Soon the entire countryside, for a hundred miles in every direction, knew that Joe Lewis was "carrying on something awfully" with Kate Goodrich.

Everybody was in the know, except poor Tom, husband of Kate, she of the voluptuous, tantalizing curves, walking to the store with insouciantly swinging hips, two thick braids of gleaming bluish-black hair forming a coronet for her proud head, an infectious smile disclosing strong, even, white teeth. Her thin, homemade dress of light cotton material revealed plainly the sturdy, shapely limbs, and the buttons of her waist were put to it desperately to hold within their jurisdiction the fullness of the firmly rounded breasts that seemed eager to burst through the bonds. Truly, a Juno of the prairies.

On the Wetherill ranch, discussion of this demonstration of the eternal triangle brought forth some interesting comments. Mrs. Wetherill sniffed scornfully and contemptuously: "No woman in her right mind would prefer that sly whippersnapper to a fine, upstanding man like Tom Goodrich; I don't believe there's a grain of truth in the whole story!"

Black Phillips "allowed" that back home, in his Kentucky hills, a meeting might be held to arrange proper handling of such a case, to prevent the culprits from giving further offense to the moral tenets of the mountaineers.

"Us folks don't stand for carryin's-on," he explained. "We take sech a woman and give her a good whippin' on the bare hide. That cures her. The man? Well, he gets a taste of the blacksnake, then we tar and feather him, and ride the fellow out of town on a rail!"

With a satisfied, faraway look in his eyes, he observed: "They don't come back!"

Palmer, the expert with the six-shooter, did not advocate physical punishment. In his opinion, marital infidelity, when it occurred in Kansas, was handled properly in the courts. However, from his remarks, it was easy to imagine that a Kansas countrywoman, divorced by her husband on the grounds of adultery, would henceforth live in a hell on earth. She would be ostracized by society, deserted by her friends, despised by her family, relations, and the community at large.

Unquestionably, this was a more lasting and bitter chastisement for the erring one than the swift, physical retribution described by the Kentuckian.

The boss was noncommittal, claiming he had no personal knowledge of the wrongdoing ascribed to the two people under discussion. He did, however, condemn in the strongest terms the breaking up of homes and the seduction of women and girls through the practices of philanderers.

Bill Finn summed up his own decision in one sentence. His cynical, unyielding eyes, and the cold, deadly earnestness of his voice made it evident that he would do exactly as he said when he declared: "I would kill a man doing that to me just like a rattlesnake!"

He did not enlighten us about the fate of the woman in the case, or refer to the potential consequences the female partner in any such affair might experience. As with the Canadian Mounted Police, Bill's sole concern appeared to be to "get his man."

Those were the expressions and opinion of 100 per cent Americans, component parts of a group including Vermont Quakers, Kansas farm people, Kentucky hill folk, and a descendant of families that explored and settled Texas. Rugged pioneer stock! Unaware of and untouched by nihilism, marxism, fascism, communism, the strange precepts of gain through destruction, thirty-hour weeks, share-the-wealth phantasms, sit-down strikes, and other phenomena that have broken out on the American body politic like festering fistulas, temporarily poisoning the entire system and devitalizing a whole nation.

These people were uncontaminated by the influx of unassimilables, those hordes from eastern and southern Europe, and elsewhere, that made of the melting-pot mixture a scummy broth. They held to ideals and ideas firmly anchored in the American Constitution, believed in the American people, and were imbued with the American Spirit!

The assembly in McGaffey's store was unanimous in supporting Tom Goodrich's action. The majority, in fact, deplored that Joe Lewis had got off so lightly; the mildest form of punishment advocated was to have been a "good kicking all over the place by Big Tom" before allowing "that skunk" to leave.

Outwardly it may appear that we have grown callous
and are indifferent to ethical laxness. Tending to support
that view is the general unconcern exhibited over wife
swapping, freak weddings, sexual crimes and aberrations.
Hollywood's inextricable tangle of multiple marriages
and divorces, fan, bubble, and nude dancers, burlesque
in its vilest and most degrading forms, lewd plays, and
other manifestations of moral degeneracy, not to mention
the unprecedented prostitution and virtually complete
corruption of political and social standards.

But that is not so; the American people, at heart, are
still committed to a course of uprightness, honesty, and
integrity. The sturdy qualities of our people, that enabled
us to build the greatest nation and the most prosperous
and happiest country in the world from scratch, out of
a wilderness, are still part and parcel of our national
nature. Some of our homespun virtues may, temporarily,
lie dormant and not produce fruit; others are, for the
moment, obliterated through the ulcerous growths that
have been grafted upon the stout trunk by insidious
foreign influences, but the American tree is still sound, the
fibre strong and free from rot, the core itself, unaffected.

The sheriff was not brought down from Gallup to take
Tom Goodrich to task for settling his domestic difficulties
in his own way. Within a week after the expulsion of Joe
Lewis, another excitement claimed the general attention,
and the affair of gorgeous Kate and her two men was
pushed into the background. This time it was an Indian,
a half-crazed Navajo, who provided local headline news.

He had come from the reservation, far to the north,
after killing another brave. The members of the slain
man's family followed his tracks to an old, abandoned
cabin within about four miles of Thoreau, and sur-

rounded the place. The killer, well supplied with ammunition, fortified himself within the decrepit shack and began firing at random at anything moving into his field of vision. McKinley County's sheriff's office was notified by telegraph, and presently a special engine, pulling a Pullman and caboose, came thundering down from the Continental Divide and screeched to a stop at the station.

The single car disgorged the great Poo-Bah, accompanied by a small regiment of policemen, some deputy sheriffs, one or two newspapermen, a beefy saloonkeeper out for a thrill, and several gentlemen of leisure whose regular habitat was the station platform at Gallup. Not satisfied with this imposing force of heavily armed men, the sheriff proceeded to swear in every male of age within sight as additional deputies. That fearless, two-gun man was not going to take any chances in this matter of capturing a lone, sick Indian.

Among the men who were pressed into doing duty for the commonwealth was a young Navajo, not more than twenty-two or twenty-three years of age, educated at some Indian school and known by the Mexican name of Manuel. Hardly had the oath been administered when this young fellow mounted his pony and rode away. In the general excitement and hubbub caused by the officious sheriff and his gang of satellites from the coal-mining town, Manuel's departure went unnoticed.

The potbellied representative of territorial law (New Mexico was not yet a state), gathered his forces in front of McGaffey's store. There a general plan of attack was evolved, the Gallup members of the coterie being most vociferous in their demands for drastic punishment to the so-and-so Indian who had dared disturb the tranquillity of the domain.

A brave showing was made when the guardian of the

law asked the men to line up; then he inspected the arma-
ment of his deputies. Every man had to be supplied with
at least fifty rounds of ammunition; those who did not
carry that much sudden death in the loops of their cartridge belts must, perforce, replenish their stock. Mc-
Gaffey's did a land-office business in cartridges that day!
Eventually, everything was satisfactory, but, the hour having advanced, it was decided to eat lunch before starting
upon the man hunt. The hungry hordes consumed huge
quantities of eatables, and the expense voucher, signed in
a flourishing manner by the great man from the county
seat, included payment not only for the food, but also for
drinks, smokes, kerchiefs, ammunition, and various other
miscellaneous items.

Finally, the posse was organized and got under way.
Horses had been commandeered for the men who arrived
in the train, and, led by the Thoreau contingent—"because you fellers know the lay of the land!"—the cavalcade
started for the place where the killer was in hiding.

In keeping with the best precepts of fine generalship,
the sheriff brought up the rear, from that point directing
"his boys." Although more accustomed to impress the
poor miners of Gallup, and to put the fear of the drasti-
cally and discriminately administered ordinances into the
Mexican portion of the town's population, he bore himself as bravely as if he were leaning against his favorite
bar and delivering speeches dripping with wisdom. True,
he did not sit his horse as well as the Indians and cowboys,
but the majesty of the law clothed him as with a regal
mantle.

The tumble-down cabin where the Indians had surrounded the fugitive slayer stood in a clearing, upon a low
knoll, within the mouth of the canyon through which the
wagon trail led to Seven Lakes and Pueblo Bonito. The

nearest pinons and cedars were fully fifty yards from the cabin, the immediate neighborhood of the shack free from trees, shrubs, and rocks, thus affording an unobstructed view on every side. The door was missing; a black opening gaped in its place. There never had been panes in the windows; originally, those holes were closed by shutters. In the course of time the boards had sagged off their hinges, leaving only the staring eyes of the apertures. The chinking that at one time had made the cabin snug and weatherproof had long ago blown out; one could put the flat of the hand between the layers of logs that formed the walls. Not much of a fortress, to be sure, but because of its commanding position still a formidable redoubt, and dangerous to approach.

Earlier in the day, scouts had reported that some eight or ten Navajos encircled the shack at a safe distance, not making any attempt to rush the old place, but apparently satisfied to hold the hiding Indian captive within the walls of the cabin. As we approached the scene we expected to see some of the sentries, but failed to notice even a single one. This was strange. Cautiously we advanced closer, and when within some two hundred feet of our objective, everybody dismounted. We formed half a dozen groups, deployed into a semicircle, then moved forward, taking advantage of every tree between us and the suddenly sinister-appearing tumble-down house.

All about us everything was quiet, the only noises those produced by our spurs and accoutrements. Unconsciously we had lowered our voices to whispers. Weren't we stalking big game? When all had reached the predetermined positions, the sheriff shattered the silence with a stentorian: "Hey there, you in the cabin!" For a moment, nothing happened, everybody was tense and expectant, then almost dumfounded by the dramatic appearance of

Manuel, who came walking slowly out of the shack. Seeing him, all hands rushed forward, meeting the young
Indian within a dozen paces of the cabin. The sheriff and
his henchmen had already shouted a score of questions
when Manuel stopped all exclamations with the three
words: "I kill him!"

The Navajo, sworn in as deputy, had ridden toward
the old cabin and there found the other Indians on
guard. He explained to them that the white men were
making ready to take the culprit, dead or alive, and told
the watchers that he would go into the cabin and talk
with the slayer. He dismounted, and while walking
slowly toward the old house, repeatedly called out in
Navajo to the one inside. Twice the demented Indian
came to the door opening and his guns blazed at the intrepid youth. Upon the third time, when Manuel was but
some fifteen feet from the shack, our young Indian returned the fire, and his first shot took effect. A bluish hole,
squarely in the center of the forehead, from which a thin
trickle of blood had already coagulated, told the end of
the killer.

Fearing the white men's incomprehensible justice, the
other Navajos had taken to their horses and fled. Manuel,
not affected by the superstitions of his people, had dragged the body of the dead Indian into the shade of the
shack, then sat down to wait for the arrival of the sheriff
and his posse. He told us some details with which we were
still unfamiliar, which explained the bountiful supply of
ammunition and guns possessed by the Navajo who had
now joined his forefathers in the happy hunting grounds.

From the other Indians Manuel had learned that, after
the slaying in the wilds of the reservation, two Indian policemen had captured the bad man. With their prisoner
they were on the road to the Fort Defiance Indian Agency

when their captive, through some trick during the rest in the night's camp, gained possession of their guns and cartridge belts. He stunned both men with blows over their heads, then escaped on the horses of the policemen, taking with him all arms and ammunition. Although pronounced mentally unbalanced, he eluded pursuit with astonishing slyness and cunning, until brought to bay a few miles north of the Santa Fe Railway tracks. There, as we had just seen, his fate overtook him.

Chapter 20

ARIZONA—BOUND

John arrived in Thoreau two days after Manuel's exploit. A letter written by him, explaining that he would be delayed about two weeks, evidently miscarried, for I never received it. Failure to hear from him had caused some anxiety and made me uneasy. Now, however, everything was rosy, and both of us celebrated a happy reunion. I took him with me to the ranch, but could not be persuaded to return to Chaco Canyon, which he desired to see.

The memories of my leave-taking were still too poignant; I was unable to bring myself to revisit the scene of Pueblo Bonito. Having left, I wished to go to other places; to return so soon to the canyon would have been an emotional anticlimax. I promised John a look into the Navajo country to the north at the end of our tour. First, however, we were to head south.

Thus we began to get ourselves ready to start upon the trip. In the following three days we were busy arranging our equipment and loads, eliminating unnecessary items, and adding others that had been overlooked in the first selection of requirements.

John spent as much time as possible in the saddle, to change his sea legs into something that could hug the ribs of a cayuse. He had never ridden on Western ranges, but was familiar with horses and, in the course of time, became a good rider.

I vetoed his suggestion to make an extended camping tour into Old Mexico. There were several reasons for my disinclination to visit that republic, the principal ones being the virtual absence of all trails beyond the border, the possibility of not finding water, and the unknown and uncalculable hazards of a lengthy trip into a country that was far from tranquil. The last consideration would not have kept us from going under ordinary circumstances. Neither John nor I were averse to taking chances, or easily frightened. However, this planned trip was to be a vacation and pleasure excursion for both of us, and we decided not to court needlessly the dangers inherent in a Mexican tour.

"After you have been on our trip for a few weeks," I told the impatient John, "you will agree with me that there is plenty to see in the good old U.S.A., and particularly in this part of Uncle Sam's domain! Let us save Mexico for another time, and take a look-see at our own country first!"

Four days after he got off the Santa Fe local at Thoreau, John rode at the rear of our pack train, arrayed in regulation cowpuncher's outfit, boots, spurs, chaps, tall-crowned Stetson, gun, everything. He had already acquired the knack of guiding his mount by neck-reining, been initiated into the mysteries of the diamond hitch, knew how to approach range-bred riding and pack animals, and could sit his horse without betraying the fact that he was more accustomed to walking the slanting deck of a heaving windjammer.

Childress, Harris, and others interested in our proposed undertaking, had offered pertinent advice about trails to follow, the location of water and feed, ranches we would encounter during the first week or ten days, and other facts that were of value or special interest. The discussions, in which everybody on the Childress ranch participated, ended in our decision to strike out in a southwesterly direction, which was to bring us toward the southeasterly corner of the territory of Arizona.

The first part of our route would take us over the Zuni Mountains into the Apache country to the south, then through the Datil and Mogollon ranges and the Pinos Altos Mountains to Silver City. Thence, we planned to follow the roads and trails by way of Lordsburg and the Chiricahua Mountains to Tombstone.

From that old mining town, in its heyday a veritable volcano of activity, we intended riding in a northwesterly direction, visiting, successively, Tucson, Phoenix, Prescott, and, continuing almost due north by Williams, hoped to reach the Grand Canyon. Then, after leaving the Grand Canyon, we would swing eastward and proceed on our tour by way of Flagstaff, completing the big circle by winding up in the Navajo and Hopi reservations.

All our plans were, of necessity, tentative only. We knew that any number of conditions and circumstances might force us to deviate from the itinerary laid down in the rather ambitious program. Too, we had to reckon with the seasonal changes, especially after returning to the northern regions of Arizona, where fall and winter set in early. Those bridges we meant to cross when we came to them; for the moment our plans were made, and only unavoidable obstacles would or should affect the carrying out of the projected trip.

The horses and mules were in fine condition, and we

had no doubt but that we could keep them so, as by far the greater portion of our route would take us through regions well watered and promising abundant feed. The mules carried light loads, consisting mainly of our camping equipment and personal effects. There was no need for taking heavy packs, as the route we meant to travel would offer many chances for replenishing our stock of staple food items and grain for the animals. Anyhow, this was not a forced march but a pleasure trip. We were going to be satisfied with making slow progress. Thus we could take good care of the animals, and the leisurely pace would afford John and me abundant opportunities to admire the beauties and interesting scenes of the country to be traversed.

Without encountering any difficulties or hardships, we carried into effect the first part of our program in accordance with the schedule that had been fixed at the beginning of the tour. Through the glorious forests that opened before us, soon after leaving Thoreau, we continued day after day, penetrating into the very heart of the Apache Indian country.

Water and feed we found in abundance, and in numerous places we took advantage of the hospitality proffered by ranchers and lumbermen. Our trip was progressing as smoothly as the unwinding of a reel, and not only John and I, but the stock, too, enjoyed every day. The horses and mules fairly reveled in the lush feed of the mountain meadows that must have seemed heavenly to them after the dryness of the desert we had left behind.

It was interesting to note the dissimilar mode of living between the Indians of the southern part of the country, principally Apaches, and those of the more northern regions, like Navajos and Hopis. Here they lived in crude wigwams, shelters constructed entirely different from the hogans of the Navajos or the pueblo homes of the Hopis. They clothed themselves in a distinct manner, affected another style of hairdress, spoke their own language, and seemed altogether a race apart, although of the same original stock as the Navajos. The Apaches appeared greasy and unkempt in comparison with the Navajos, but, possibly, I was prejudiced. In any event, they did not carry themselves as proudly and independently as the friends I had made and learned to respect while in Chaco Canyon.

Between the Zuni Mountains and the Pinos Altos Range, near Silver City, we skirted the bases of scores of tall peaks, rising from eight to ten thousand feet toward the skies. The scenery held us enthralled. John, who had never before seen the southwestern part of the United States, exhausted the superlatives during the first week of our ride. After that he was dumb, overcome by the wonders he saw.

He was ready to concede the correctness of my prediction that he would not hanker for any Mexican excursion after getting well started on our tour through that part of New Mexico and Arizona. I did not tell him that I was saving the visit to the Grand Canyon for the tail end of our long trek; that was to be the *pièce de résistance* of the thousands of scenic marvels we would encounter.

In Silver City our horses and mules were taken care of by a blacksmith. Several of the animals had cast shoes, due to the rough traveling over that part of our route where we had to cross lava beds and rocky ground. We knew that we could not avoid additional stretches of difficult going before reaching Tombstone, and meant to be prepared for them. The camp outfit, too, required attention. We needed a few new tie ropes, and our supply of flour, bacon, coffee, and sugar was low. To make sure that we would not overlook anything, we established camp in the outskirts of Silver City and spent three days checking and rechecking supplies, equipment, ammunition, and other items.

Through the Burro Mountains we continued our trek, and soon after Lordsburg had been left in our rear, entered Arizona, moving into a country entirely different from that of the Hopis and Navajos, the Lukachukais and Canyon de Chelly. It was still the land of immense distances, of flawless skies and incomparable vistas, yet altogether unlike the northern part of the territory.

The air was milder, due to the more southern latitude and the generally lower altitude. The vegetation, too, had changed. The scrubby pinons and dwarfed cedars had made way for an innumerable variety of trees, shrubs, and bushes that possessed one thing in common: all were prickly leafed if not downright thorny. Cacti of scores of species flourished, growing in fantastic and tortured shapes. Air currents caused fine sand and dust to whirl sky high, and heat waves shimmered over the endless plains and produced most realistic mirages.

In the dim distances to the south could be seen the peaks of the bald ranges that cross Chihuahua. Those, as well as the mighty mountain barriers closer at hand, presented a barren, desolate appearance. They thrust their bulk upward out of the seemingly limitless expanse of flat prairie land like so much rock, lava, and slag piled on high. The Almighty plowed some tremendous furrows when He created those ranges!

In color, the hills and cliffs showed every variation from light gray to nearly black. Some were slate colored, others a rosy tan, and still another one would present a greenish tint that resembled cloudy jade.

John and I, with our horses and pack train in fine shape, arrived in Tombstone. For both of us it marked the first visit to a "ghost city," and our impressions of the place were not particularly favorable. True, we knew that this had been the setting for some memorable occurrences, but the stark reality of deserted and abandoned shacks and houses, nearly obliterated corrals and stables, closed-down mines and dead shafts, and the general air of decay and dissolution were hardly conducive to re-creating the atmosphere of wild Western romance.

Nevertheless, almost everything that had been told, or was in future to be said about Tombstone, was based upon fact.

One could write a book of a thousand pages about Tombstone and not begin to exhaust the material. We haven't any spots in this country where things happened consistently, for hundreds of years on end, as, for example, in London, but to offset that we have places where in a short period of time more real history was enacted than took place elsewhere in a century. It may not come amiss to tell just a few things about this Arizona town which John and I were visiting, and, first of all, how Tombstone happened to spring into existence.

The enormously rich silver fields that led to the founding of Tombstone were discovered virtually by accident. Ed Schieffelin, a civilian scout who accompanied a flying column of troopers during the campaigns waged against the marauding and murderous Apaches, stumbled onto the wealth that literally split the ground to the very surface. This happened in 1877.

Cattlemen undoubtedly resented the invasion of what they had come to consider their own private territory by prospectors, miners, settlers, and others who interfered with their accustomed, particular ways of living. However, the news of the strike traveled with the speed of wildfire, fast, irresistible. From every section of the country flocked the eager hunters after fortune. They were augmented by the horde of gamblers, saloonkeepers, desperados, prostitutes, and the plain riffraff that constitutes an inevitable contingent in every mining town's boom days.

They came by ox wagon and mule team, others used pack trains or rode horseback, some walked every foot of the bitter trail. Yuma was the the terminus of the railroad approaching the location of the sensational strike from the west; in the east, steel had been laid as far as Deming. The intervening hundreds of miles between those two points and Tombstone were a veritable hell to cross, what with a lack of passable roads, a scarcity of water, savage attacks by the Indians, the terrors of the burning desert and the biting cold of the high mountain passes. Many of the adventurers died in the rush for El Dorado; their bleaching bones became trail markers.

The discovery of whole mountains actually bursting with silver wrought a transformation that was all but incredible. Barren mesa lands, naked hills, and cactus-covered desert became the site of Arizona's largest town almost overnight. Although situated in the isolation of a wilderness of badlands, it enjoyed all the amenities of civilization that riches could purchase. Paradoxically, it was a wild and woolly cattle country that gave birth to the queen of mining camps. The entire region was hardly more than a barren desert, yet, within two years after the initial discovery of silver, Tombstone had grown to be a good-sized town, boasting between 12,000 and 15,000 inhabitants. Phoenix, at the same time, had a population of a mere 1,800.

The Tombstone mines produced silver ore assaying

$15,000 to $20,000 a ton! Schieffelin, who had formed a partnership with his brother Al and a man named Richard Gird, staked out several claims. All those parcels of ground developed into enormous producers.

The three partners sold one claim, the Contention, for $10,000; the new owners got *millions* out of it. The two Schieffelins disposed of their interest in the Tough Nut mines for a million dollars; later, Gird sold his third share for an equal amount. The three partners let go of a half-interest in the Lucky Cuss, but the other half-share in the mine, retained by them, provided a steady stream of wealth for the fortunate men over a number of years.

By the end of 1879 one Wyatt Earp had arrived in Tombstone, wearing the badge of a United States deputy marshal. Tombstone had its man for breakfast every morning, according to the boastful legend, but there were many who desired law enforcement and a curb upon the wanton killings. The better or more responsible element was fed up and disgusted with the cold-blooded, ruthless ways adopted by the high and mighty factions of organized outlawry that were then giving Arizona the unenviable reputation of being the wildest, toughest, and most lawless territory in the United States.

The heads of the unruly mob included the Clanton gang, the McLowerys, Curly Bill, and Pony Deal, but there were, in addition, a number of others who openly asserted their belief and conviction in the adage "Might makes right!"

Acknowledged killers hobnobbed with the sheriff and his deputies; stagecoach robbers operated so frequently and openly that they came to be known by their voices. Cattle thieves and holdup men and crooked gamblers stood elbow to elbow with bankers and merchants, patronizing the same bars.

Into this atmosphere came imperturbable Wyatt Earp,
assisted by his brothers Virgil, Morgan, James, and War-
ren. The quintet's right-hand bower was "Doc" Holliday,
a consumptive dentist who had given up practicing his
profession for the, to him, more entertaining and enjoyable pursuits of gambling and killing. He left behind him
a reputation of having been the top-notch performer
among the assembly of remorseless killers and experts
with the six-shooter that made life interesting, if uncertain, in the Tombstone of silver-boom days.

Wyatt Earp's term of office lasted during his entire stay
in Tombstone. It was marked by the relentless Earp-
Clanton feud that had its flaming climax in the battle
of the O. K. Corral. This queer warfare witnessed some
unusual alliances on both sides. The faction of law and
order, personified by Wyatt Earp, gained the allegiance
of various characters that would anywhere be classified as
decidedly "shady," while the notorious outlaw machine
of the Clantons, desperados of the worst type and ruthless
killers, was consistently shielded and even openly supported by Sheriff "Johnny" Behan.

Historians will probably decide that this sharp division
and paradoxical line-up was brought about through political aspirations, charges, and countermoves of the two
principal actors. Earp had declared to run for sheriff in
opposition to Behan, and the latter, an astute politician,
experienced no qualms about enlisting his adherents and
securing their votes where he could find them. Behan was
of the type that would approve gleefully of a postmaster-
general acting as distributing agent for millions of dollars extracted from the Federal treasury for the thinly
disguised purpose of swinging votes. He believed firmly
in the concept that the end justifies the means.

Despite the bitter and unyielding feud, the two main

actors in the bloody warfare, Earp as well as Behan, came
to their end in a peaceful manner. All about them men
were cut down in their prime; the song of the six-shooter
was the leitmotiv. But Wyatt Earp closed his earthly
career at a ripe old age in his home in Southern California, while Behan, after having served in various political
offices, died in Tucson in 1912.

Old-timers related to me stories of the fights and battles
that produced the daily drama of Tombstone. They told
of personal encounters with the Earps, Sheriff Behan,
some of the Clanton boys and Old Man Clanton, of meeting "Doc" Holliday, the McLowerys, Buckskin Frank,
John Ringo, and others. One of my friends spoke of
Sheriff Bat Masterson, he of Dodge City fame. None
dramatized the men he spoke of, or the turbulent times
in which those characters played major roles upon their
particular stages.

"Yes, Wyatt Earp sure was one fellow that was not afraid
of man or devil," would be the comment. Or, said another, "that there 'Doc' Holliday was faster with his gun
than any other man I ever saw," in genuine admiration of
a real gun fighter. But none eulogized, nobody waxed
dramatic or resorted to superlatives. Simply, and without
emotion, they described occurrences and people that had
been a part of the daily life, exciting for the moment, but
not extraordinarily out of the common, or unexpected.

Possibly the ones telling the tales lacked proper appreciation; retrospectively it is, quite likely, easier to establish true values or to obtain a more accurate viewpoint.
The fact remains that the narrators did *not* make heroes
or gallant gentlemen of those tough *hombres* and killers
who in later years were to furnish material for many
lurid stories foisted upon an unknowing and gullible
public.

To those eyewitnesses of gun fights, holdups, gaming and whoring scenes, saloon brawls and rowdy bagnio and dance-hall mix-ups, there was nothing dashing or audacious in the manner of their contemporaries. All they admitted and thought worth remembering was the facility with which some bad man could get into action "He sure was handy with a gun!"

Wyatt Earp was, unquestionably, the outstanding figure of the time and place, and several writers have made more or less successful attempts to depict the man and his life. They made generous use of such facts as were furnished by old files, public documents, the tales of old-timers, the editorials and reports of the newspapers of the period, and other sources of information. For the rest, they allowed their imaginations free rein. That they dramatized and embellished their tales was probably inevitable, only human—and therefore, excusable. Even authors keep an eye cocked to the interest their product will evoke in hoped-for readers. Storytelling is but a business, and must earn bread and butter for the writer.

That at least some of the narrators were not altogether careful in stating nothing but the truth can be gleaned from the following item, taken from the Bisbee *Daily Review*, February 21, 1937 which I quote verbatim:

MRS. WYATT EARP VISITS TOMBSTONE

Tombstone, Feb. 20 (AP) Mrs. Wyatt Earp, widow of the famous pioneer peace officer, visited Tombstone today where her husband as town marshall kept law and order during the silver boom days of the 80's.

Mrs. Earp, modest and soft-spoken, said she had fought writers, publishing companies and film concerns in an effort to establish the truth about her famous husband's career.

Mrs. Earp's indignation is probably the best indication that many of the stories written, and purporting to be true accounts of the old Tombstone days, are overdrawn, if not deliberately falsified for the sake of creating a still greater luridness.

One peculiar circumstance that gives food for thought may be found in the fact that *two* bonds were filed by Virgil Earp, brother of Wyatt, upon his appointment as chief of police in Tombstone.

The old records contain both of those documents, and it appears that the first bond, dated June 24, 1881, in which Wyatt Earp assumes surety for one thousand dollars of the total amount of five thousand dollars, was never accepted by the city. The second bond, dated June 29, 1881, and July 2, 1881, respectively, shows two other bondsmen, J. M. Vizina and C. R. Brown. According to the stamps and endorsement, this, the second bond, was accepted.

Whether some petty political jealousies or personal chicaneries were involved, or whether the first bond was rejected merely because it happened to be at variance with exact legal requirements, may never be known. Apparently, the first bond was kept because it also contained the oath of office, sworn to by Virgil Earp. In the second bond, the oath is missing, and presumably the later instrument was accepted only for its indemnity value to the city of Tombstone.

Chinamen were employed by a number of mines in the old Tombstone days. The resurrected pay roll of the Compromise Mine lists six Celestials and three white men. The standard rate of wages for Chinamen appears to have been $1.50 a day, regardless of occupation, if we accept this old time sheet as a criterion. The mine superintendent received the munificent salary of one hundred dollars monthly, while the mine engineer was paid $2.50 a day. One of the miners, James Harris, toiled for three dollars daily. Everyone's pay was computed by the number of days actually worked, except the superintendent's remuneration, which seems to have been fixed on a monthly basis.

An interesting thing to come to light is the fact that the Chinese cook, Ah Gin, contrived to put in thirty-five working days during the month of October, 1885. I am unable to decide whether to call this an example of brazen pay-roll padding, or to consider it merely a clerical error.

What a splendid field modern agitators and sit-downers would have found in the mines as they were operated in and about the Tombstone of those days! The wage scale, with its obvious discrimination, would have furnished all the excuse necessary to begin unionizing, to resort to strikes, tieups, sympathetic walkouts, violence, intimidation, and all the other unlovely demonstrations that mark labor troubles at this time, especially when scientifically and expertly handled and staged by professional labor leaders (!) and organizers.

However, that was more than sixty years ago, and at that time the scum of Europe and Australia had not yet migrated to the United States, and self-appointed *leaders* hailing from abroad had not taken control of the workers' destinies in American mines and industries. In any event, if only a small portion of the reports concerning the old hard-rock miners of that era is founded upon facts, then the Australians, Russians, and other foreign agitators of our days would have met with an uncomfortably short shrift in Tombstone.

As for strikers through the "sit-down" taking possession of other men's mines, claims, or other property, well, that idea would have been both preposterous and suicidal.

Any attempt at such procedure could have had only one result: an immediate addition to the occupants of Boot Hill, Tombstone's official burial ground.

Sic transit gloria mundi might well be written under the name Tombstone. The lights that blazed in the gaudy saloons and gaming houses of the boom days have been extinguished these many years. Tea, yes, tea, is being served in the Bird Cage Theater of unholy renown! The *Epitaph*, whose news columns and editorials chronicled in vivid fashion the happenings of the hectic days of the feud, is still being published. But no longer does it contain reports of the nature that used to make men run for their horses and guns, that caused the clans to gather, and that made the entire territory of Arizona sit up and take notice.

A large, wooden billboard has been erected at the edge of town, overlooking the site of Boot Hill, the graveyard. This sign welcomes the traveler, tourist, and sightseer to Tombstone. On it are reported the names of those whose remains lie buried in Boot Hill. Of five men it states, with unconscious naïveté, that they were hanged "legally"—a nice distinction.

The highway connecting Tucson with Douglas and beyond to El Paso, or, leaving town at the other end, with Phoenix, traverses Tombstone in a straight line, a matter of some few blocks of disintegrating and dilapidated adobe buildings. The few remaining inhabitants bask in the reflected glory or notoriety of the hardy characters that strutted the stage more than half a century ago.

A not-too-alert clerk in the corner drugstore sells postcards and photographs, depicting the locations that were the scenes where history was written in glamor, heroism, hardship, privation, and blood. From all around the spot that was once the most notorious mining camp of the

Southwest, the hills look down upon the confined area where excitement ran high. Those hills witnessed the rise and fall of a Tombstone of unceasing activity, hectic excitements, and virile, if raw, life. Now they guard the somnolent town that is not even the shadow of its earlier and lustier self.

Chapter 21

ARIZONA

Well over four hundred years ago, long before the landing of the Pilgrims on Plymouth Rock marked a common milestone in American history, the first white men visited what we know now as Arizona. Historians still quabble over the question as to whom belongs the honor of actually having been the very first. It is so long ago, and of such relatively small importance, that one hardly need worry over the point.

Just as happened in New Mexico, the newcomers were Spaniards, and there is abundant proof that in those days they were a much more progressive and aggressive race than are their present-day colonial descendants, most of whom seem to be afflicted with the hookworm habit of *manana*.

Those hardy adventurers of the sixteenth century, whether knights and soldiers, mariners, traders, or friars, must have been possessed of wonderful endurance and matchless courage. They started their search from Florida, looking for golden cities, vast domains sheeted with precious metals, fabled realms and other fantastic goals. Suffering every conceivable setback, their protracted

voyages along the coasts and their weary journeys overland were one unbroken chain of privations, hardships,
and disasters. Some trailed through the country that was
later to become Texas and New Mexico, others reached
Arizona by way of Mexico, entering the waterless wastes
through blistering Sonora and Chihuahua.

They came buoyed with the hope of repaying themselves for the dangers encountered and the privations endured in a country where even the cooking utensils of the
natives were made of silver and gold. Hadn't Fray Marcos
de Niza, who started on a tour in March, 1539, accompanied by Friar Onorato, reported back to Mexico City
that "they (the natives) use vessels of gold and silver, for
they have no other metal, whereof there is greater use and
more abundant than in Peru!"

The glowing expectations of the adventurous pioneers
were destined to be dashed to the ground; the Pueblo
Indians, and others whom they encountered, possessed
neither yellow gold nor shining silver. The fabled Seven
Cities of Cibola were, in reality, plain, unimportant
pueblos, containing no golden or silver dishes, and the
streets were not surfaced with precious metals, as had been
reported. There was untold wealth slumbering in the
ground beneath their feet, but of that the Spaniards had
no actual knowledge.

According to the reports made by the various missionaries, and practicularly by the Jesuit fathers who were
active in the country, it was not until about the middle of
the seventeenth century that mining had a small beginning in Arizona. But that was more than a hundred years
after the undaunted, even though sorely disappointed,
first adventurers and discoverers plodded wearily over the
tremendous expanses of desert and towering ranges in
their hunt for the imagined mines of the natives. How

were the proud cavaliers, the common soldiers, and the zealous friars to know that in the course of time hundreds of millions of dollars' worth of gold, silver, and copper would be taken from the many mines which later comers opened up and developed?

No matter where one goes in our wonderful Southwest, the Spaniards were there long ago. Even the Grand Canyon, so far from the colonies in Mexico and undoubtedly nearly inaccessible at that period, had for its first white visitors a group of Spanish gentlemen. This band consisted of Don Garcia Lopez de Cardenas who, with twelve cavaliers, and guided by Hopi Indians, came to the magnificent gash in 1540.

Father Time chalked off many decades before seeing the first American whites arrive in Arizona. It was in 1824, only a few years over a century ago, when trappers and hunters explored the Gila, Salt, Colorado, and other rivers. They reported that, in favorable sections, they had found many beavers, and a variety and abundance of game virtually everywhere.

Hunting, trapping, exploring, mining and stock raising, or any form of agriculture, were hazardous undertakings in the territory until even beyond the middle of the last century. The foremost danger, almost impossible to guard against, was the bloodthirsty Apaches with whom plundering, raiding, torturing, and killing were part of the routine of life.

One of the most notorious of Indian chiefs, perhaps the worst of the lot, who delighted in the most inhuman and abominable atrocities, was Geronimo. Eventually his reign of terror was brought to an end; he became a prisoner of Uncle Sam's troops, but instead of shooting or hanging the monster out of hand, an addlepated government pensioned him, kept him in comfort for the rest of his life, and even paraded him in Washington and other places for the delectation of gawking crowds. What a parody on justice!

In the year 1846 General Kearny marched to California, traversing parts of present-day New Mexico and Arizona. Kit Carson, one of the ablest scouts and pathfinders of the West, guided the column. Kearny's force, including the Mormon Battalion, left Council Bluffs, Iowa, on July 20, 1846. It reached Santa Fe on October 9 of the same year, and after incredible hardships and sufferings arrived at San Diego Mission in California on January 27, 1847.

Over half a year was spent to accomplish the march; today, almost any automobile can cover the same distance within a few days.

Less than ten years after the memorable performance of General Kearny and his troops, James Gadsden, then United States Minister to Mexico, arranged for the purchase from that country of a large strip of land, now forming a part of Arizona and New Mexico, for the sum of ten million dollars. If the United States had increased the ante to twenty-five million dollars, we could have bought not only what we have within our borders today, but also the greater part of the present Mexican states of Sonora and Chihuahua, *with Lower California in its entirety thrown in!*

What a bargain that would have been, considering the tremendous natural resources of those vast territories with their timberlands, their mineral wealth, the untouched, rich agricultural sections, the important outlets on the Gulf of California, plus the unimaginable possibilities represented by, and lying dormant in the whole of Lower California, as yet not even partially classified and catalogued.

It is not likely that the chance we passed up at that time will ever again present itself.

The land acquired by the Gadsden Purchase became part of New Mexico Territory on August 4, 1854, making the already extensive area even more cumbersome.

One of the amusing incidents connected with the history of Arizona occurred in 1856 when the War Department decided to inaugurate a camel service. It had been reasoned that the "ships of the desert" would solve the problem of transportation and communication in the arid wastes of the vast territory. Consequently two army officers, Major Wayne and Lieutenant Porter, were commissioned to purchase a number of those Arabian and Bactrian beasts. The two men traveled to Asia Minor and bought the camels in Smyrna. The strange brutes were shipped to Arizona and put into service, but the venture proved to be as much of a comedy, although decidedly less expensive and not nearly so burdensome to the taxpayers, as more recent Washington experiments and alphabetical bureaus.

President Abraham Lincoln approved the act making a political entity of Arizona on February 24, 1863. The boundaries of the new territory, fixed at that time, remain virtually unchanged to this day.

The new commonwealth had to be properly represented in Washington, of course, and so, on July 18, 1864, in the first election after Arizona's organization, C. D. Poston was chosen for the job. He polled 514 votes, his nearest competitor for office, Charles Leib, receiving but 224 endorsements.

The newly elected representative traveled by way of Panama to reach his post in the nation's capital. Upon his arrival in Washington he presented the handsome bill of seven thousand dollars for mileage, covering this one journey!

Delegate Poston made a speech in Congress in which he referred to the Hopi Indians as a people "supposed to be descendants of the Welsh prince Madoc, who sailed from Wales to the New World in the eleventh century." We don't know how much truth there was back of that supposition, but it is fairly safe to assume that no Welshman ever succeeded in talking with a Hopi by speaking his native tongue.

The Mormons, however, must have taken Poston's statement at face value, for it is a matter of record that they took with them a man able to converse in Welsh when they started a missionary party to the Hopis in after years. The Mormon expert failed to gain converts through his linguistic accomplishments; one may surmise that the Hopis were ignorant of the Welsh phase of their descent.

Governor McCormick, the first chief executive of the newly created territory, stated in his message to the third legislature that the Arizona treasury had the imposing balance of $249.50! Although burdened by so much wealth, he advised economy, thereby putting himself in a class apart from later administrators.

The seat of government changed location nine or ten times, switching from one town to another and back again, until in the late 1880's Phoenix became the capital of Arizona. Since then, there has been no change.

Licensed and unrestricted gambling, which had been one of the most flourishing "industries" of the territory from the time Americans first settled there, was officially abolished by an act of the legislature in 1907. We may take it for granted that this law was just as effective as the Prohibition Amendment that in later years transformed all Americans into teetotalers with one stroke of the pen.

President William Howard Taft signed the proclamation which made Arizona a state. This was on February 14, 1912. It is the youngest of the forty-eight members of Uncle Sam's family, but ranks fifth in size. Nearly 114,000 square miles of land are within the boundaries of the state, and only 146 square miles are water-covered. On that basis, Arizona is an arid country, indeed. California, for example, with some forty thousand square miles more of land, boasts nearly twenty times the water surface of Arizona. Other states are even more generously provided with the liquid element in the way of streams and lakes and other bodies of water.

Arizona altitudes present a remarkable variety. In the sections adjacent to Yuma, it is about 150 feet above sea level, while in the Grand Canyon region the average of the level rises to over seven thousand feet. A large number of peaks tower to heights of over ten thousand feet.

Here is a fact that will make you sit up and take notice: At the present time Arizona has more standing, merchantable timber than any other state in the Union, and within its borders can be found the largest virgin pine forest in the United States! In the forests of the Kaibab Plateau alone, stretching from the northern rim of the Grand Canyon toward Utah, are millions of trees, mostly firs, yellow pine, spruce, and birch.

This must come as a shock to many people who still consider Arizona nothing but "a vast desert." It should be one more argument in favor of "seeing America first."

There are a number of substantial coal deposits in different sections of the state. One of the largest of these, as yet unmined, lies in the Black Mesa region, mostly within the boundaries of the Moqui (Hopi) Indian reservation. Enormous quantities of black diamonds, billions upon billions of tons, are in Nature's storage for the time when America may require this additional source of heat and power. Tests and assays prove that the coal thus awaiting mining operations is of equal quality with that produced in Gallup, New Mexico.

Originally, approximately half of the seventy-five million acres that comprise Arizona were available for grazing purposes—quite a fair-sized pasture. Now the open range, except for much-diminished portions in the foothill country, is just about a thing of the past. Small and large farms and ranches cut up the country; barbed-wire fences crisscross what used to be free and unrestricted grazing land. Most of what is left of real range is now within the confines of national forest preserves carefully supervised and regulated by forest rangers who fix the amount of stock that may be grazed upon the public domain and levy the established charges for each head of stock so pastured.

Cotton has become an important crop in Arizona. Various growers, notably Dr. A. J. Chandler, experimented with the plants. From the best strains of Egyptian cotton was developed the so-called Pima variety, claimed to be the longest-stapled cotton in the world. Through a subsidiary, at least one of the principal tire manufacturers of the country grows large quantities of Pima cotton, utilizing the product in the making of fabrics for automobile tires.

Where longhorn steers used to roam, and bands of Indians prepared for attacks upon wagon trains, the farmer now raises lettuce, cantaloupes, citrus fruits, cotton, dates, wheat, oats, alfalfa, and other products. Several huge dams impound the waters that were wasted in former years, insuring abundant supplies for the needs of intensive irrigation.

Mining is still carried on extensively, but it lacks its former picturesque aspects—the Tombstones are a thing of the past. Bear in mind, however, that Arizona produces one half of the total output of copper in the United States, which is equal to one-fourth the quantity of the supply of the entire world. Gold, silver, and other precious metals continue to be brought from the bowels of the earth, although not in such sensational quantities as when Wyatt Earp packed his guns and tried to make rough men toe the mark.

There are more Indians in Arizona than in any other of the United States, except Oklahoma, and Uncle Sam's largest Indian school is located in Phoenix. But the red man has buried the tomahawk; no longer do the echoes ring to the blood-curdling war cries of the Apaches, and the white people's scalps are safe upon their heads.

Chapter 22

THE END OF ONE CAMPING TRIP

The Dragoons flanked our right and on our left marched the Whetstone Mountains as we rode toward the Rincon and Santa Catalina ranges. After leaving Tombstone John and I had decided to forego the visit to Tucson. Instead, we would ride in a slightly more northerly direction, heading for Superstition Mountain. From there we planned to branch sharply westward, thus reaching Phoenix. The few days spent in Silver City and Tombstone had given us all we wanted of civilization for the time being, and Tucson did not attract us like the ghost of the old mining town, where we had camped sufficiently long to see everything that proved of particular interest.

Traveling across country by pack train and horseback was more strenuous now; the water and feed conditions were not nearly as good as they had been during the first few weeks of our trip. In several instances, we were forced to make extra-long marches in order to reach water and grazing. In much of the country, and especially in the long valleys between mountain ranges, the vegetation was scorched and burnt by the terrific heat of the sun. The only plants that appeared to thrive in that blastfurnacelike desert were the numberless varieties of cacti and chaparral.

To overcome those handicaps which Nature herself had placed in our way, we routed our direction to follow as closely as possible the lay of the ranges, keeping to the more elevated levels of the foothills. In the higher altitudes we found more congenial temperatures and, of greater importance, better grazing and springs or small streams of cool water.

Despite the fact that we had covered a distance of hundreds of miles, the horses and mules were still in excellent condition. Not quite so fat and round as they had been at the time when we left the Childress ranch, it is true, but tougher, seasoned, and better able to withstand the harder demands we made upon them at this stage of the tour. Whenever there was a chance, we stopped with ranchers, paying for the hay and grain consumed by the stock. Not one of these hospitable fellows would accept reimbursement for the meals we enjoyed in the cookshacks or for the use of beds in the bunkhouses. When we reached one of those oases affording a break in the camp routine, we simply slipped the packs off the mules' backs and, instead of opening up, left the duffle just as it was.

John had become a hardened campaigner. The long rides under the broiling sun did not bother him; he bore whatever hardship the hike entailed with happy grins. My partner's longing to have some dry land under his feet after the half-year-long voyage around Cape Horn in a windjammer was being satisfied; at times, we had almost a bit too much "dry" land for comfort.

It turned out that John had a natural knack for cooking, so most of the honors of the culinary department were thrust upon him, while I busied myself, in the mornings and evenings, with taking care of the horses and mules. However, both of us shared the chores of cleaning up camp, washing dishes, getting firewood, and suchlike duties that are part of every camping tour.

Mount Lemmon, the high peak of the Santa Catalinas, rising upward to a height of about 9,200 feet, had long since disappeared in our rear, but we were still a good three days' ride from Superstition Mountain. The intervening space became the most uncomfortable distance we covered during our trek. Our animals suffered noticeably from lack of water, and by the afternoon of the third day, when we established camp in the shadow of the huge rock mass that is called Superstition Mountain, not only the saddle horses and pack mules, but the riders as well, were gaunt.

We camped in that spot two full days. Near by was the one-room stone-and-log cabin of a prospector, but he was the first and only man we encountered during the whole of our trip who was a bit stand-offish. We were not encroaching upon his water or grazing— his livestock consisted of an old Indian pony and a scarred, diminutive burro—but when we made what was intended to be a friendly, neighborly call in the evening, he was barely civil. His contribution to the conversation consisted of monosyllables, and it was obvious that even these were given grudgingly. Neither John nor I could account for the strange behavior of this chance acquaintance. Were we trespassing upon his own domain? Was he perhaps suspicious about our open declaration that we were traveling just for pleasure? Did he, by chance, guard a secret strike?

His cool reception did not induce another visit; John and I had no desire to call on the old fellow a second time. I felt sorry that we did not engender a more sympathetic mood in our neighbor, for nothing would have pleased me better than to pry some stories out of the man. His weather-beaten face, the long grey hair and beard, and those gnarled hands that showed plainly the bluish-black powder-explosion marks, all bespoke the real old-timer. the wanderer over the wastelands, the confirmed prospector and miner, who never loses the hope of finding the fabled mother lode. How often had he been led by a Fata Morgana, how many times had this desert hermit followed some *ignis fatuus* to its disillusioning reality?

In many previous encounters I had been successful in unloosening the tongues of uncommunicative, solitary men, but here I failed miserably. What a pity, I thought, not to be able to obtain at least part of the history of the aged prospector.

That section of the territory we found dotted with thousands upon thousands of saguaro, the huge cactus that grows twenty to thirty feet tall, generally in the forms of gigantic candelabra. The entire region between Tombstone and Superstition Mountain was one immense park of those striking plants, interspersed with dozens of other species of cacti.

Since leaving Tombstone, we had killed five rattlesnakes and two Gila monsters. Ordinarily, neither John nor I would kill any animal, bird, or reptile, and during the whole of our tour we had not shot any rabbit or deer except for food, although upon many occasions we could have done so with ease. But we would not have taken pleasure in killing just for "sport's" sake, and preferred to watch the graceful movements of the wild denizens of forests and plains without frightening them with gunshots. We even spared several mountain lions that crossed our paths, slinking away upon soft, padded feet.

At one time, one of those tawny felines watched our

procession from an overhanging sandstone ledge, not more than a dozen feet above the trail we happened to be following at the moment. He was so thoroughly blended into the background of tannish rock that only the twitching of his long tail betrayed the presence of the killer. I suggested to John that he pitch his rope at the cat when he should be abreast, just to make him jump, but he became so interested in the lazy beast, unperturbedly blinking through half-closed eyes at our train, that he rode past the animal before realizing that he had missed his chance.

Rattlesnakes, bull snakes, and a great variety of horned toads and bright-colored lizards slithered away in many places. As a rule, the rattler would give us a gentlemanly warning not to disturb him, and we respected his *noli me tangere*. Nor would we have killed those others, had it not been for the fact that they were uncomfortably close to our camp sites. To allow them to live might have resulted in injury to us or to the stock.

Fully recuperated from the wearying ride over the scorching flats, we struck out for Phoenix and experienced no difficulty in reaching the city. To give ourselves a change from camp chores, we placed the horses and mules in a feed corral, adjacent to a livery stable, and John and I treated ourselves to a few of the conveniences of civilization. These included a long overdue trip to the barbershop, the purchase of some shirts, socks, and overalls, restaurant meals and service, hot baths and real beds in the Adams Hotel.

Our funds were running low—the trip was costing more money that we anticipated while casting up figures on the Childress ranch. John carried an account with a San Francisco bank that also attended to other business for him, and he sent a letter to the institution, asking for a remittance. He gave instructions to forward the letter and check to Prescott, there to await our arrival. That proved to be the factor which eventually brought our wonderful trip to a sudden end, but, happily, we were unaware of that when John mailed his request for additional cash.

We had spent several days in Phoenix, reveling in the "fleshpots of Egypt," and it was not until fully two weeks later that we got to Prescott, the town which nestles among the pines, high up in the hills. The ride from Phoenix to Prescott took us through marvelously beautiful country, although we had difficulty keeping to the trail. There were, literally, hundreds of turns and twists and cutbacks that had us almost dizzy.

First the sun would be on our right, then on the left, now directly in front of us, blinding our vision, then, all of a sudden, shining upon our backs. Never before had we seen Phoebus behave so erratically.

Our camp was established near a lovely little lake within about three miles of Prescott. The stock showed its happiness over the tall, green grass and the abundance of water. Indeed, the change from the lower and hotter altitudes proved very agreeable to all of us, and we looked forward with zest to the final stages of the tour which were to bring us into still higher levels of country and correspondingly cooler atmospheres.

John had ridden into Prescott to make inquiry for mail at the post office. He expected the letter from the San Francisco bank with a draft or check, and intended converting the paper into cash. It was the middle of the afternoon, and I began to feel impatient, as he had left camp soon after breakfast. I thought that he should have returned hours ago, and yet there was no sign of him.

The sun had set and it was dusk when John and his

horse came into view. From the very attitude of my pal as he came riding toward camp, I sensed that something was amiss. Instead of shouting a happy greeting he rode into camp and dismounted without saying anything more than just a half-hearted hello. With every moment I was feeling more uneasy; an iron band seemed to be pressing upon my heart, leaving me squeamish. What could have happened to John?

His horse unsaddled and taken care of, John came to the place where we had spread the tarpaulins and arranged our beds. He sat down upon the blankets, sighing, deeply, and then told his story. His first words were: "Well, I shall have to leave you!" and then he continued with his explanations.

He had found the answer from the San Francisco bankers in the post office. It contained the money asked for, but also the sad and startling news that John's only brother had died suddenly, a victim to some tropical disease. The bankers, not having any idea where to locate him, had been trying in every possible way to find him, it was John's letter that gave the people in San Francisco the first inkling of his actual whereabouts. Charles, John's brother, had been established in business in Iquique, Chile. The dead man's affairs awaited settlement, and the letter of the California bank insisted that it was imperative for John to proceed immediately to South America, to take charge of the unfinished matters which were looked after jointly by the consular officials and the Iquique courts.

Charles had been a bachelor and was without a business partner, hence the job of winding up his business and private affairs could not be delegated to a widow, or children, or other relatives on the spot. The shocking news had caused John to spend virtually the whole day in Prescott, telegraphing back and forth in an attempt to arrange matters with the bank in such a manner as to allow a third party to take care of the Chilean affair. It turned out that this was not feasible. John must go in person, and he had been urged to make preparations to leave as quickly as possible.

We discussed the sudden change in the situation until the middle of the night, both of us stunned by the sad news which would mean, unavoidably, the breaking up of our trip. By the following morning, however, we were able to look at the bitter reality with more calm. While not at all reconciled to the blow, we conceded that it would be to the best interest of John to go to Chile and claim his brother's estate, Charles's will making him sole heir. We had discussed the chances of undertaking another trip on horseback after his return from South America, planning at that time to finish this one which was so unexpectedly interrupted; John felt cheated out of the best part of the tour as I had talked at length about the wonders of the Grand Canyon while riding to Prescott.

John left the next day. He had insisted upon me taking half of the money sent by the bank, and the entire camping outfit, as well as his horse and the mules. However, I did not care to continue the proposed trip alone. Consequently I disposed of most of the equipment during the following week, keeping only one pack mule, my personal effects, and my own horse. It was my intention to get back to the more familiar ranges of northern New Mexico, although I had decided against returning to Chaco Canyon.

It had been arranged between us that John and I would keep in close touch with each other, writing letters frequently, and thus not lose sight of one another. He had promised to send full directions before sailing, but I waited in vain for John's letters; I never heard from him or saw him again after he left our camp near Prescott. Whether he sailed from San Francisco almost immediately after reaching there, I was never able to ascertain. In fact, I am to this day in ignorance whether or not he got there at all.

John had not told me just which bank in San Francisco carried his account. When he mentioned the connection at all, he simply referred to "the bank in 'Frisco," instead of calling it by name. Today, I would know better how to handle matters of that sort; then, I was a youngster with but little business experience. In any event, the letters I sent to different San Francisco banks failed to bring any enlightenment, and no answer came to various letters that I addressed to him at Iquique. He should have reached the city by the Golden Gate about the eighteenth of October; exactly six months later San Francisco was destroyed by earthquake and fire.

My own plans, like those of Burns's men and mice, went agley. Instead of returning to my beloved ranges, I became a wanderer upon the face of the earth and over the seven seas, emulating Eugène Sue's famous Jew, and the Flying Dutchman. A number of years rolled by to join the unrecallable past before I again came to New Mexico and Arizona. By that time I had given up cowpunching and broncobusting, and turned to trading. For a while I lived in Albuquerque, engaged exclusively in buying and selling Navajo Indian blankets, but not long after I took over the management of a regular, full-fledged Indian trading post in Sanders, Arizona, discharging at the same time the duties of postmaster of that small settlement.

When the opportunity presented itself, I acquired the famous old Hubbell post in Keams Canyon, the same one I had seen and admired many years before when Bill Finn and I made the trip for Wetherill through that part of Arizona on our way to the Hopi Indian Snake Dance. My friends, the Navajos and Hopis, traded with me to such an extent that I prospered, and this enabled me, after several years, to branch out by building another trading post in the heart of the Navajo country, some twenty miles farther inland.

There, in Keams Canyon, surrounded by the beauty and serenity of the uncontaminated Indian domain, I spent nearly a decade as Indian trader, deputy sheriff, postmaster, and notary public.

Chapter 23

LIFE AT A TRADING POST

It was while a member of Wetherill's outfit that I cut my eyeteeth in the trading game. Barter meant the soul of existence for the boss; everybody on the ranch, of necessity, was involved in the acquisition of stock, wool, pelts, hides, and rugs. It followed inevitably that we should become lesser traders under Wetherill, than whom it would have been difficult to find a better-qualified mentor. He must have inherited the trading proclivities from his eastern home and forefathers, but at Pueblo Bonito, in the desert of Chaco Canyon, dealing with Indians, Mexicans, and Americans, those faculties came to full blossom.

He was a keen bargainer, a typical "Yankee horse trader," but always and painstakingly fair. He knew every trick of the trade, besides several others of his own invention. No use trying to hoodwink him— he knew the answers before the questions were put. Of course, he possessed intimate knowledge of values, but over and above that he was a master psychologist. That, perhaps, more than the actual trading knowledge and experience, was the reason for his success.

Under Wetherill's critical and scrutinizing tutelage, most of the boys evolved into more or less full-fledged traders, becoming proficient dealers, able to conclude transactions independently. The boss's criticisms helped to perfect each one's technique; his good-humored chaffing over some slip-up in the trade left lasting impressions. Mr. or Mrs. Navajo might get the better of the green trader in one or two deals, but after that they would probably find that the master had taken the neophyte in hand and imparted to him special knowledge to offset their wiles and cunning. Every trading transaction was a battle of wits, but none was allowed to have recourse to unfair means, to cheat, falsify weights, or in any other manner take advantage of the illiteracy of the Indian. Fair play was the rule of the game, and each deal had to leave a pleasant taste in the mouth of everybody concerned. The Indians were our hosts as lawful occupants of the reservation, they were our good neighbors, and we wanted them to be more than that; we desired their friendship!

Maybe it will not come amiss to quote what Dane Coolidge and Mary Roberts Coolidge, in their book, *The Navajo Indians*, have to say about the Indian trader. Let me quote from it:

The most important personage on the Navajo Reservation aside from Government authorities and Indian headmen, is the trader. Licensed by the Indian Bureau and strictly regulated in his dealings with the Indians of his district, he is a unique and influential man. A few traders are merely transients, either because they are unsuccessful in trade or because their wives cannot endure the hardships and isolation of the country; a larger number are about like other businessmen on the outside. But the majority are men of ability who have been in the country for years, whose fathers, perhaps, were among the first white men to settle there, who speak good trading Navajo, and who enjoy bargaining with their critical and whimsical customers.

For these Navajos have a very shrewd system of playing one trader off against another and, time and distance being of small account with them, they take pride in getting the better of a trader in a bargain. Some traders even acknowledge that many Indians have as good business sense as white men. If the Indian likes the trader's personality, and if he is known to pay fair prices and give fair credit, they will often take their products and livestock long distances, passing by the posts of traders in whom they have no confidence.

The trading-post serves the purpose of a local newspaper. Birth, marriage, divorce, the selling of livestock, the gossip of the white settlements, are matters of as much interest to the Indian as to the trader. Often the trader is called upon to bury some dead person whose superstitious family are afraid to touch the body. They call on him to bandage their wounds, and get from him their colic cure, liniment and eye-water, whatever simple drugs they need. If he is a friendly fellow with an interest in his clientele, he becomes their adviser, patching up family quarrels, persuading them to go to the hospital, or to invest their surplus in more sheep.

Nominally, his principal business is to sell groceries and merchandise—everything from candy to tools and dry goods— but, as there is no money circulating among the Indians, he must take his pay in sheep, wool and pelts, blankets and pinon nuts; and he must be prepared to take in pawn, on long time, thousands of dollars worth of jewelry, turquoise, silver and saddlery without interest. He does a heavy credit business.

The Government permits him to sell the pawn after six months, with proper notice, but the Indians do not like it if he does so. They may pay a little on account now and then, and the trader often holds a valuable necklace or belt for years until the owner dies or moves away. And rather than lose their goodwill, he will refuse to sell it to the tourist who would sometimes pay far more than its pawn value. The trader must hold it, not at its sale value, but according to how much he thinks the owner of his family will ultimately be willing to pay in trade to reclaim it.

Since the Government regulations permit him to buy sheep and wool only during two months of the fall and two in the spring, the Indians expect the trader to give them the necessities —groceries, flour, shoes, and dry goods—on credit for the six-months intervals, and he must judge in advance how much they are likely to be able to pay when the next settling time comes around.

To Government employees his cooperation and knowledge
are indispensable. An expert sent out to build a small dam for
Indian farmers generally speaks no Navajo, does not know what
Indians he can get to work, may not even know what the
sources of water are nor how much can probably be developed.
Inevitably he must depend on the trader for getting the cooperation of the Indians and frequently for interpreting his directions.
The trader must cash the Government order for wages, under
strict regulation, otherwise the Indians would have to wait at
least a month for their pay. And on the walls of every store are
posted up from time to time all Government decisions and regulations, couched in elaborate English, which he interprets to
Indians who read with more or less difficulty.

He must be strong, patient, good-humored, able to fight and
shoot straight; a social adviser to the Indians and an intermediary
with the Government. He must be both a good salesman and a
good buyer to make a profit; incidentally something of a
mechanic and handyman. But imperatively, he must please the
Indians. If they prosper, he prospers.

This is high praise. Some smart-alecky Indian agents
overburdened with the weight of their own importance
may not agree with it, but in the main it is a correct and
unbiased summary.

The trading post in Keams Canyon is one of the oldest
and best known in the entire Navajo country, dating its
establishment back to Kit Carson's time. Prior to my
taking over the place, it had had but two other owners—
I was the third proprietor and trader in that particular
store. Every Indian family within a radius of some two
hundred miles was acquainted with the Keams Canyon
trading post. Through successive generations of trading
Indians, it had become well and favorably known. The
accumulated good will of a large clientele was something
intangible, but very valuable.

I arrived at the post in the middle of winter, coming
from Gallup, New Mexico, by way of St. Michaels,

Ganado, and Steamboat Canyon, riding in a heavy-duty, open buckboard. The trip consumed two days, and in many places the road was obliterated by the snowdrifts. From Gallup to Ganado, it was fairly easy traveling, the road being kept open by the mail stages. After stopping overnight at Ganado, where Lorenzo Hubbell, Sr., was a gracious host, the trip was continued early in the morning, but instead of having just a two-horse team, the second stage of the journey was behind a doubled-up outfit, the buckboard now drawn by four horses.

Hubbell was mail contractor between Gallup and Keams Canyon, and furnished our conveyance and teams.

While mail between Ganado and Gallup moved every day, except Sunday, the stage came to Keams Canyon only twice weekly. That meant obscured roads should a snowstorm cover the trail between trips, and since the going was a harder job at the farther end of the route, extra horses were necessary.

Few passengers availed themselves of the stage service; generally, the buckboard arrived carrying only the Mexican driver and the mail pouches. However, the stage was important—it was the only link with the outside world, there being no telephone or telegraph, or other public means of communication.

The nearest railroad towns to Keams Canyon are, in the order of their importance, Gallup, New Mexico; Winslow, Arizona; and Holbrook, Arizona. At the time of my residence in Keams Canyon none was closer than approximately ninety miles. The distance has been shortened since then through the building of bridges, cutoffs, and other road improvements. In my time not even so much as a single culvert had been installed, and bridges were to be found only at the very outskirts of the town.

Toward evening of the second day we reached our destination. My wife and our young baby boy accompanied me on the trip, although I had tried to keep them in Gallup until the weather would be milder. But she, descendant of South Dakota pioneer stock, could not be persuaded, but insisted that I take her and the baby with me, winter or not. In the manner usual with wives, she won the argument.

Throughout the long day it had snowed intermittently, and a cold wind swept across the mesa lands. Occasionally, and for all too brief moments, we would enjoy the shelter of some dunelike rises, or have a bit of protection when crossing smaller canyons and arroyos. Then, for a few short minutes, we were out of the cutting breeze, but as soon as we got into the open again, the numbing cold penetrated the blankets and robes wrapped around us. Woolen scarfs left only the tips of noses exposed, storm boots and fur-lined gloves protected feet and hands. The baby was bundled up in soft pelt-lined robes and so many fleecy blankets that I was afraid the poor fellow might suffocate. Strangely enough, he did not seem to feel the discomforts of the trip at all, snuggled down in his cocoon-like nest, and waking only for his feeding times.

Fresh teams had been substituted at the stage station in Steamboat Canyon, where the four horses that had brought us from Ganado were left in the warm stable for a well deserved rest. The new teams struck out with a will when we started upon the last lap of our journey to Keams Canyon, but as the afternoon wore on, they tired from the exertion of breaking through the many breast-high snowdrifts that the wind had piled in our path. Several times during the last two hours of the trip we found ourselves straying away from the snow-obliterated trail, and had to grasp the headstall of one of the leading horses and pull the team back onto the almost invisible roadway. The heavy clouds, pregnant with as yet unshed snows, caused the murky darkness to bring evening early, and while it was not so very late by clock time, nevertheless, we seemed to be traveling in an almost impenetrable obscurity. The driver, my wife and I, were stiff from riding in the open, uncovered buckboard for so many hours, and, despite the heavy wrappings, we were numb from the cold.

Our driver was a Navajo, taking the place of the regular stage driver, a Mexican, who had fallen ill. He was a stranger to this region, having come from the neighborhood of Shiprock, New Mexico. This was his first wagon trip over the trail between Steamboat Canyon and Keams Canyon and his unfamiliarity with the road became more evident with each succeeding mile. The directions he had received at the stage station covered only the main points, and, apparently, he had already forgotten them by the time we were out of sight of the relay station. He knew the general direction in which we were to travel, and if he had been on horseback would have been able to make a much better job of it, but the only thing that kept us from getting lost was the absence of any other road. Since there was no choice, all we had to do was to follow the road indicated, provided we could see it. We did not have to worry over losing the *right* road—our trouble was to hold onto the *only* one there was.

I tried to engage the driver in conversation, but failed to get more than a "yes" or a "no" to some half-dozen questions, after which I left him to the solitude of his thoughts. Strangely, I never saw the man again after he left Keams Canyon on the return trip to Steamboat Canyon—a rarity in the Indian country where the natives travel without letup and where everybody is engaged in making the rounds of trading posts, sings, dances, and similar gatherings.

A slight bend in the road prevented us from seeing the lights which could have told us that we had about reached the goal. The trader's residence was upon a knoll and some fifty feet to the upper side of the trail, and the trading post itself on the opposite side of a depression, hence we did not realize that we had arrived until we were practically upon the very doorsteps of the store. Our driver's shout brought several men to the door, and when that swung wide and let out a bright stream of light, we began untangling ourselves from the robes and blankets wound about us. Cold-stiffened fingers made that a difficult job, but there were willing hands to assist us.

We were pretty well frozen, a tired and hungry lot by the time the stage pulled up in front of the Keams Canyon trading post. However, once being assisted from the buckboard, and supported for a moment or two to allow the numbed bodies to regain their own abilities, we thawed out quickly. One of the store clerks led the way to the residence. There, a Hopi girl, who was both cook and housekeeper, showed us to a bedroom. It boasted a fireplace, with a fire already laid and waiting the touch of a match. In a short while the flames dispersed the refrigerator-like chill of the unused room and spread welcome warmth.

Lorenzo Hubbell, Jr., the trader, had remained at the store to take care of the unloading of the mail and our baggage, assisted in that by one of the clerks and his bookkeeper, Elias Armijo. The Indian driver, and, of course, the teams, were looked after and properly provided for. Then Mr. Hubbell joined us at the residence to make sure that we were comfortable. By then, thoroughly thawed out, and after putting the baby to bed, we were ready to enjoy a hot supper prepared by the young Hopi woman. Soon after having refreshed ourselves, we retired to our bedroom and a much-needed and most welcome rest.

The general terms and conditions of the sale of the trading post had been agreed upon in Gallup some weeks previous to our coming, but the evaluation of the stock on hand was, of necessity, postponed until our arrival. With that work, Mr. Hubbell and I started early the following morning, and for two days we continued listing the amounts of goods in the store, basement cellar, in the warehouse and adjacent storage spaces. Then the completed inventory had to be priced and figured, which required an additional two days. After that was done, we spent another day arranging the matter of several thousands of dollars' worth of Indian pawns. Between the various matters to be attended to, it took nearly a week in which to complete the business of turning over the post and residence with all stocks and other possessions.

While I was familiar with the usual assortment of trade items to be found in trading posts, I was dumfounded when confronted by Mr. Hubbell's stock of Hopi Indian pottery. He had stored the accumulation of years of trading in a long, shedlike room, putting the pieces as he received them into cases of every shape and size, and when he showed me this immense quantity of pottery there were at least thirty or more large containers filled to the very top. He had taken large dry-goods packing cases and used them to store away the pottery. From the floor to the roof of the room, every square foot of space was occupied, leaving just enough room to walk.

There must have been tens of thousands of pieces in that lot— I never learned the exact amount. In size and shape they ranged from small pieces of finger-bowl shape to large ollas; others resembled punch bowls and urns,

and many pieces were of tall vaselike appearance. Several
large cases were filled completely with shallow, platelike
plaques. For many I could not find a suitable description;
Mark Twain might have classified them as Etruscan tear
jugs. All were decorated by hand with the characteristic
Hopi designs; many were real showpieces, and of decided
artistic value. But what to do with a stock of that size, in
a place remote from the railroad, without any regular
tourist trade or other means of selling the stuff? It would
have been a wearisome job just to count the lot, or to
segregate the mass into respective cost values and appraise
the accumulation in its entirety.

Hubbell, who was moving to a new location, some forty
miles away from Keams Canyon, did not relish the
prospect of carting the fragile pottery over badly rutted
winter roads and then cluttering up his new post with it.

That was quite evident, and helped to bring about his
resolve to turn the whole lot over to me at a round sum,
a nominal valuation of just a few hundred dollars for all
of it. To that offer I agreed, figuring that I should surely
be able to turn the pottery at a profit, even if some time
might be required to do so.

In that I was not mistaken, as each year at Snake Dance
time, the visitors from the outside world would pick up
dozens of pieces, to take with them as mementos of their
trip to the Hopi Indians. Throughout the year a steady
sale disposed of single pieces, or just a few at a time, to
tourists, salesmen, government employees, and others.
The biggest sale of pottery, however, was made to B.
Altman & Co., New York, whose vice-president came to
Keams Canyon one day and bought three thousand
assorted pieces, all sizes, leaving the selection to me. That
one transaction netted me twice the original cost of the

entire stock, and still left thousands of pieces of pottery in my possession.

Eventually, the work of inventorying was accomplished, the figuring completed, and the final papers signed. Mr. Hubbell, accompanied by Elias, the bookkeeper, and another one of his clerks, left for the Hopi pueblo of Oraibi, where he meant to continue in his trading activities, and I was, at last, in full possession of Keams Canyon, one of the best-known and most influential Indian trading posts in the country.

Many Indians had flocked to Keams Canyon while we were engaged with the work of making the transfer of ownership—all were curious to see what was going on, to take a look at the prospective new owner, and to learn about the disposition of their valuables, left as pawn in the past. Hubbell introduced us to each other, bespeaking their continued patronage for the newcomer and assuring them that their silver, buckskins, beads, and other pledged items were in safe hands and would not be sold by me, but guarded carefully until such time as they could redeem them.

That same guaranty was given the Indian agent, to whom I was introduced, and who had already been approached by several Indians who were uneasy over the possibility of losing their family jewelry and other valuables among the pawned articles.

I was owner of a large stock of Indian trade goods and other miscellaneous merchandise, as well as furniture, fixtures, and similar equipment, and in possession of a well-established trading post, but not, as yet, a trader! And until such time as my application for a trader's license was granted by the Indian Bureau in Washington, I was not permitted, legally, to engage in actual trading with the Indians. This had been foreseen by Hubbell and me, and to remedy that situation, Hubbell left one of his licensed clerks with me to carry on the trading activities until I, myself, should be granted the required license from Washington.

A complete history of my background accompanied my license-application form, also references and recommendations from private and professional friends and acquaintances. Too, there were letters from wholesalers and banks, attesting my business integrity and financial responsibility. All those, with the character references and sworn affidavits, went to the Indian Bureau, with a lengthy statement from the agent in charge of the reservation explaining the details of change of ownership proposed for the Keams Canyon trading post.

None of this had been necessary in Chaco Canyon, where Wetherill traded, or in Sanders, Arizona, where my trading post was just outside the Indian reservation boundaries. But here, in Keams Canyon, I must comply with all the requirements of the Indian Bureau, and was under the strict supervision of the Indian agent in charge of the reservation.

The chief clerk of the agency had informed me of the almost unlimited power of the Indian agent, how he could, at will, make or break any trader, how important it was at all times to observe to the letter every regulation and directive issued by the Indian Bureau's representative. He gave the impression of being awed by this virtually absolute power vested in the person of the agent—the little man holding in his hands the destinies of Indians and traders alike. While a lot of his discourse sounded farcical, I kept a serious face, and let him gain the impression that I was truly convinced and in complete agreement—in fact, that he was but voicing my own ideas and opinions. And never afterward did I allow any member of the agency's office to think that possibly I held mental reservations, or agreed to their dictums with tongue in cheek.

With rare exceptions, the entire lot of agency employees, from the agent on down, and including clerical staff, mechanics, stockmen, medical workers, teachers, and just plain, everyday help, appeared suckled on bureaucracy—all were hopelessly narrow-minded and, consequently, imbued with the weight and importance of their own jobs. I am not speaking of the Keams Canyon agency alone, but of every other agency that I had come to know in the Indian country. All were tarred by the same brush, and that I was not prejudiced was borne out in generous measure by the freely voiced opinions of others who had business or official dealings with those benighted underlings of one of the most flagrantly autocratic divisions of the Department of the Interior.

Nevertheless, my years of trading in Keams Canyon passed without any interference by, or disharmony with, any agency employees; at all times I managed to be *persona grata* with the powers that had temporary charge of the reservation and its inhabitants.

After weeks of waiting, the trader's license arrived, and was given to me through the agency. At last I could consider myself a full-fledged trader! Hubbell's clerk was sent on to join his employer, and I took independent charge of the post.

The same amount of red tape had to be unwound in the matter of arranging licenses for clerks and assistants. All had to secure Washington's special O.K.

A trading license is valid for twelve months only, hence it is necessary to apply for a renewal once a year. The clerk's licenses, too, must be renewed annually. However, after the original permit has been granted, the request for a new license is a fairly easy matter to handle, since it does not involve making new statements, furnishing references, and going through all the vexatious details that accompany the securing of the initial authorization to trade.

An Indian trading post's stock of merchandise makes one think of the old-time country store, where just about everything was to be had. The post is not merely a grocery store, but also a hardware store. Too, it carries dry goods, clothing, hats, shoes, notions, patent medicines, harness, saddlery items, fencing, nails, horseshoes, and stock salt. The larger posts, such as Keams Canyon, also have on hand several types of wagons, suited to the country, up to and including the heavy freighters. Thus, anything the Indian customers may want, from a needle to a big freight wagon, is to be found at the trading post.

One item of Hubbell's stock which was turned over to me was something I had not previously seen in an Indian trading post: several wooden cases with nursing bottles, and a corresponding number of rubber nipples!

I did not know what to make of that, knowing that the Indian mothers had no scruples about nursing their babies, and were not conscious of having to "save their figures." But here were hundreds of bottles and nipples, in a country that recognized no wet nurse.

When Hubbell saw my astonishment over the presence of these items, he explained that the Navajos trading in Keams Canyon were steady customers for bottles and nipples, using them to feed lambs which had lost their mothers. This I found to be true, and over the course of years brought in many more cases of those nursing utensils. Apparently, loss and breakage was high in the lambing camps, which helped swell the turnover of bottles in the store.

The sale of firearms and ammunition is forbidden in the licensed trading post, but this does not keep the Indians from obtaining them. Generally, they buy these prohibited articles in the railroad towns when engaged in freighting, or when somebody indulges in a bit of bootlegging of cartridges and shells. The hardware stores off the reservation are, of course, permitted to sell the guns and ammunition to Indians as well as to Mexicans or Americans. That creates a situation which penalizes the licensed trader. The regulations restrict him, and he is not allowed to supply the demand for certain items. If he, too, had the right to deal in these articles, it would, automatically, give him a chance at some control. As the matter stands, no control is exercised, and nobody knows what is sold to the Indians or brought onto the reservation.

The sale of any and all alcoholic beverages is strictly forbidden. A trader loses his license if he is proved guilty of an infraction of that regulation. This, of course, is a very sensible precaution, as Indians are notoriously unable to "hold their liquor." As a consequence, drunkenness is rare on the Indian reservation, although now and then an Indian does get a bottle of whisky, usually through the connivance of some careless Mexican or indifferent white.

To combat the Indian's craving for alcohol, the Indian Bureau frowns upon the sale of patent medicines, because the larger portion of them contains excessive amounts of alcohol. The more innocuous types of home remedies do not come under the official ban, and are part of every trader's stock. In this connection it may be noted that the trader is also prohibited from bringing alcoholic beverages onto the reservation for his personal use. He can not alibi his action if a bottle of whisky is found upon his premises, even if that were kept by him for "strictly medicinal purposes!"

Both the brave and the squaw are good shoppers, and as "brand conscious" as the whites. It is difficult to introduce new brands, particularly in the food and dry-good lines, and I learned through costly experience that it does not pay to go against the stream in the matter of attempting to substitute unknown goods for articles in long-established demand.

To make this clearer, I shall name some of the preferred brands, although this is not to imply that other goods are not just as good, and possibly even better. However, the Navajo shopper *insists* upon certain brands, and the trader simply *must* supply them.

That applies to Arbuckle's "Ariosa" coffee, both the whole bean and the ground product. Navajos and Hopis alike prefer this particular brand above all others. At different times I tried to introduce other coffees, packaged in a similar manner, but had no success. For the occasional white trade, the post carried Hills Bros., Maxwell House, Iris, Edwards, Folger's, Sanka, and one or two other coffees, but those brands did not appeal to the Indians. If for some reason or other they could not get "Ariosa," they would take none. Incidentally, price did not influence the customers. At different times, less expensive brands were tried, but "Ariosa" remained the preference.

The men would not buy any other but either "Star" or "Horseshoe" chewing tobacco, and only "Bull Durham" suited them for smoking.

The squaws had similar well-defined preferences for the brands of flour and baking powder. At one time we were forced to resack several hundred bags of flour because the mill had stamped a wolf's head on the white bags. To the Navajos it looked like a coyote's head—enough to make that flour taboo!

The accepted brands included Stetson hats from Philadelphia, Levi Strauss overalls from San Francisco, and Indian robes and shawls bearing the blue and gold label of the Pendleton Woolen Mills in Pendleton, Oregon. The latter consisted of the selvage robes worn by the men, and the gorgeously fringed shawls which were bought by and for the squaws.

Heavy stock saddles, both plain and hand-tooled, came from famous makers in Miles City, Montana, and Pueblo, Colorado. They had to be "double-rigged," meaning that they were equipped with both front and rear *cinchas*, and not too large-skirted, as the Indian ponies are mostly short coupled. The round-skirted, three-quarter rig, favored by many cowboys in that section of the Southwest, did not appeal to the Indians. The saddle horn had to be leather- or rawhide-covered. When a saddlery had shipped several saddles with bright, nickled horns, I had to hire an Indian to cover them by braiding rawhide over them. Those smooth, shiny metal surfaces do not allow a satisfactory grip to the reata when roping stock. Still more objectionable is the blinding reflection upon the eyes when the rider is under the sun's rays.

Manufacturers in Houston, Texas, supplied most of the harness, horse collars, collar pads, hame straps, and similar saddlery items.

Shoes and boots for the Indian trade came from St. Louis, Missouri; cowboys and ranchers would, occasionally, leave orders for bench-made boots to be forwarded to a certain bootmaker in Texas.

Flour was bought in carload lots from various mills in Colorado. Oats, corn, and corn chops, too, came in carloads. To haul such quantities of freight, each carload weighing from 50,000 to 60,000 pounds, demanded many teams and wagons. The Indian teamsters and freighters never managed such large or heavy loads as we had freighted for Wetherill from Albuquerque to Chaco Canyon, hence a long train of wagons was required whenever carload shipments had to be moved.

Regardless of the nature of the load, the cost of hauling was the same: a flat rate of $1.50 per one hundred pounds was fixed and paid for every pound of merchandise or other freight that arrived in Keams Canyon. The rate dropped to $1.00 per hundredweight for outgoing freight, such as hides, wool, skins, pelts, blankets, and similar goods, to be carried to the railroad.

Several wholesale houses—devoted entirely to supplying Indian traders, and located in the various towns along the Santa Fe Railway between Albuquerque at the eastern extreme and Flagstaff at the western end—competed for the business of the trading posts. Some El Paso dealers, too, sent out salesmen, but at rarer intervals.

Goods purchased from the more distant supply houses were sent by freight, express, or parcel post. If freight or express, they would be addressed to Holbrook or Winslow in Arizona; or to Gallup, New Mexico, as requested in the order. From the respective freight stations or express offices, the packages would be picked up by the first freighter sent into town, and brought out to the canyon with other freight.

Generally the Indian teams would go into Gallup, or Holbrook or Winslow—all of these points being approximately equally distant from Keams Canyon. There they would unload the wool, hides, or other goods they had taken in, then load up with the merchandise ordered from the wholesaler. That would include calicos, unbleached muslin, canned goods, notions, gloves, quilts,

wool cards (for carding wool, preparatory to spinning),
hardware items, stock salt, dyes, and the thousand and
one other items in regular demand in the trading post.
Sometimes, wagons were loaded with just one single item,
as once when an order included four thousand pounds of
salt. At different times, the wagons carried solid loads of
lumber, used for repairs, rebuilding of counters and
shelves, and for the erection of new buildings.

I recall one time when the wagons coming from the
railroad carried two hundred cases of one hundred pounds
each of Arbuckle's "Ariosa"—ten tons of coffee! The total
weight, in fact, exceeded that because each wooden case
added some twenty-eight pounds to the weight of the
contents.

Many staple grocery items, both dry and canned, had
to be bought in large quantities to insure a stock supply
through those months when weather and road conditions
made freighting impossible. The heaviest freighting took
place in late summer and early fall, when the summer
cloudbursts had ended, insuring good grazing and plentiful water along the trail, and before the coming of snow-
storms. After the first snows, freighting came, automatically, to a standstill.

Upon arrival in Keams Canyon, the wagons would
pull up to the unloading platform of the main warehouse,
if the freight was to be stored there. Or a wagon might
drive up to the very front steps of the store, where the
goods were taken directly into the store and piled on the
floor or laid on the counters, until unpacked and checked.
Still other merchandise was taken to a side door, leading
down to the large basement of the store. There heavy,
wide planks placed over the stone steps made a convenient
slide for the cases of canned goods and similar items that
were kept in the lower part of the building. Kerosene,

and, in later years, gasoline, were put in a special storeroom, entirely apart from the other buildings, as a fire
precaution.

Each load had to be checked carefully against the in-
voices and bills of lading of the wholesaler. Frequently,
yes, almost invariably, there was some small shortage,
particularly if the load included such goods as flour,
coffee, canned goods, and so forth. The freighter might
have been loaded out with one hundred sacks of flour,
but the count upon arrival at the post would show only
ninety-two bags. The missing eight bags had been left at
his hogan, where he camped one night, he would declare.
Similar shortage might show up in other articles, although
friend Navajo would not bother to explain that he had
opened a case of canned tomatoes, taken out several of
them, and then renailed the box after carefully stuffing hay
into the space formerly occupied by the cans of tomatoes!
Weeks, or even months later, the theft would be discovered when the box was opened, too late to hold the pilferer
responsible.

The readiness with which the freighters accepted de-
ductions for "short" items was proof that the missing
goods had not been lost off the wagons or been stolen en
route, but had been taken by the drivers for their own
use. In many years of trading, no Indian freighter ever
argued about this point.

The interior of the Keams Canyon post did not differ
from the conventional arrangement of other trading
stores. Upon entering, one saw counters running the
full length of the store at both right and left sides, and also
at the rear, forming a large U. Back of the counters,
shelves ranged upward to about eight feet from the floor,
while the space above the shelves was used for suspending
various articles of merchandise. From nails and pegs

driven into the walls, and also into the exposed roof
beams, dangled pots and pans, pails, galvanized tubs,
slickers, assorted saddlery and harness items, lengths of
rope, wool cards, tanned buckskins, whips, quirts, canvas
water bags, a piece of oil-tanned calfskin from which are
cut narrow strips for latigos, and in one section a bar
made of an old broom handle holding "dead" pawn, the
designation for unredeemed pledges.

When pledged silver belts, beads, bracelets, saddle
blankets, or other articles are not redeemed after a specified period, or after wool season or sheep-selling season, the
trader will take out of his pawn closet the items which are
"dead." Those he will string up or otherwise put on
display in the store, which action automatically notifies
the owner that unless he redeems his valuables quickly,
they will be sold. Friends, acquaintances, or members of
his family or relations, who happen to see the display,
promptly inform the owner that his treasurers are now
offered for sale. Usually he comes to the trading post in
a hurry, either to redeem the pledges, or to persuade the
trader to grant him an extension.

The trader holds the pawns with the understanding
that they be redeemed when the sale of rugs, wool, or livestock gives the Indian enough cash to take care of his
obligations. However, if he finds that his faith has been
misplaced and that the customer who used him for a
convenience when broke, goes to some other trader when
he has a load of wool to sell, then the trader is justified in
disposing of the "dead" pawn. Generally, such pawned
articles are snapped up by other Navajos, since the trader
does not sell them at a profit, but at the actual amount of
the loan. Of course, if unredeemed pledges are disposed
of to chance tourists, or sent to some of the wholesalers or
Indian-craft specialty shops who are always on the lookout

for such items, they bring their legitimate market value. However, traders generally "lean backward" in the matter of holding pawns, and often carry some article for a long time, taking on-account payments, and increasing the loan through additional advances if the owner finds it necessary to ask for more credit. The Indian considers the collateral a sort of bank account, drawing against it, when need arises, and paying off in convenient installments as he is able.

It is impossible to carry on a trading business without handling pawns, although that means tying up considerable sums. The capital invested does not accumulate interest, since a trader is not permitted to charge that. The sole benefit the trader derives from the pawn business is the profit from the sale of the merchandise (since no cash is advanced on pawns) and whatever good will accrues to him for accommodating the Indians. At all times the trader has to be careful that the pawn is not "sold" to him. If he advances too much credit against the value of the article, he will find that the Indian who pledged it does not come back, neither as a customer nor as a redeemer of the pawn. The trader is simply stuck with something that he finds has been overvalued.

The counters in the store were about forty inches high, and fully three feet wide. That was to discourage shoplifting and pilfering from the shelves. It was virtually impossible for anyone to reach across the high and wide counters and span the equally wide aisle back of the counters to grasp any of the merchandise displayed on the shelves. Experience had proved that these precautions were necessary, virtually all of the Indians being kleptomaniacs, to use a polite term.

In a number of trading posts some sections of the counters were protected by close-mesh wire screens. All posts that I ever visited had heavy iron bars across the window opening to discourage burglary. The store in Keams Canyon was similarly protected. Doors were double locked and equipped with stout drop bars, all of which demonstrated that the traders did not place too much reliance in the nobility of the red man. In the James Fenimore Cooper "Leatherstocking" tales and in the Karl May series of "Old Shatterhand" Western stories, we are introduced to some noble redskins endowed with wonderful qualities and characteristics. It is unlikely that any Indian trader ever encountered the living counterparts of those Cooper and May heroes. After some disappointing and disillusioning experiences, the trader discovers that the milk of human kindness is about to turn to clabber in his breast. Thereafter he puts his trust in divine protection and strengthens that faith by employing stout bars and strong locks.

The trader has to trust in the iron bars, heavy padlocks, the barred doors to safeguard his goods against burglary. but that still leaves him without the comfort of fire insurance. In those isolated posts, far away from organized fire departments, without adequate water supply and in the absence of hydrants and sprinkler systems, fire insurance companies do not issue policies. If they did, the premiums would be so high as to be prohibitive.

We had several fire extinguishers in the store and main warehouse, and one in our dwelling. They were of the type that releases a powerful stream through a rubber hose and nozzle when turned upside down. At periodic intervals, they were emptied and refilled with the chemicals and water necessary for a new charge.

The thought that he will suffer a complete loss in case of fire tends to make every trader doubly careful in handling lights and heating equipment. No matches are thrown away carelessly, no cigarette stubs allowed to burn into wood or other inflammable substances. Everybody in and around a trading post is vigilant to prevent fires, and in the many years I spent on reservations, I never found a trading post featuring a fire sale!

The trader is both buyer and seller. In order to sell his trade goods to the Indian, who but seldom has money, it becomes necessary first to buy whatever the Indian offers for sale. That may include a wide variety of commodities and articles. Throughout the entire year the Navajos have blankets used for rugs. Too, there is a steady trade in sheep pelts and goatskins, since the meat of those animals are part of the staple foods of the Navajos. The pelts and skins of the slaughtered animals are pegged out, or hung up to dry, and later taken to the most convenient trading post where they are exchanged for coffee, sugar, flour, and other necessities.

In years when the pinons produce a good crop of pinon nuts, the trader will take in varying amounts of those delicious nuts. At the end of good seasons, the Hopis may take large quantities of shelled Indian corn to the trader. While the pinon nuts are shipped to the railroad towns and sold to the supply houses, the trader usually stores the corn and resells it to the Indians in smaller amounts through the winter months, both for human consumption and for stock feed

The Navajo silversmiths trade the products of their forges and anvils; the Hopis bring in many specimens of their pottery. Wildcat and mountain lion skins are brought in by hunters, baskets and plaques by the Hopi squaws who are experts in basketry.

The really big trading seasons are the periods during which the wool clip is brought in, and the one which sees the sale of sheep, lambs, horses, or cattle. At those times the Indian receives hundreds of dollars in a lump sum, and as a rule will spend virtually the entire amount in the trading post. First, he redeems his pawns, then he loads up his wagon with quantities of foodstuffs. After that, he may buy a new wagon or saddle, or make other purchases of the more expensive goods, such as Pendleton robes and shawls, Stetson hats, many yards of velveteen for squaw skirts and shirts for both men and women, and other items bought rarely at ordinary times.

The trader purchases all and everything that is brought to him, paying for it in silver dollars. Paper money is held in disfavor by the Indians. Many do not know the difference between the various denominations of bills, and paper is too easily destroyed. Therefore, silver is the universal medium of exchange. However, since the Indian has no safe place in his hogan, he is inclined to spend nearly all of the money received, keeping only a nominal amount for future needs.

In times past some traders made use of so-called "seco" money, which designated brass trade chips, stamped with the name of the trading post, and saying: "Good for 50 cents," or whatever value it might have at that particular store. This practice is now outlawed. To persuade the Indian to accept this one-store "money," it was customary to offer a premium for trade in "seco." For example, the trader might offer eight dollars for a blanket if taken in silver, but would go to ten dollars if the Indian agreed to accept "seco."

The usual procedure of a big transaction is something like this: After the price has been agreed upon, trader and customer return from the warehouse, where the wool was weighed, to the store. If he has a private room or office, the trader goes to that—the Indian preferring to do business where hungry onlookers cannot watch over every phase of the deal. The amount due him for the wool (or whatever else it may be) is counted out to him in stacks of silver dollars. Often the money is divided between the brave and squaw, and maybe even into three or more parts, each taking his or her share. Just how the division is arrived at, is difficult to understand, since it is not on a fifty-fifty or other proportionate basis.

After the money has been paid over, the Indian will take it into the store and begin buying, or he may, as happened often, shove a stack or two of the silver back toward me, and say: "Flour!" On a memorandum I would mark the number of sacks of flour the money would buy, and tell him just how much he had bought. Another stack of dollar pieces would come, with the single word "Sugar," which meant another notation on the shopping slip. More stacks followed for coffee, baking powder, canned goods of various kinds, all noted down on the slip. Eventually, the Indian and his squaw and family would follow me into the store and begin looking over the dry goods or other articles they might wish to buy. The slip prepared in the office was then taken care of by one of the clerks. All goods listed thereon as already purchased were piled on the counter, from where the buyer, assisted by his family, would take them to his wagon.

However, the first matter to be disposed of would always be the redemption of the pawns. Even well-to-do Indians, owners of large herds and other worldly goods, pawn jewelry and other items of value through the winter months. The pawning of pledges does not cast any derogatory reflection upon the Indian—it is an accepted and legitimate business procedure, free from the social stigma that ordinarily accompanies the white man's transactions in a pawnshop.

If the Indian receives his money over the counter, he may, and usually does, give a few dollars to any of the onlookers present in the store. He will take two or three dollars and hand them to the man or woman standing at his elbow, and everybody in the store usually shares in the returns from his sale. And it is not an' infrequent occurrence that in the end the just-redeemed pawns are pledged anew to cover purchases for which there does not remain sufficient cash!

The trader must, of necessity, have an accurate knowledge of the values of wool, pelts, skins, livestock, and other things or commodities offered in trade by the Indian. Unless he buys right, and is able to dispose of his accumulated stock at a profit, he will lose money. He has to take chances on market fluctuations that govern the price of wool and skins, which are likely to change rapidly. It is humanly impossible always to buy at the bottom and sell at the top, hence the trader will incur losses and may even go bankrupt, unless he is exceptionally careful.

Navajo rugs and other products of Indian handicraft are a fairly stable investment of trading funds. Those things possess an intrinsic value not affected by stock market or commodity market fluctuations. For the finer grades of rugs there has always been a steady demand— in fact, the supply of the best-grade Navajo rugs is insufficient to take care of the orders.

In summer as well as in winter, a large pail with fresh water stands at one end of the counter, with a long-handled enamelware dipper resting alongside or standing in the pail. That is drinking water for the Indians, and every man, woman, and child coming into the store refreshes himself. There are no individual cups—the Indians make use of the common dipper, but are clean and careful in drinking.

During the winter the store must be warm and cozy. Most of the trading in inclement or stormy weather is done by the men. They do not like it if they have to transact business in a cold place after riding through chilling rains or stinging snows. The trader sees to it that the big cast-iron stove in the middle of the floor between the counters holds a good fire, to welcome the frozen fellows when they enter the place. Quite often they unwrap strips of cloth or sacking or pelts wound about the mocassins (which will absorb water like a dry sponge), to dry out by the stove while they attend to the shopping.

Canned salmon and sardines were part of the stock, but only the white trade would buy them. Occasionally, someone would open a can of the canned fish and eat it in the store, and might offer an Indian part of the contents of the can. That, however, was something he would not eat—not he! In fact, he was astounded to see the white man relish the "snake meat"—he could not be convinced it was anything but canned reptile.

On the counter of the store was to be found a shallow wooden box, fastened down by screws, and holding some loose smoking tobacco, cigarette papers, and a few matches. Long, slender nails had been driven to about half their length through the bottom of the box into the counter. That was not to hold the box more securely to its place but to prevent the Indians from scooping up handfuls of tobacco. The nails allowed thumb and forefinger to take a pinch or two of tobacco, enough to fill the cigarette paper, but did not permit a cleaning out of the box, as would have happened quickly if it were not for obstructing nails. A trader learns many tricks!

At every trading post can be found a substantial hogan, which is a camping place for the Indians who stay at the post overnight. It has been built by the Indians, is constructed in accord with their own ideas, door opening facing east, and has been properly blessed by a medicine man. If the customers arrive at the post late in the afternoon, or weather conditions force them to remain overnight, that hogan becomes the guesthouse.

The trader furnishes firewood for the hogan, and is also expected to supply such camping equipment as coffeepot, tin cups, fry pan and water bucket. He is often "touched" for coffee and sugar, or anything else the Indian can persuade him to donate.

The cooking utensils require frequent replacement—for some reason or other they disappear, piece by piece, until out of the entire assortment there remains perhaps one battered tin cup!

During my trading years in Sanders and in Keams Canyon Arizona, I developed a steadily increasing mail-order business in Indian arts and crafts. Choice pieces of Navajo silverware, Hopi basketry and pottery, and—foremost—Navajo rugs, were sent by me to all parts of the country. The major portion of the business was with New York, where B. Altman & Co., the Fifth Avenue department store, was one of my largest customers. Specialty shops on Madison Avenue were always in the market for the finely made old-time Navajo silver jewelry, and eagerly bought any "dead" pawn of that nature.

Elbert Hubbard furnished all rooms, the lobby and recreation hall, and so-called chapel of his Roycroft Inn at East Aurora, New York, with fine Navajo rugs purchased from me. He also had me send him several large shipments of rugs to be sold by his Roycrofters to the many visitors to the inn. To make this business mutually profitable, I had the Roycrofters design and make for me business stationery and check forms. In addition, I bought several beautiful pieces of Roycroft handmade

furniture, including a large bookcase, a handsome desk
and big chair to match, which I had personally selected
when I spent some six weeks in the inn at East Aurora.
Those choice examples of Roycroft handicraft gave a rare
distinction to my office in the Keams Canyon trading post.
It tickled my vanity to consider mine the only trader's
office furnished so regally.

Visitors to the Snake Dance generally bought up all
the choice rugs I displayed in the store at those times.
Prize specimens were bought by the president of the
Pennsylvania Railroad, who came out to the Hopi
pueblos upon one of those occasions. Other rare rugs
went to Phoenix, Arizona, having been selected by Governor Tom Campbell. The president of the Southern
California Edison Company, who was in Governor
Campbell's party coming to see the Snake Dance, also
acquired some extra-fine rugs. Many others became part
of private collections, such as that of Mr. James W.
Young, advertising executive of Chicago who thus furnished several rooms in his home in Winnetka, Illinois.
Another advertising man, Mr. George Roebling, of New
York, received some extraordinarily well-woven rugs for
his fine country home in New Jersey. He introduced me
to several other New York businessmen at the various
times when we lunched together in the Lotus Club, and
I had the privilege of filling orders for them, too.

During our stay in Keams Canyon we entertained
many well-known persons, who were glad to accept our
hospitality. There were no hotel facilities in Keams
Canyon, the nearest accommodations of that sort being
some ninety miles away, hence it became virtually oblig-
atory for us to shelter and feed the visitors from the outside world. We were glad to do that as those contacts
were not a bother, but a pleasure. The visitors would

bring a fresh viewpoint into our lives, and give my wife and I some new interests.

Scientists, geologists, archaeologists and others came to study the Indians, the pueblos of the Hopis, the desert, the queer natural formations, the rocks, and everything else that exerted a peculiar charm for them. Artists found inspiration in the always changing lights and shadows, in the strange Indian types, in the daily life of the trading post. W. R. Leigh, the famous painter of Western scenes, made Keams Canyon his headquarters and studio for months on end. Several writers, whose subjects were Indian lore, came to gather local color and authentic information.

Douglas Fairbanks arrived with a large troupe to "shoot" some scenes for one of his pictures whose locale was laid in the desert country. Mary Pickford and Miss Pickford's mother were members of that party. Mary Roberts Rhinehart, the writer, came as a visitor, and the result of her impressions of that trip were later published in the *Saturday Evening Post* under the title "Lorenzo the Magnificent."

An interesting character appeared upon the scene one day when Tom Smith rode into the canyon, driving before him a string of seven pack mules. I watched him and his animals coming up the trail, and at first thought that his mules were carrying loads of firewood. As he drew closer, I saw that it was not wood he was bringing, but still I could not distinguish what was in the strange-looking packs until he reached the store. Then I was able to see and inspect the queer cargo at close range.

The mules were loaded with deer's horns, and not just single sets of horns. All were double sets, coming from the heads of bucks which had locked their horns during a fight. Inextricably bound together by the spreading

horns, the animals perished from hunger or were devour-
ed by mountain lions. Tom Smith had gone up into the
Kaibab Forest, at the northern edge of the Grand Canyon,
and gathered up the horns. He had, at the same time,
killed some twenty mountain lions, and the tawny hides
of the big cats were a part of his pack.

He was on his way to the railroad. He planned to sell
his trophies to lodges, barrooms, and private homes, and
after resting in Keams Canyon for several days, during
which time he told us tales of his hunting experiences in
the high forest country, he proceeded on his trip.

Some time later, Douglas Fairbanks came to Arizona,
and Tom Smith made himself acquainted with Fairbanks.
The latter gave him a job taking care of his horses, and
took him along to Hollywood. Eventually, Tom became
a member of the Hollywood movie colony and had a part
in many Western pictures.

Indian agents, salesmen, tourists, ex-Governor Hager-
man of New Mexico, missionaries, cowpunchers, hunters,
adventurers, freighters, congressmen and senators, Mormon bishops, the sheriff of the county, postal inspectors,
Indians of various tribes, Mexicans, agency employees—
a never-ending stream of callers came, each one a type
with problems of a particular nature. All helped to bring
spice into our existence, to furnish us with new thrills,
just as we, very likely, were something new and strange
to them.

Invariably, the eastern visitors would arrive at the
question: "Don't you get terribly lonesome, out here all
by yourselves and away from civilization?" Most of them
failed to differentiate between lonesomeness and solitude,
and did not appreciate the fact that our lives were so full
as to leave no time in which to feel loneliness. True, we
lacked the conveniences of modern towns, such as electric-

ity, gas, telegraph and telephone, daily news and mail service, and, most missed of all, modern plumbing. But those hardships, as they appeared to others, were not considered too tough by us, but were put up with and taken in stride. We consoled ourselves with the thought that all pioneering involves the giving up of certain comforts, and we reflected that the builders of this nation and the western-bound travelers who crossed the prairies and mountains in ox-drawn wagons managed very nicely without tiled bathrooms and electric switches.

White neighbors, of course, were few and far away, but an Indian trader and his wife soon learn that their real neighbors are their customers, the Indians. Many times we would saddle our horses and go a-visiting, riding to the different camps and hogans to make friendly calls. Arrived at a hogan, we would dismount, secure our horses, then squat down upon a sheep pelt or blanket and join the family in talk, or share a meal with them. We would, in that fashion, keep track of the progress of some fine blanket that was still on the loom, or would with our own eyes verify the lamb crop. But many trips did not have any ulterior or interested motive—we simply went for the ride to be sociable, to enjoy the visit with our friends, and to create good will and happy understandings.

An Indian trader's wife foregoes the contacts that mean so much to women in more civilized surroundings, but my own, and the wives of other traders who I knew, did not seem to care a lot about missing town gossip, church socials, bridge parties, *Kaffeeklatsches,* sewing bees, matinées, and other gatherings of the ladies. The women who helped their men in the ranches and trading posts of the Western country soon learned to develop self-sufficiency, and it was they who really enabled the men to carry on. Without their loyal and unselfish help and love and devotion, ranching and Indian trading would have been a sorry chore, indeed.

Naturally, a trader's wife has to become accustomed to an entirely different way of living. She has no meat market to go to, nor is there a bakery around the corner. Fresh vegetables are, in most cases, an unknown or unobtainable luxury—planning meals and cooking means more than just making up a menu and then ordering the required items over the telephone.

There is no laundry within a hundred miles or more. Servants cannot be had—white girls want to be where they can go to dances and other entertainments, and where they can meet young men who are not buried in trading stores. Indian girls can be trained to do some of the things in a white household, but it is a tedious job, and often, for no reason at all, the jewel that has been polished and is just beginning to take on the right gloss decides to return to her hogan!

Small children and babies are a real problem under those conditions, but, with a fortitude that mere man could not match, the women in the wastelands accept the responsibilities and carry on with the raising of families.

Radio had not yet been perfected when we lived in Keams Canyon, and thus we did not enjoy the pleasures which it could have brought to us in our out-of-the-way post. For music we had a phonograph and a good-sized library of records embracing everything from popular songs to opera, and from light dance music to symphonic compositions. Sitting in front of a cheerful cedarwood fire in the open fireplace and listening to some fine records gave us a fair imitation of Carnegie Hall or the Metropolitan. And we could listen to those lovely airs without the deadly "commercial" breaking in at the most enjoyable moment of the concert or opera!

On pleasant summer evenings we would place chairs outside and watch for the moon to rise. The rosy flush of the sunset would change gradually to orange and paler yellow shades, the sky and horizon finally merging into one against the dark-blue mountains. The last flashes of color break through the fringe of evening clouds, but cannot stem the ineluctable advance of darkness. Then the moon rises and peeks over the canyon walls, and, when full, fills that dark void with a silver radiance that is unearthly.

There are no night birds—not a sound disturbs the serenity. The stars glitter with a fire that not even the brightness of the moon can dim; the vault of the heavens is translucent compared with the deep shadows cast by mesa walls, rocks, and eroded pinnacles. No Indians are abroad—there are too many *chindees* at large when darkness takes over. It behooves the brave to be in a safe place when the hobgoblins and ghosts cavort—one can not afford to displease those powerful beings.

As wonderful and soul stirring as the moonlit nights are the sunrises. Dawn brings an ever-fresh wonder into the beauty of the canyon country. The sky darkens from a pearly-green to the serene blue of a hue that is associated with the Mediterranean Sea. Glorious sunshine fills the world, and where wagon wheels have packed the hard adobe, blinding reflections from the bone-white road dazzle the eyes. Each object stands out in sharp relief, and the visibility is almost unlimited.

Cactus flowers in a great variety of delicate hues splash a touch of beauty on the desert; cedars and pinons let us admire their ragged bark and dark, pinelike needles. Many square miles are covered with sage boasting wide color variations from olive gray-green when viewed close by, to dark, hazy purple where it blends into the far horizon. Stretches of shimmering white sand alternate with pink and rose-colored sandstone formations—a veritable kaleidoscope of colors and visual sensations.

The air in this rare altitude (Keams Canyon is well over seven thousand feet above sea level) is as invigorating as wine, but can be as cutting as a knife in the crackling, frosty winter nights. Even during the summer months the desert temperature drops rapidly after dark, and woolen blankets and heavier bedding are as welcome in July and August as in the colder seasons.

At Christmas time, Indians from far and wide make the post their rendezvous. For days prior to the great event, everyone, including the wife, has been busy with preparations. Paper bags are filled with candies and apples and peanuts, chewing gum and similar confections and sweets. Other bags hold smoking tobacco and cigarette papers. Several cases of Cracker Jack have been opened, and the little cartons with their prizes are piled with the other things. There are larger packages, especially put up for the regular customers, containing some coffee, sugar, soda crackers, a can or two of fruit or tomatoes, and perhaps some Nabisco, Fig Newtons or other packaged cookies.

Everybody that comes to the store on Christmas Day receives a gift of candy and other delectables; the Indians who are the regular patrons of the post get the bigger packages which were made ready for them. In addition, those of the children who may be in need of them are fitted out with new stockings, or little sweaters, and any and everything that can be spared from our own wardrobe—used, it is true, but still very acceptable because clean, warm, and serviceable.

It is a day of little trade—the object of the Indians is to receive gifts, and, if time allows, to make a hurried trip to the nearest mission or other trading post to repeat the performance and share in the gifts offered at those places. If that means a ride of twenty or thirty miles, it does not discourage anyone—distance must lend enchantment!

The missions maintained through Navajoland by the different churches also prepare for the Christmas holidays. Usually they distribute large quantities of clothing, shoes, overcoats, and other wearables which have been donated by the denominations supporting the missions. They call upon the nearest traders to help out with assortments of fruits, candies, cookies, and peanuts, which means that the trader near a mission carries a double burden. However, nobody frets over that—the yuletide spirit is strong, and to play Santa Claus is about the only chance the trader has to do something for his friends and customers.

Merchants in towns and cities contribute to community chests, to churches, the Salvation Army, to welfare organizations and other causes. None of those benevolent institutions make any demands upon the Indian trader, far removed from civilized communities, hence he feels it is but fair to make the celebration at Christmas a real affair for his Indians. The time and effort and money for the gifts and donations earn big interest in good will— the recipients of the Christmas packages spread the word wherever they go and praise the generosity of their trader friend.

My friend, Captain O. A. Burtner, for long years a resident of Albuquerque, New Mexico, who had retired and made his home in Pomona, California, asked me to bring an exhibit of Indian crafts to the Los Angeles County Fair. I decided to do so, but in addition to a representative collection of rugs, silver jewelry, pottery and baskets, also took two Navajo blanket weavers and two silversmiths along.

Our exhibit at the fair, at that time shown under a huge tent, was one of the principal attractions, and the sale of the rugs and other items repaid me for nearly the total cost of the trip.

The four Navajos never tired of telling of the wonders of the journey into the setting sun. They related to disbelieving friends and members of their families the high lights of the trip as they had appeared to them. They spoke of having to pay a dollar for a small piece of mutton in the butcher shop in Pomona, when a whole lamb's carcass could be bought for that amount on the reservation.

But the outstanding and most unforgettable thrill of the whole trip was their visit to the Pacific Ocean. I took them down to Santa Monica and Venice, by electric car, and gave them their first glimpse of the Big Water. That was almost too much to believe, even when their own eyes saw the expanse of ocean. They went down to the very edge of the water and scooped up a little in their hands to taste it. To have proof of this wonder, only dimly understood by the rest of the tribe, they filled several bottles with ocean water and carried them back to the reservation.

Quite a few times during my trading years I was called by Indians to come to their camp or hogan to see a "sick" person. That might mean visiting a place long miles away, perhaps in the dead of winter with snow piled high on mesas and in the canyons. However, in the absence of doctors or other professional help, the trader must of necessity assume the role of physician. Our first-aid kit contained many remedies, antiseptics, germicides, bandages, salves, ointments and similar items that might be needed at any time. Out of that stock, a traveling kit would be assembled and taken along, securely tied back of the saddle.

Arrived at the hogan, one would find—well, almost anything from a swollen jaw due to bad teeth to broken legs or arms. In every case, rough-and-ready first aid was administered, and such is the vitality of the Indians that the effects were frequently more than gratifying. The trader begins to wonder whether he may not have missed his calling—it seems quite evident (at least to himself) that he is a natural-born doctor!

However, upon some five or six times, the "sick" person turned out to be a squaw in labor! That was an illness or accident not covered by the first-aid instructions, but could not be dismissed on that account. Something had to be done, but what does an Indian trader, even if he is married, know about obstetrics? But here is a young woman, in much pain, and in fear of the unknown. It is her first baby, and there is no Indian camp or hogan within miles. The trader happens to be the nearest other human, so the husband has come to the white man, who knows everything!

Had the brave said that his wife was about to give birth to a baby, the trader's wife could have come along, bringing towels, linens, and other desirable things. But all he said in the store was that a sick person needed immediate attention.

The young squaw is resting upon some sheep pelts, laid flat upon the floor. From one of the poles of the roof, a twisted rawhide rope hangs to within a foot or so of her chest. She has grabbed this rope with both hands, and pulls and strains against it. Now and then a little moan escapes from her lips. She is in great pain, but only the fathomless depths of her eyes give the real indication of her suffering. Fortunately, the first-aid kit has a small bottle of chloroform, and I give her a quick whiff of that at frequent intervals to numb the agony of her pains. That is just about the extent of the assistance I am able to render, until finally the baby makes its appearance.

The husband helps to cut the umbilical cord, to clean the baby as well as the meager facilities permit, and, in the absence of proper oils, assists in rubbing some pure white vaseline over the wrinkled skin of the newcomer. A strip of fairly clean calico or unbleached muslin is tied about the little one's middle, protecting the navel cord, its little eyes are washed and cleansed with an antiseptic solution, and then, after the mother has been removed to some dry and clean pelts, the performance is over. The baby rests by its mother, and she manages a wan and shy smile. Even the father looks as if he would recover!

The trader-doctor is likely to be the most exhausted one of the lot—it has been a nerve-racking job, and the utter helplessness of the male when confronted by a situation like that is without compare. Even after repeated experiences of that sort, it remains a terrible task.

Many Indians came to the post to get injections of Argyrol, the antiseptic compound which has practically become a specific in the treatment of trachoma. A pathetically large number of Hopis and Navajos are afflicted with this highly contagious disease of the eyelids, and the inflammation results in many cases of total blindness. Conditions in the camps and hogans are ideal for transmitting trachoma and as a consequence it happens frequently that every member of a family is affected. We did what we could to alleviate the cases that came to us, and both the wife and I ministered to the sufferers by dropping the Argyrol solution into the granulated eyelids. In every case, we advised the patient to go to the nearest Indian agency hospital, or to the clinics maintained by some of the missions, for more prolonged and professional treatment.

The flu epidemic that ravished the entire country at the end of the first World War was especially virulent in the form that struck the Indians. Without any medical safeguards, and entirely sans prophylactic or curative agents, hundreds of Indians perished. Whole families were wiped out—in some hogans the dead rested in a circle, occupying the entire space of the structure.

Assisted by the Baptist missionary, I buried some thirty Indians, young and old, whom we found in abandoned hogans. It was pitiful to see the conditions in the camps that had been decimated by the scourge—sometimes there were but one or two survivors out of a large family, and those resembled corpses more than living persons.

Yes, a trader's life is not just standing behind a store counter and selling merchandise at exorbitant prices to untutored savages, as some people seem to believe. It embodies many other phases, but from whatever angle it is viewed, the trader sees life in capital letters. There is fun and pleasure and profit, to be sure, but also pathos, misery, and tragedy. The trader has to be an adaptable person—he is called upon to face many situations that never trouble one off the reservation. At all times he must be self-reliant; there simply is no one else to whom he can delegate unpleasant and dangerous tasks. Unless he is willing, ready, and qualified to do his share, and to accept the responsibilities, he had better look for some less exacting calling.

Chapter 24

EXIT OF AN INDIAN TRADER

The years rolled by and we flourished. Encouraged by the good trade built up in Keams Canyon, I applied for a license to operate a second post some twenty miles distant. It was to be in a spot where there had never been a store despite the fact that many Indians made the locality their almost permanent camping grounds. I convinced the Indian agent that the proposed post would benefit a large number of his charges. Many of my prospective customers were at a decided disadvantage during those months of the year when road and weather conditions made going to a trading post for supplies virtually impossible. Due to the agent's favorable recommendation, no objections were raised by the Indian Bureau in Washington, and presently a license was issued, permitting Joseph Schmedding & Company to conduct a trading business at Low Mountain, Arizona, within the confines of the reservation.

The store was built by Indian labor, under the supervision and with the help of my brother, who had joined me in the trading venture. Lumber, windows, doors, hardware, cement, and other necessary materials were freighted from Holbrook.

The walls of the building were of rock, quarried and hauled to the site by Indians. They also worked as stone-masons, and quickly laid tier after tier until the roof line was reached. Corrugated, galvanized sheet iron formed the roof.

Even before the roof was in place, and such things as shelves and counters had been put up, the Indians started a brisk trade. They bought coffee, sugar, flour, baking powder, and other staples that had been hauled over to the new store but were still on the freight wagons and as yet not unloaded. By the time the shelves were stocked with goods, and the store looked like a trading post, there was already a sizable accumulation of skins, pelts, and wool, taken in exchange for commodities handed down from the freight wagons. From the very beginning, the branch of the Keams Canyon establishment proved a pro-fitable undertaking.

I was postmaster of Keams Canyon, in charge of the fourth-class office, which occupied a section of the store. The revenue derived from that source amounted to a thousand dollars annually. I also held commissions as notary public, one signed by Governor Tom Campbell, the other bearing the signature of Governor George W. P. Hunt. The duties of deputy sheriff rested lightly upon my shoulders—crooks and criminals evaded the fastnesses of the Indian country. And, in any event, lawbreakers and other miscreants were the rightful prey of the native Indian police, maintained by the Indian agencies and peculiarly well fitted for the job of tracking down evil-doers and bringing them to justice.

Thus, from a material point at least, all appeared well, but there were two considerations that caused us to give up the posts and leave our beloved Navajoland. The first was the matter of the children, the baby boy having been joined by a sister.

My wife insisted that it would not be fair to the two youngsters to be reared in the wilds of the reservation, away from all contacts with white children, and without the possibility of having them enjoy the benefits of proper education. We circled the question for a long time, and found excuses for staying, but inevitably, sooner or later, came up against the unsolved issue. We did not want to send the children to relatives, and still less to strangers. To have them go with their mother, and leave me behind, did not appear to be the answer—neither my wife nor I would agree to a separation of long years. But all those perplexing aspects of the situation would not have prompted us to give up our trading posts quite so soon if it had not been for a happening that occurred in the winter of 1923.

Snow was hiding the trails in and out of Keams Canyon, the mesas and mountains glistened under the cover of the winter's mantle. Trading was light, travel almost wholly confined to horseback riding. No freight could move over the obscured roads; mail reached us by horsemen who could bring only the locked pouches containing the registered and first-class mail. Papers, magazines, parcel post, and other bulky matter piled up in the post office at Holbrook, to await the opening up of the roads.

It was then when the agent in charge of the reservation made an evening call. We were sitting by the fireplace and enjoying some music when his knock came upon the door. He entered with a more sober mien than usual, being, ordinarily, quite jolly. For a little while he sat and talked with us, but it was obvious that something weighed on his mind.

Eventually, he reached into his coat pocket and brought out an official letter. With a deep sigh, he opened it, and said to me: "I would rather take a beating than deliver this letter to you—better prepare yourself for some mighty bad news!" With that he handed me the sheet of paper. It was a communication from Washington, D.C., and read as follows:

71569—18—

DEPARTMENT OF THE INTERIOR
WASHINGTON

Feb. 14, 1923

Mr. Joseph Schmedding,
   Through Supt. Moqui School
Sir:

For administrative reasons, your license as Indian trader at Keams Canyon, on the Moqui Reservation, is hereby revoked, effective immediately. You will be given thirty days from the date hereof within which to remove your goods and close up business.

Respectfully,
Albert B. Fall, *Secretary*

A bombshell dropped into our midst could not have caused greater consternation than that message, signed by the Secretary of the Interior in person. We were stunned and dumfounded. For some moments, none spoke. Then I asked for an explanation of this astounding and shocking order, but the agent was unable to enlighten me. He had received the letter with instructions to transmit it to me personally, and was as amazed over the contents as we were.

The term "for administrative reasons" did not convey anything to him, since he was not aware of any valid reasons for cancelling my license. He was powerless to intervene in my behalf, and could only express his deepest sympathy. What caused Secretary Albert B. Fall to issue the peremptory order was a mystery—neither the agent nor I had the slightest idea as to what to attribute the action of Fall.

The agent himself had always been very friendly, and subsequently jeopardized his official position when he wrote to the Indian commissioner that "the removal of Schmedding from the post in Keams Canyon will result in grave injury to the Indian Department and the Indians." During my entire time as trader there had never been any friction between myself and my customers, or any disagreement between the department and myself. Repeatedly, I had been cited as a model trader, and I was in the belief that I enjoyed the confidence of not only the Indians but also of the government officials with whom I had to deal.

Fall's order was impracticable to obey—it was a physical impossibility to transfer the entire stock of a large trading establishment and every bit of our household and personal effects in the middle of the winter, over snow-covered trails and treacherous washes, canyons, and mesas. However, I had no intention of quitting. What I wanted to know of the Indian agent was : What am I to do next? and where can I go to find out what this is all about?

Then was brought home to me the autocratic power of the Indian Department, which I had considered a sort of bombastic claim when the chief clerk of the agency enlarged upon it at the time when I first came to Keams Canyon. I learned that Secretary Fall did not have to explain or give any reasons or justifications for his act. His order was the last word—there was no recourse! He was not accountable to anyone in the whole country, except to the President of the United States, and in this case, President Harding was his personal friend! Only the President could intervene in my behalf, and that was poor consolation to an Indian trader whose complaint would, in all probability, be filed away in some dusty corner of one of the multitudinous bureaus and commissions.

Nevertheless, and undismayed by the staggering news, I made arrangements to ride to the railroad upon the following morning, to set in motion such efforts as I could devise to secure a hearing, if nothing else.

The store, of course, had to be closed, but one of the clerks was left in charge as a watchman, and, with the permission of the agent, allowed to dispose of perishable goods, such as butter, meats, and so forth. Strangely, nothing was said about the other trading post, operating under the name of Joseph Schmedding & Company, and some twenty miles from Keams Canyon. I wondered by just what circumstances I could be considered unacceptable to the Indian Bureau as trader in one place, and still be in good standing and a proper person, fit to trade, a few miles distant. That was a paradoxical question that kept going through my mind as I made the long ride over the snow-swept trails to Holbrook.

The horseback ride took two full days, broken by an overnight stop with the trader at the Smith's Lake post, but early upon the third morning after leaving the canyon, I began to get busy. Of the thirty days allowed me for removal of goods from my store, ten were already gone, since the order read "thirty days from the date hereof." That meant I had to work quickly if I wanted to save anything out of this wrecking attempt, put in action by persons or for reasons unknown to me.

One of the leading attorneys of Holbrook, the county seat, listened to my story. He, too, expressed grave doubts that we could get any satisfaction out of a complaint against Fall. He had no faith in the efficacy of any appeal to the Secretary for fair play—his estimate of Fall did not leave a shred of respectability to the Secretary of the Interior. He advised me to get all friends and acquaintances of any importance, whether social, commercial, or political, to intercede for me. It was his belief that if enough pressure were brought to bear, we should at least secure an extension of the time limit given in the order. That we could bring about an outright revocation of the order seemed exceedingly unlikely to him.

Acting upon his advice, I wrote numerous letters to friends and acquaintances in almost every part of the country. I also sent night letters by Western Union, and made several long-distance telephone calls. Locally, in Holbrook, I interested the Chamber of Commerce and the mayor of the town in my case, causing them to send telegrams of protest to Washington. Similar action was taken by the Chambers of Commerce of Albuquerque, New Mexico; El Paso, Texas; and Pueblo, Colorado.

As a result of my letters and other appeals, and through the help of friends everywhere, congressional delegations from seventeen states were instructed to add their complaints about the highhanded methods of the Secretary. Eleven senators, including the ones from Arizona, New Mexico, Colorado, California, Iowa, South Dakota, New York and Michigan were enlisted in my support. Personal letters and telegrams were received in Washington by Indian Commissioner Burke, Secretary Fall's office, and even by the White House from friends, relatives, and acquaintances in all parts of the country, and from as far away as the Philippine Islands.

The most important contribution to the fight, however, was made by my friend, James W. Young, of New York and Chicago, executive of one of the world's largest and most influential advertising agencies.

Jim Young had visited Keams Canyon several times.

He liked the Western country, the Indians, and everything pertaining to the great outdoors. He and I together
had made a horseback-and-pack-horse trip to the Rainbow
Bridge, the glorious natural wonder in southern Utah.
In the course of years, a strong friendship had developed
between us. When the hour of need arose, Jim proved
to be a staunch helper, and his efforts toward securing
justice for me amounted to almost as much as the combined exertions of all others who came to assistance.

Upon receipt of my detailed letter, Jim got eight of the
nation's biggest news agencies in Washington busy on
the case. The reporters swarmed into the office of the
Secretary of the Interior, into the sanctum of the Indian
Commissioner, and even interviewed President Harding's
secretary, Christian. They demanded the details of the
"Schmedding story" that was about to break, and were
persistent in their efforts to get a "scoop."

Jim had engaged the services of a big Washington law
firm, and representatives of that concern tried repeatedly
to interview Secretary Fall. They did not see Fall, but
his secretary informed them that so far as Fall was concerned, the Schmedding case was closed, and would not
be reopened!

Commissioner Burke of the Bureau of Indian Affairs,
and Assistant Commissioner Merritt, declared that my
record as a trader was free from blemish. They said that
the Indian Bureau did not know of any reason for the
revocation of my trader's license. According to them,
Secretary Fall had sent for the Indian Bureau's file containing my license applications, findings of inspectors,
periodical reports by the agent in charge of the reservation—in fact, my complete history. Nothing contained in
that could by any stretch of the imagination be considered
derogatory.

That record, the entire file, disappeared in Secretary Fall's office. Whether he destroyed those papers or just dumped them into a wastebasket remains a secret. We learned, eventually, that he had handled the whole matter by himself, without consultation with the officials of the Indian Bureau, and even without the knowledge of his secretary.

Fall was under a cloud and already on his way out as a cabinet officer. He had been involved in the Teapot Dome oil scandal, and the public knew about the notorious $100,000 carried in the black satchel. Nevertheless, as a personal friend of the President, he was still a powerful figure, and it looked like a hopeless struggle to force a reversal of his order. That would have been like a slap in the face of the Secretary of the Interior, and without a precedent in Washington political history.

Despite those obstacles, congressman, senators, reporters, lawyers, and private individuals continued to exert pressure. Jim Young threatened to splash the story of the maltreated Indian trader across the pages of every newspaper in the country. Several of the congressmen and senators declared that they would take the matter onto the floor of Congress or the Senate, unless I was given an impartial hearing and an opportunity to hear the charges against me, and to defend myself. The President's secretary, Christian, was told that this affair could be used to embarrass the administration.

From various sources we got to the root of the matter and found out just what prompted Fall to issue the peremptory order. As in several other shady deals perpetrated by the Secretary, so in this case: money, graft, and dirty politics were the basis of his action.

As I said earlier in this narrative, for a while there was considerable excitement in the Navajo country when geologists discovered the presence of oil. Many could already picture the Navajos in the role of millionaires, very much in the manner of the Oklahoma Indians who fell heir to untold wealth in oil royalties. To those smart men it was plain that any trader in a well-located post could reap golden harvests should the boom in oil flower into the bonanza they visualized.

One of Fall's old-time friends and political cronies, a wholesaler in Gallup, New Mexico, had been casting envious eyes upon the Keams Canyon post. He probably figured that, holding such a strategic position, the store would presently be a gold mine to the trader running the place. Therefore, why not acquire it before the rush started—all that was necessary was to kick Schmedding, an unknown trader, out of there, and make application for a trader's license to take over the post. A letter to friend Fall and the thing would be done!

Secretary Fall issued the order revoking my license. He did not have to explain his reasons for the act—the phrase "for administrative reasons" covered all that. Anyhow, he was leaving the Department of the Interior, so why not do this last little favor for his friend?

That he was stirring up a hornet's nest of public indignation which would cause a flood of protests to swamp Washington could not have been foreseen by him. After all, the order affected only a small unknown Indian trader, stuck away in the wilderness of a Western reservation. The fellow could not possibly do anything against a peremptory order issued by the Secretary of the Interior, but would simply pack his goods and get out, convinced of the hopelessness of fighting a man situated next to the President. That would leave the field clear for Fall's friend who could then take the required steps to gain possession of the coveted post.

I made several trips to Albuquerque, New Mexico, to El Paso, Texas, and other places, always returning to Holbrook, and, eventually, to Keams Canyon, awaiting the result of the efforts put forth in my behalf by the various parties who had been interested in the case. However, it became imperative that I plead my case in person, and both Jim Young, and the lawyers in Washington recommended that I come to the nation's capital to speak in my own behalf.

Following the statement that it was an impossibility to move my goods and family in the winter season, an extension of thirty days had been granted me by the Indian Bureau, but that time, too, was rapidly drawing to the expiration date.

Congressman Carl Hayden, of Arizona, had constituted himself a one-man investigating committee, and came to Keams Canyon to get details on the ground. He consulted with the agent in charge of the reservation, talked with others, and got my side of the story. After he had assembled all pertinent data, he wrote the following letter:

> Keams Canon, Arizona,
> April 3, 1923
>
> MY DEAR MERRITT:
> I have examined into the facts of the case against Mr. Joseph Schmedding and am convinced that the revocation of his trader's license is more than an injustice, it is an outrage!
> I hope that you will do everything possible to assist him while he is in Washington and if I can aid in any way, do not hesitate to let me know.
>
> Yours as ever,
> CARL HAYDEN.
>
> TO THE HON. EDGAR B. MERRITT
>   ASSISSTANT COMMISSIONER OF INDIAN AFFAIRS
>   WASHINGTON, D.C.

I started for Washington, by way of Chicago, where I was met by friend Jim Young. He, in turn, took me to Judge Stephen A. Foster, who talked with me at great length concerning the case. Judge Foster had received a complete resumé of the case as handled by the Washington attorneys, and from it quoted the following part, contained in a letter sent by one of the associate members of the law firm:

> . . . regarding the Schmedding case . . . and to advise that this morning I saw Mr. Merritt, Assistant Secretary of Indian Affairs, who was as non-commital as the various other officials I have seen in the Interior Department regarding the case. They all tell me that it was a matter handled entirely by Secretary Fall personally and that the case was closed. Yesterday I attempted to see Secretary Fall but his secretary told me that Mr. Fall had closed the case and did not desire to discuss it further.

Fall had left Washington for Hot Springs, Arkansas, and the new Secretary of the Interior, Dr. Hubert Work, was now in the position formerly occupied by Fall. However, being altogether unfamiliar with the affair, and unable to judge the reasons for Fall's order, he must have felt very reluctant to overrule or set aside what was virtually the last order of his predecessor. What he was asked to do was without precedent—naturally, he hesitated despite the pressure from all sides to correct this manifest wrong.

Arrived in Washington, I had some long consulations with the attorneys working on the case. I also visited the offices of Senator Cameron (Arizona), Congressman Hayden, and others. Several of the staff members of different news agencies interviewed me at my hotel and discussed the details of the case, preparing for the eventuality that the press would be turned loose in the matter.

Accompanied by Senator Cameron, two congressmen, and two members of my lawyer's firm, I was ushered into the White House. Secretary Christian announced our party to the President and made the introductions. President Harding looked as if he failed to understand why he should be annoyed by us, but listened to a much condensed history of my case. I started with the conciliatory and "face-saving" statement that it was my belief that Secretary Fall had acted under a *misapprehension* and continued by saying that I was ready to accept the judgment if the actual charges (if any) were substantiated and justified the drastic action, and asked that I be accorded the privilege of a fair and unbiased hearing.

Senator Cameron and one of the attorneys spoke briefly, touching upon the fact that nothing was known of the underlying reasons for my license revocation, and adding their plea to mine that I be given a chance to answer whatever charges there might be.

The President had listened carefully and attentively throughout the interview. At last he rose from his chair, and, turning to me, said: "We shall see that you get justice, Mr. Schmedding." He then shook hands, and the audience was over.

Two days later, I met Dr. Hubert Work, the new Secretary of the Interior. Again there were some five or six influential people with me. Dr. Work must have studied the submitted reports and findings thoroughly—he was familiar with the various phases of the controversy, and asked me numerous questions. At the end he said:

"I believe you have given me the true story, and I do not see why you should not be allowed to continue in your trading business in Keams Canyon. A new license will be issued to you at once, and you may return to the reservation and join your family!"

The bitter struggle against long odds had been won! I sent a telegram to my wife to relieve her anxiety, then packed my bag and left Washington by the first train. About ten days after I arrived in Keams Canyon, a new license was in my hands, typed in Secretary Work's office, bearing the seal of the Department of the Interior and signed by Hubert Work personally!—undoubtedly the only Indian trader's license of the kind.

Fall never regained political power or influence. He was indicted by a grand jury and subsequently became a numbered convict in a Federal penitentiary. The one-time El Paso lawyer passed out of the picture, broken in health and ruined financially.

For several weeks after returning from Washington my mail was loaded with letters of congratulations. Everybody that had taken any part in the fight was notified by the Indian Bureau that a new license had been granted, and many of those notifications were forwarded to me with cheerful messages. Here is a sample:

30296-23

DEPARTMENT OF THE INTERIOR
OFFICE OF INDIAN AFFAIRS
WASHINGTON

April 34, 1923

MY DEAR SENATOR:

In the absence of Commissioner Burke in the field, and referring to the letter addressed to you on March 26th by Mr. Joseph Schmedding, Indian trader at Keams Canon, on the Moqui reservation, Arizona, you are advised that, upon reconsideration of this case on April 16, 1923, the Secretary of the Interior rescinded the order of revocation and issued Mr. Schmedding a new license effective April 1, 1923.

Cordially yours,
E. B. MERRITT
Acting Commissioner

HONORABLE RALPH H. CAMERON,
UNITED STATES SENATE.

The scores of congratulatory letters and telegrams had a heartening effect and helped to overcome the strain of those bleak days when the going was hardest. But nothing could make me forget this experience of bureaucratic misrule and stupidity that came so near being disastrous to our tranquil existence. To appreciate just what the loss of the license would have meant, it is necessary to understand that while a trader occupies his post and enjoys unrestricted possession, he cannot sell or convey title to any buildings or other improvements he may erect.

Store buildings, warehouses, sheds, family dwellings, wells, and any and all other improvements become, automatically, government property when erected upon Indian lands. The trader has the right of occupancy, but when he leaves he can not sell the buildings. Nor is he allowed to wreck them for salvage of materials that could be used in some other location—he is obliged to leave everything in good order.

During our years in Keams Canyon we had spent thousands of dollars for improvements, additions, and changes. The post at Low Mountain, too, had proved an expensive undertaking. Thus, I should have suffered a heavy financial loss if I had been forced to leave the reservation suddenly. While licensed posts are restricted in number, and considered highly desirable by many, yet it is not easy to find a buyer able to handle a deal of the magnitude involved in transferring a place of the size and importance of Keams Canyon, still more valuable through having an independent branch trading post.

When I acquired the Keams Canyon post, the buildings and other improvements were not sold to me as such, but listed as "good will." That same procedure I would have to follow in making a deal for turning over the post, as well as Low Mountain, to a new owner. Only in that fashion could I reimburse myself for the money spent on improvements.

The Fall controversy had crystalized our intentions to remove from the reservation—it now became important to find a buyer able to take over our combined interests in Keams Canyon and Low Mountain. For weeks and months I made inquiries, and let it be known in several quarters that I would entertain offers for the two posts. Meanwhile, of course, we carried on our trading activities.

Another year went by before we found a buyer—then Mr. Halderman, an Indian trader who had spent his apprenticeship in an Indian traders' wholesale house in Winslow, Arizona, began negotiations. Finally, we agreed upon the terms and conditions of the sale, and at last saw the day coming when we would leave Keams Canyon, to return no more.

The Indians who, of course, had heard the news of our impending departure, were just as curious as they had been when we took the place. They wanted to know why I wanted to sell—how could I bring myself to leave my many friends—if I would not change my mind and remain. A big lump would rise in my throat when some old fellow, bent and wrinkled, placed his hands about my shoulders and laid his head against my chest. Much older than I, he would, nevertheless address me as *sheeyeh*, "father":

"*Sheeyeh,* who will take care of us when you are gone . . . Who will give us flour and coffee when we are hungry? . . . To whom shall we bring our wool and pelts and blankets?" Tears rolled down the leathery cheeks; he would not be comforted.

Many of our Indian friends and customers came to bid us good-by—all expressed the hope that soon we would open another trading post, not too far away. They would all come and trade only with me!

Since then, nearly a quarter of a century has joined the past. At different times, I approached the outskirts of the Navajo reservation when traveling across country by car or train. From reports that have reached me I learned that my successor prospered. The trading post in Keams Canyon continues to flourish—it is still the nerve center of the Navajo country and can measure the heartbeats of its people.

Modern progress has affected both traders and Indians. Bridges span deep arroyos and treacherous washes that once were impassable barriers during the rainy season. Roads have been graded and even hard-surfaced in parts. The journeys that required days and weeks for the slow freight wagons can now be accomplished within a matter of hours. Freight and mail moves by automobile and truck. Telephones connect formerly isolated places. Some of the trading posts have individual electric light plants. Oil and gasoline are dispensed to the tourist from pumps that are becoming standard equipment of many trading stores. Tires, tubes, and spark plugs take their place on the trader's shelves. The Indians, too, have adopted the modern transportation, and cars of every brand and all vintages can be seen alongside the hogans where hobbled ponies used to doze. Blankets are peddled to the curious travelers from roadside camps adjoining transcontinental highways; the fine art of the silversmith is in a rapid decline.

Some distance from the highways that parallel the railroad tracks, off the beaten paths, and in the remoter portions of Navajoland, conditions are as they were twenty-five or even fifty years ago.

The Navajos have been there for hundreds of years and their conservative nature does not incline them to change. They look with suspicion upon innovations that appear foolish or useless to them. The *Dinneh* are reluctant to turn from the ways of their forebears. It is difficult to persuade them that "improvements" really do mean a betterment when those changes having nothing to recommend them except being of today.

One cannot retard the march of time; change is the only thing that is constant. To bewail the passing of old customs will be considered by many as undue sentimentality. What we term "modern" today is classed with the "good old times" almost before the present generation makes way for the next one. All this is called logic and reason. None of it, by any name, alters the fact that my heart overflows with nostalgia for the carefree and unhampered life on the ranges and in the Indian country, for the return of the observance of sturdier American habits and characteristics. Many of our heritages from founding fathers and pioneer days are in danger of being uprooted and discarded. If something finer or better were offered to take their place, all would be well, but our hectic jazz days do not hold out much promise for an improvement. Is it any wonder then that I have a deep-seated longing for the revival of the simpler and more truly American ways, so frequently belittled by unassimilated aliens, and put in jeopardy by cynical elements contemptuous of our cherished institutions?

If the tale makes this sentiment understandable, my labor has not been in vain.